Joinery, Joists and Gender

Joinery, Joists and Gender: A History of Woodworking for the 21st Century is the first publication of its kind to survey the long and rich histories of women and gender non-conforming persons who work in wood. Written for craft practitioners, design students, and readers interested in the intersections of gender and labor history—with 200 full-color images, both historical and contemporary—this book provides an accessible and insightful entry into the histories, practices, and lived experiences of women and nonbinary makers in woodworking.

In the first half the author presents a woodworking history primarily in Europe and the United States that highlights the practical and philosophical issues that have marked women's participation in the field. Research focuses on a diverse range of practitioners from Lady Yun to Adina White.

This is followed by sixteen in-depth profiles of contemporary woodworkers, all of whom identify fine woodworking as their principal vocation. Through studio visits, interviews, and photographs of space and process, the book uncovers the varied practices and contributions these diverse artisans make to the understanding of wood as a medium to engage spatial, material, aesthetic, and even existential challenges.

Beautifully illustrated profiles include Wendy Maruyama, one of the first women to earn an MFA in woodworking in the US; Sarah Marriage, founder of Baltimore's A Workshop of Our Own, a woodshop and educational space specifically for women and gender non-conforming makers; Yuri Kobayashi, whose sublime work blurs boundaries between the worlds of art and craft, sculpture, and furniture; and Folayemi Wilson, whose work draws equally on African American history and Afrofuturism to explore and illuminate the ways that furniture and wood traditions shape social relations.

Deirdre Visser is a curator, educator, visual artist, and woodworker in San Francisco's Mission District. As Curator of The Arts at the California Institute of Integral Studies (CIIS) since 2010, Visser connects history to the present to look for common themes and engage historical context in a deeper understanding of the challenges we face today. She also has an active visual practice engaged with the arts as a form of civic participation, working collaboratively for the past decade with the Skywatchers Ensemble in San Francisco's Tenderloin District.

Visser started woodworking as an undergraduate in the sculpture studio, learning to build furniture from old growth Douglas fir scavenged from dumpsters. She later worked as a finish carpenter on residential remodeling sites. Mostly self-taught, Visser continued to pursue woodworking; in 2015–2016 she studied furniture making at the Krenov School in Mendocino.

Visser is co-curator with Laura Mays of *Making a Seat at the Table: Women Transform Woodworking*, the survey exhibition that grew out of this research process, which debuted in 2019 at the Center for Art in Wood in Philadelphia, featuring contemporary women and gender non-conforming woodworkers.

Joinery, Joists and Gender

A History of Woodworking for the 21st Century

Deirdre Visser

Routledge
Taylor & Francis Group

LONDON AND NEW YORK

Cover image: © Ivy Siosi

First published 2022
by Routledge
4 Park Square, Milton Park, Abingdon, Oxon OX14 4RN

and by Routledge
605 Third Avenue, New York, NY 10158

Routledge is an imprint of the Taylor & Francis Group, an informa business

British Library Cataloguing-in-Publication Data
A catalogue record for this book is available from the British Library

Library of Congress Cataloging-in-Publication Data
Names: Visser, Deirdre, author. | Mays, Laura, author.
Title: Joinery, joists and gender : a woodworking history for the 21st
    century / Deirdre Visser with contributions from Laura Mays.
Description: Milton Park, Abingdon, Oxon ; New York : Routledge, 2022. |
    Includes bibliographical references and index.
Identifiers: LCCN 2021044780 (print) | LCCN 2021044781 (ebook)
Subjects: LCSH: Women woodworkers. | Gender-nonconforming
    woodworkers. | Woodworking—History—21st century,
Classification: LCC HD8039.W6 V57 2022 (print) | LCC HD8039.W6
    (ebook) | DDC 331.4/868408—dc23/eng/20211103
LC record available at https://lccn.loc.gov/2021044780
LC ebook record available at https://lccn.loc.gov/2021044781

ISBN: 978-0-367-36340-6 (hbk)
ISBN: 978-0-367-36341-3 (pbk)
ISBN: 978-0-429-34541-8 (ebk)

DOI: 10.4324/9780429345418

Typeset in Trade Gothic
by Apex CoVantage, LLC

Every effort has been made to contact copyright-holders. Please advise
the publisher of any errors or omissions, and these will be corrected in
subsequent editions.

Printed in Canada

Work doesn't care who does it.
—Mary Perpetua Maloney, "Grossmutti" (1901–1983)

This book is dedicated to the incredible artists/designers/woodworkers who have participated in this project, whether through interviews or in the exhibition. Each was generous beyond measure with their story; in moments when my energy flagged, their lives and work inspired me to continue.

Contents

Contents

Contents

Figures

Acknowledgments

A casual conversation over Thanksgiving dinner in 2015 would never have turned into this book without many friends, family members, colleagues, and scholars whose support, conversation, questions, research, and opinions have made indelible contributions to its realization.

I am indebted to Laura Mays and Phoebe Kuo, my early partners in crime. At that dinner on the Mendocino coast, I asked Laura about her experience in a male-dominated field of practice. Her initial reticence about that question was the catalyst for a years-long conversation that became this book. As my co-curator for the *Making a Seat at the Table* exhibition in 2019 at the Center for Art in Wood, she was also my travel, research, and conversation partner; her deep knowledge of wood and woodworking history and her generosity in sharing it is evident all over this book. Phoebe's experience in ethnographic interviews shaped our collective approach to our primary research with contemporary makers. Her guidance in the interview process fostered a climate and culture of warmth that is manifest throughout. When I was deep in the writing process, Kristi Williams stepped up to help pursue permissions, research sources, and bring her wonderful drafting skills to creating an illustrated glossary.

As the writing process developed, I turned to Carla Williams—writer, photo historian, photographer, editor, friend, and sometime collaborator of two decades—whose deep pleasure in language fills our conversations with laughter and the editing process with joy. This is a vastly better book for her participation. Jennifer-Navva Milliken and the wonderful staff of the Center for Art in Wood made it possible to realize *Making a Seat at the Table*; thank you! In the many dozens of exhibitions I've curated, this stands out among my favorite experiences for its extraordinary sense of community on top of the staggering array of talent. Cheryl R. Riley and Tom Loeser were wonderful jurors for that exhibition; their distinct professional and creative paths came to the table in a rich conversation and selection process. Donald Fortescue, Stephanie Hanor, Glenn Adamson, and J.D. Sassaman were early and generous supporters, helping us garner the critical financial support from The Center for Craft, Creativity, and Design, The Krenov Foundation, and Autodesk at Pier 9.

I would be remiss if I didn't give a shout out to Suzanne Ellison, whose wonderful writing is found on the Lost Art Press blog. Her passion for illuminating the hidden histories of women in the woodshop from the medieval period through the World Wars has been invaluable in this work. Merry Weisner's work on labor in medieval and early modern Europe places the woodshop into a larger social and economic framework in a way that is dynamic, contextual, and relatable. Marianne Mays was an early, supportive, but rigorous reader. I also want to thank Amy Epstein, Carolyn Cooke, Carol Sauvion, Megan Fitzpatrick, and Sarah Carter for conversation, support, and thoughtful scholarship at many critical junctures. Jillian Elliott, my colleague at CIIS, was supportive in ways both practical and philosophical. Jim Christiansen catalyzed my own love of woodworking many years ago when I was an undergrad in the sculpture studio at Mills College and returned in the final stages of this project's completion to reinforce that lifelong love affair.

My sister Maura brought her decades-long teaching experience to holding her younger sister accountable to deadlines with a balance of candor and humor. Many other friends and loved ones—particularly Briana, Jodie, Pam, Anne, Shamus, Sonya, Kim, and Jen—listened and asked questions as I pondered approaches, wrestled with ideas, fell apart in exhaustion, and celebrated successes. And not least, my cousin Patrick and his family offered me their beautiful home on the northern coast of Oregon to sequester myself and finish the book! I'm grateful beyond measure; there can be no doubt this wouldn't have happened without each and every one of you.

Foreword

Navva Milliken

During my first conversation with curators Laura Mays and Deirdre Visser about *Making a Seat at the Table*, I envisioned an exhibition in the gallery of the Center for Art in Wood that would translate their research into a navigable spatial presentation. What resulted was the most celebrated and visited program ever organized by the Center. The excitement and wonder generated during the run of the exhibition was a confirmation of the core beliefs that energize the Center's mission: that an inclusive, truth-based approach simultaneously bolsters scholarship, excellence, and innovation among all practitioners in our field.

A work of great care, this book is a foundational text that lays the groundwork and fills the gaps of documentation upon which a discourse is built. Much is said about the power of representation—in positions of leadership, education, and professions that are dominated by cis-gender men and white-racialized people. The challenges faced by woman-identifying or gender-non-conforming woodworkers discourage meaningful advancement in this field, but have also motivated people with skill and know-how to construct platforms for self-learning and community-building that are nurturing and broadening this ecosystem. Shining a light on the faces and stories of the overlooked in a field that offers so much creative inspiration and empowerment is an act of joy and restitution.

The craftspeople here tell their stories, importantly including their paths to work and the many people along the way—family members, instructors, mentors, partners—who helped them get there. As in all forms of craft practice, their biographies are intimately and finely "dovetailed" with their bodies of work. Each account is individual, with its diversions and idiosyncrasies. Like trees, they change course to seek the light, enduring infestations and spalting, and expanding root systems and canopies all the while.

This project is a critical mechanism for engaging in deeper narratives around craft, wood, and the gender experience. When I learned of this documentation effort, I was intrigued by its promise to bridge deep chasms in the creative and vocational woodworking communities. It emphasizes the important relationship between the crafted object and the community being built around it. This work highlights the ways that woodworkers are creating and deploying their tools to change—from the center and from the margins—models of education, production, entrepreneurship, and distri-bution, while building toward a more sustainable, equitable future from which all can benefit.

Introduction

The exhibition

In fall 2019, *Making a Seat at the Table: Women Transform Woodworking* (MASATT: WTW), opened at Philadelphia's Center for Art in Wood), featuring forty-seven innovative and diverse original works by forty-three women and gender non-conforming persons from nineteen of the United States, two Canadian provinces, and Australia. The show was timed to coincide with the centennial celebration of the Nineteenth Amendment that granted (but didn't yet guarantee) women the right to vote in the United States. CAW Artistic Director, Jennifer Navva Milliken, had invited Laura Mays, woodworker and Director of the Krenov School at Mendocino College, and me, a longtime woodworker, curator, and arts educator in San Francisco, to translate the work originally conceived as a book into an exhibition. Never before had a survey exhibition of contemporary women woodworkers been mounted with so broad a reach; in 2011 the exhibition *Furniture Divas* at the Fuller Craft Museum in Massachusetts included the work of fifteen women makers, not all woodworkers, and prior to that the most recent exhibition of women in woodworking was in the 1980s. We put out a call for submissions and invited Milliken and woodworkers/designers Cheryl R. Riley and Tom Loeser to jury the selection with us. To keep it manageable and focused, we decided to show contemporary makers whose work—while diverse in concept, material, and approach—has roots in the furniture tradition, rather than the related fields of carving, turning, or carpentry

DOI: 10.4324/9780429345418-1

and trades work. It was an exciting opportunity to assemble in one space both iconic works by artists whom we greatly admired, and new works by emerging and mid-career makers who together addressed a broad range of conceptual and material questions.

The first question we asked ourselves in this process was why, in the second decade of the twenty-first century, is it necessary to highlight gender while examining a decidedly genderless art form and medium? Despite a full fifty years of significant creative output by women makers, and centuries of history in woodshops throughout the world, there simply has not been commensurate attention granted—and credit given—to the contributions of women woodworkers. Women and gender non-conforming woodworkers are still largely invisible on bookshelves and in woodworking magazines. Thus, we sought to illuminate that history and examine the breadth and richness of practices engaged by these makers so that the work can ultimately speak for itself. As exhibiting maker Laura Kishimoto would recently attest, it remains necessary and vital to recognize and acknowledge the realities women and gender non-conforming makers continue to face in the field, and to never assume that the work is done:

> *Making a Seat at the Table* remains the most significant and emotionally gratifying show I have participated in. It made me realize how power-fully being a woman in woodworking has shaped my identity. When I first began woodworking professionally in Ireland, I felt so isolated and discouraged. All of my coworkers were older men and considerably more experienced. One sexually assaulted me multiple times. But now being a woman in woodworking is a source of empowerment and community to me. Thank you very much for telling our stories.
>
> (2021)

From the outset we grappled with the use of the terms "woman" and "women" to frame this project. Two decades into the twenty-first century, as queer and trans activists continue the liberatory work of disrupting the gender binary and expand the boundaries of our understanding, we are conscious of honoring self-identity without positioning it as a foil to other descriptors. KG MacKinnon (Profile pp. 243–252), for example, who identifies as queer and trans, is profiled in this book; they didn't respond to the open call for MASATT: WTW because they did not see themselves included within that framework. Likewise, Sean Desiree, also profiled here (Profile pp. 185–196), identifies as non-binary. But as we spoke with makers, including those who identify as women and were sexed male at birth, their stories and reflections further illuminated the role of sex and gender expression in the woodshop, and it was essential that we included those makers in this survey.

It's the wood that makes it good

A second question arose which we did not expect, perhaps because it seemed too obvious: What do we mean by wood? We had never actually asked that question, though some sustainable alternatives sit at the threshold but are not themselves wood. Rattan, for example, is a woody climbing plant—technically a *liana*—derived from the bark of a vine that is part of the palm family and has characteristics of wood, while **bamboo** is a tree-like grass without woody material in its stem. Bamboo is widely used as a sustainable alternative to wood, particularly in contexts calling for sheet material; the stems are edge-laminated into broad sheets that can be worked much like wood. Many makers utilize whatever they need for the best results and don't limit themselves by these definitions.

But beyond the cell structure or biology of the plant, there is the cultural significance of wood: More than any other single material we use, for most communities around the world wood is the literal foundation of home, both its structure and its furnishings. We cleave, carve, and join wood to make the world habitable, to create the objects that make it possible, for example, to sit down for a meal with friends and family around a table, or to make a room that is safe and comfortable in which to sleep. The spatial organization and relative scales of furnishings can invite and constrain, blur boundaries, suggest intimacies, or determine and reinforce relations of power. Objects and structures illuminate the world of fabrication, shedding light on the maker and the means of production. While factory manufacturing models divide the production process into small-scale component parts on an assembly line, we fundamentally understand the integral relationship between the craftsperson and the work.

When we consider woodworking, we also take a deep dive into the implications of resource consumption. There are no simple answers to the questions of sustainability as we humans—a species with outsized impact relative to our biomass—use and exploit this plant material with ratios of strength to weight and workability that make it irreplaceably useful. Trees not only provide us with the means to material objects, to build structure, but also to heat, and to cook, one of a few things that distinguishes us from other species. It completely changes our ability to extract nutrients from food, thus making it possible to support our energy-consuming brains. Most importantly of all, trees provide us oxygen necessary for life.

As a gateway to habitation and domesticity, woodworking is also a portal through which to view the world. Furniture is its manifestation, as symbolic as it is utilitarian, and woodworking forms a web of interconnectivity so deeply embedded in our collective consciousness that nature and culture are virtually indistinguishable. It can convey history and the present, access and welcome, wealth and power. It can also reveal a narrative rooted in geography, climate, and migration, or provide an entryway into ideas about agency and the agent.

Now "craft" is a place where the individual maker interacts with systems, whether technological, material, or economic. The body of the craftsperson is afforded mastery of the machine, and their labor is valued outside the imperatives of late capitalism. If mass production divides the fabrication of goods into small-scale interchangeable component parts, each separate from the next, from the maker(s), and even from the end user, then the craftsperson creates a web of interconnection in creating form and satisfying a functional need. This craftsperson at their bench, we imagine, signifies the integral relationship between the maker and their materials, an entryway into a conversation about place, rootedness, and the movement of global capital and material goods across this shared planet.

The book

When we first embarked on the project in 2017, Laura and I envisioned that it would be rooted in the personal stories of the nearly forty exceptionally talented and inspiring woodworkers, furniture makers, and artists working in wood across the United States and into Canada with whom we conducted intimate and lengthy interviews, rounded out with a history of women makers in the field through the last few decades. We anticipated contrasting their contemporary narratives with a history, as written, in which women were—with relatively few exceptions—denied access to the shop until the latter half of the twentieth century. We interviewed makers who exhibit within traditional fine art networks of museums and galleries; makers who have sold their work through commercial channels for private consumers; makers who have and are continuing to transform the field by becoming leaders in craft education; makers who are bridging their knowledge with community engagement to advance inclusive and community-driven design and fabrication; and serious and committed emergent makers who exert an important influence over how women and gender non-conforming makers in woodworking have come to be understood in this moment. We shaped the questions so that stories of their lived experiences emerged. The makers we profiled are diverse, ranging in age, ethnicity, region, and experience, and were selected to help illuminate the pluralism of histories and practices among makers in this field; to represent the breadth of concerns and questions that define the practice today; and to speak to contemporary women and non-binary makers in woodworking while not attempting to reach tidy or packaged conclusions.

With more than forty combined years of experience in the arts and woodworking, Laura and I initially divided up the work to emphasize our respective expertise, fully expecting to flesh out the historical sections with those individual and well-recognized makers who had set the stage for what we saw as the current pluralism in the field. After all, women and gender non-conforming woodworkers were everywhere we looked, making exciting work, shaping university programs, and coordinating conferences for makers and artists. Eventually the project morphed into each of us playing to our strengths: I became the sole author while Laura became a contributing expert with her comprehensive knowledge of twentieth-century woodworking makers and movements.

The book and the exhibition each tell a part of this story, offering different pathways into the history, present, and future of women and gender non-conforming makers in this medium. Makers are daily, weekly, and for their careers choosing this practice. What draws them? What is the experience like? And what does the future look like? My hope is that this first history of women in woodworking inspires more scholarship and research into movements and moments that give us a deepening knowledge of our own complex and overlapping histories, and that more women and gender non-conforming makers walk into the woodshop with the certain knowledge of the rich story and history they carry with them. Although many of the exhibited artists from the CAW show are also included in this book in some way, this is not an exhibition catalog but rather a stand-alone volume. It is structured to address core conceptual and material questions and to examine how the field was founded, developed, and transformed over the years. The first half is a history of woodworking in (predominantly) the United States and Europe, from the earliest documented makers to the present, and the second half is selected profiles of sixteen contemporary US-based makers, including educators, functional furniture makers, conceptual artists, and hobbyists turned social media influencers.

In writing a history of women and gender non-conforming makers in woodworking, I am conscious of the risk of eliding difference in the name of creating a coherent and manageable narrative that centers sex and gender. While I write about the specific and various histories that happen(ed) generally within a binary model, I also embrace the growing complexity of gender identities and everyone's right to self-identify. Throughout the text I attempt to make clear the ways that class, ethnicity, and race intersect with gender to shape experience. Each of the stories here is relevant in illuminating the field, and our assumptions, about agency in making and the social construction of gender. I adhere in all instances to chosen pronouns; in historical instances when no preference is known, I use she/her.

Research methodology

The overarching framework for this discussion is a cultural history of European and North American makers that is focused through the lens of changing social and economic imperatives through time, in no small part due to the availability of source material supporting this history. In the existing history books, important narratives were buried because they didn't conform to normative conceptions of sex and gender. For example, women who did trades work and labored in medieval guild shops were left out of painted and written records of the period because they didn't fit the prevalent cultural narrative. Casting a wider net in this research, new names quickly began to emerge, which allowed me to draw connections between moments and movements that had not previously been connected. What was evident is that I would write a new history; not as a counterpart to the male maker but as an independent, stand-alone narrative that encompasses the relevant discussions as I identified them. Between the history and the profile conversations, it became clear that there were four significant lines of inquiry to follow through time: education, economics, sustainability, and community.

To manageably weave together the diverse histories of women in woodworking, I center the discussion around a lineage that started in the mid-nineteenth-century Arts and Crafts movement in England through the transformative writings of John Ruskin and William Morris. I looked at the various ways women have worked in wood across Western Europe and the United States, from medieval guilds to the Cincinnati Art Carvers at the turn of the twentieth century to England's Lumberjills in the Second World War. Each of those paths illuminate the constructions of gender that informed how and when women have had access to the woodshop.

Organization

This book is divided into five broadly chronological sections that map the terrain of the field at large, integrating the voices and experiences of many makers to create a coherent and accessible narrative. Chapter 1 is a history of women working in wood-related fields from the late medieval period (sixteenth century) to the Victorian period (late nineteenth century). This chapter contextualizes woodworking and its changing narratives, from a guild-based society to an individual exploration of creativity and artistic practice. The social and aesthetic foundation of the mid- to late nineteenth century Arts and Crafts movement links woodworking in the United States to England and Western European medieval culture. These craftspeople brought theories of making and expression—even morality—into the construction of quotidian objects. A reaction against the dehumanizing conditions of industrial production, Arts and Crafts celebrated the maker who brought the work from conception to completion, an expression of their identities, and a celebration of the integrity and authenticity of their labor.

One of the more interesting examples of Arts and Crafts idealism which took root in the US is the Cincinnati Art Carvers. These carvers were virtually always depicted as wealthy women with time on their hands to pursue carving before Roberta A. Mayer's essay "'Against the Grain'? Perspectives on Women and Woodcarving in Cincinnati, 1873–1925" rendered their history more complicated and thrilling; in reality, some of the women made commitments of seven to ten years to learn the craft and then pursued it professionally.

Chapter 2 takes a close look at the emergence of the manual training educational model in the late nineteenth century and continues up to the First World War, exploring the transition from manual to vocational education in this country. While the use of these terms varies in the scholarship, and both can be considered mechanical or industrial—or even manual—education, I am making a distinction between a manual pedagogy that emphasizes the education of a whole student regardless of future career path, and vocational training, which explicitly ties pedagogy and course offerings to one's job or vocational trajectory. Career-driven vocational education mirrored gender- and class-based assumptions about what life paths were open to male and female students, and as such reinforced the exclusion of young women from educational spaces tied to masculine social and economic roles. The history of shop class and vocational education comes up throughout the twentieth century as we consider the distinct pedagogical values of the art classroom versus the trade skills training program in the development of woodworking education and trace the social locations and opportunities that lead a maker into those divergent educational settings. These distinct experiences can result in quite different ways of conceiving of wood as an expressive or utilitarian medium.

European Arts and Crafts-based models such as Educational Slöjd (Sloyd) found purchase in schools in the late nineteenth century from North Bennet Street in Boston to historically Black colleges and universities (HBCUs) throughout the South. The embrace of manual education and the writings of John Ruskin at HBCUs adds critical dimension to what has too often been a privileging of a Western European legacy that traveled from England to New England.

Chapter 3 "Shifting economies" begins with the First World War and extends through the Second, the post-war period and 1950s-era retrenchment into what had been understood as white, middle class, normative gender roles, and then into the cultural upheaval of the 1960s. This section also explores the doors that opened for women in trade skills during the first and second World Wars. Echoes of and direct references to the Arts and Crafts movement between the wars are evident in Works Progress Administration (WPA) projects from New Mexico to Milwaukee. Arts and Crafts appears once more, with a relatively small group of named male makers, including George

Nakashima, Sam Maloof, and James Krenov, who, with their almost spiritual reverence for wood and their modernist conception of the singular maker at their bench, defined a field of practice as the worlds of craft and the arts grew closer, and galleries began to privilege personal expression over utility.

The institutionalization of art education in colleges and universities across the US—in part due to the GI Bill—and the large-scale shifts in the US economy and manufacturing, destabilized union labor and changed the economic imperatives to pursue college education. This period also marks the beginning of second-wave feminism and the ways that women were reshaping their lives through the 70s, increasingly entering non-traditional fields and creating networks of support in the face of employment discrimination.

Chapter 4 "The American studio furniture movement" begins amid the countercultural movements of the 1960s and 70s with the 1972 passage of Title IX, which barred schools receiving federal funding from discriminating on the basis of sex. This section explores the landscape-changing contributions of a generation of women who broke into the field of fine woodworking and furniture making in the mid to late 1970s in the United States, and continued to alter the field as makers, advocates, and educators in art schools and craft programs across the country. Their motivations and aspirations are foundational to the emergence of studio crafts and woodworking in the twentieth century. This section covers nearly forty years, from the post-Title IX educational landscape to the collapse of the US economy (and of most countries around the globe) in 2008, which took with it the formal mechanisms that supported the Studio Furniture movement, irrevocably altering the economic model in which makers created and exhibited.

The last section, Chapter 5 "Contemporary profiles" focuses on the group of makers selected to speak to the pluralism of practice and idiom today, framed by an introduction that looks at some of the driving questions that emerged from the interview process: Resources and sustainability; the economics of production in the twenty-first century; education and equity; and collaborating with community and building community-centered spaces. From the forty interviews conducted, sixteen were selected for the complexity and diversity of both their lives and practices.

In a territory that sits between art, design, and craft, I was interested in the edges and overlaps, and in work that seemed to straddle the boundaries, to push, extend, or question them. Most of the makers have wrestled with identifying as artists, craftspeople, or woodworkers; the categories can be mutable, and many use more than one, often strategically changing their selection through time and according to location, identifying what's useful about each choice in a particular context. Some choose "artist" because the tent seems bigger, allowing a blurring of boundaries and creating fruitful tensions. None of the work can be viewed solely as art—it all retains a grounding in the languages of furniture—material, technique, utility, and the body—as a key part of its genesis.

~

Though many of our subjects were hesitant to adopt the appellation "woman woodworker," all had stories to tell of gender-based treatment, whether in the workplace or the lumberyard. From the overtly dangerous to the subtly belittling, the experience of bias was almost universal. While horror stories persist of gender bias and righteous indifference within the world of woodworking and craft education in the twenty-first century, I have made the conscious decision here not to give those attitudes any further attention by constructing these makers' accomplishments as measured against the opinions of men. Rather, any comparisons made, or incidents of bias, hostility, and denial of access cited are done so only as it pertains to the work and specific history itself, where they advance a personal narrative of a given maker or contextualize the limitations of a particular movement.

Finally, in a time when many artists and artisans of all genders have another income stream, the book speaks to the diverse ways that these makers make a living, and the experiences particular to women and gender non-conforming makers in the marketplace. While not all make their income solely from woodworking or the objects made in the shop, for everyone it is a key part of their professional identity. The question of economic sustainability has implications for our understanding of the value ascribed to art versus craft, the possibilities of small batch production relative to singular works, and the small-scale implications of the internet-based global market.

Reference

Kishimoto, L. (2021). Email with the author. Denver.

Figure 0.1: Shop class, Seattle, 1974, young girl trying to hammer a nail. (Unattributed, Author's collection)

Chapter One

Early histories of women in woodworking

Early histories of women in woodworking are shaped by the ever-shifting dynamics between the public and private spheres. Whether in early modern Europe or in the twentieth century, women's participation in the public sphere is contested and circumscribed; when constrained for fear that it threatened to upend the concepts of family and home, women exerted more power in the private sphere, often as consumers. In times of economic hardship, men have taken steps to further constrain women's economic participation in the public sphere. There is, however, often a gap between narrative and reality, and even between policy and reality. The persistent cultural narrative that women are best suited to lives rooted in home and family, for example, is at odds with the reality that many women either have to, or choose to, work outside the home. Yet amidst these large-scale patterns and norms—often despite them—women have always shaped their own stories.

The legacy of Lady Yun

The earliest known woman credited in woodworking is Yun Shi, more commonly referred to as Lady Yun, who lived during China's Spring and Autumn period (770–476 BCE), which corresponds to the first portion of the Dong (Eastern) Zhou dynasty (Britannica, 2011), a time of diminishing power of imperial rule, emergent intellectual life symbolized most vividly by Confucius' writings, and a growing significance of merchants and craft-speople. Lady Yun worked alongside her husband, Lu Ban (also called Gongshu Ban), who is recognized for his foundational work in Chinese

DOI: 10.4324/9780429345418-2

woodworking and is widely revered in China as the father of carpentry and masonry. An illustration from the fifteenth-century carpentry manual *Lu Ban Jing* shows Lady Yun wielding a mallet, working side by side with Lu Ban. Significantly, she is the active maker in the image; Lu Ban stands by, observing. As their legend grew, it was frequently said that "What Lu Ban invented the Lady Yun would improve," and that she possessed a talent in woodworking that exceeded that of her husband (Taylor, 2009–2021):

> So is it not excellent and grand how our master, starting from the objects, mastered their manufacture and in the course of their manufacture fully perceived the spirit behind it? And his chaste spouse, Lady Yun …, was also blessed with heavenly skill. It is hard to enumerate one by one the objects she made, but if we compare them with those of the master, they may be even still more beautiful. Husband and wife helped each other, and thus they were able to enjoy a great and everlasting fame.
>
> (Ruitenbeek, 1993)

It is a remarkable acknowledgment of and respect for a woman woodworker at a time when few woodworkers were ever individually credited for their work. Lady Yun's inventive mastery and skill is evident to this day, as she is credited with, among other things, the invention of the umbrella; her best-known contribution is an object for personal use, neither furniture nor decorative but absolutely functional. It is reasonable to conclude from Lady Yun's example that it was not entirely exceptional for there to be a woman woodworker in the field; indeed, she is noted for her mastery, not her mere existence. Yet while Lady Yun is an important forerunner, no other such early examples have endured to provide us with a more complete understanding of women's roles in the woodshop. It is not until the late medieval period in Europe that more documented examples of women's work with wood emerged.

Public and private: Economics and social formations

Medieval: Private versus public

The transition from medieval (fifth to the late fifteenth century) to early modern Europe (late fifteenth to late eighteenth century) provides written

（ 9 ） 鲁班把这带盖的斧片装上木座，便成了第一把刨子。他叫妻子云氏在对面抵着，用刨子把一块又一块的木料刨平。云氏很会动脑筋，在作凳上钉了个橛子顶住木头，这样刨起来更稳当了。这橛子后来就被人们叫作"班妻"。

Figure 1.1: Illustration from *Lu Ban Jing*. Translation of comic strip text: "Later on, Lu Ban created a wooden frame on this tiny sharp axe and invented the first wooden plane. Whenever he needed to plane wood, he would ask his wife, Yun, to hold the other end of the wood so it wouldn't slide off the bench. Yun found it as troublesome because it involved two persons for a task. She came up with a clever solution to the problem: She nailed a small piece of wood on the bench to prevent the wood from moving forward. This action makes wood planing job so much easier. Thus, successors named this device as ban qi (qi is a Chinese word for 'wife')." Hand drawing from *Lu Ban Jing*, "Luban Comic Strips – (P67–70)." (Johru Bahru Furniture Association, 2012, https://jbfurniture.com.my/jbfa/index.php/en/about-us/aboutluban/lubanxiaozhuan, last accessed 12/2020)

and material histories for tracing the relationship between women, labor, and the woodshop. Huge social and economic upheavals rocked Europe in the late medieval period, including famines, plagues, wars, and catastrophic weather. Much as we see today, the impulse to control women's participation in the public sector and the economy intensifies in challenging times. While conventional histories of these periods comfortably concluded that the work of women was purely ancillary to and in support of their male counterparts, researcher Suzanne Ellison argues that the lives of women were much more complicated than those histories suggest. The medieval European family workshop was the engine of the economy; crafts and trades were family businesses, and all members were involved. The economic system was based around the household workshop; both men and women participated in all facets of the family business, including fabrication in the woodshop. Women might have been seen working as stonemasons, blacksmiths, and bakers, as well as textile and woodworkers (Ellison, Women in the Workshop, 2016). Craftsmen were expected to be married, and marriage to a master craftsman conferred some social status on their wives, who worked alongside their husbands managing accounts and sales, overseeing both journeymen and apprentices in the shop, and managing the household. As part of a web of interconnected trades, from sawyers and lumber dealers to toolmakers and apprentices, the family woodshop supplied furniture for domestic and public spaces; it was a way of providing for the needs of not only one's family, but also one's neighbors and community. Woodworking and furniture were solidly knit into the everyday world of commerce and the production of goods for use.

Ellison invites her readers to think about the employment of women through the frame of the public versus private spheres. It was easier and safer for wives and daughters to take up the trade of the master craftsman at the head of their household, thus remaining in the private, family sphere. Even if incomplete training or household demands meant that a woman couldn't get to journeyman level, she could contribute to the household income and production in the shop. However, if that master craftsman of a given family did carpentry on a building site, the women in his family were less likely to work at that site. There *were* women working as laborers on building sites, but those who were there were more likely related to unskilled male laborers rather than the master craftsman. They might also have been poor single women, widows, or enslaved persons (Ellison, Craftswomen and the Guilds, 2016).

When demand was high, young women might be hired to do **piecework** and even formally enter an apprenticeship in some cities, particularly in wood **turning**, one arena in which women were often allowed full participation since it was deemed more decorative than structural. Widows could continue to run the shop after a master's death and as such participated fully in the guild. Despite few formal provisions for hiring daughters as apprentices—as there were for hiring sons—there *were* opportunities, and in fact, skills in craft work helped make girls and young women more marriageable. In the last quarter of the thirteenth century, the *Livres des Métiers*, which documented codes of the traditional Parisian crafts, indicated that five of the one hundred traditional craft guilds were headed by women, and *some* women were employed in almost all of them; participation in these guilds was at the high end of respectability (Weisner, 1993). For her doctoral thesis in 1995, Janice Archer did extensive work on the *Livres des Métiers*, creating databases and deciphering obscure terms which allowed her to illuminate more of the work done by women. Archer's research indicated that one-third of women worked in food and clothing production—more traditionally considered feminine—and two thirds worked in the same jobs that men did (Ellison, Craftswomen and the Guilds, 2016).

The medieval craft guilds—groups of artisans in the same occupation who joined together for mutual aid and protection—dominated the organization of material production and distribution even into the early modern period. They came to hold exclusive local rights to practice and trade in that craft. In images of labor from that time, working class women were sometimes pictured doing the arduous work of farming, tending animals, and working in the fields, but when they are represented in a woodworker's shop, they are typically pictured doing needlework at the side of their male partner's bench and/or tending to children. Women's employment did not fit religious or socially conservative norms and so were largely invisible in works of visual art from the period. Neither drawing nor painting from life at that time, artists were tasked with representing the social *ideal* for wealthy patrons who were not necessarily interested in realism, and they were generally silent on women's role in the economy. A rare exception to this is the *Balthasar Behem Codex*: Printed in 1505 and published by the Guilds of Krakow in Polish, German, and Latin, it includes images that place women *next to* men in guild shops. In the carpenter's shop, a woman is using a bellows to keep coals under a glue pot warm (Figure 1.3), and in the cooper's shop women are working on casks (Figure 1.4).

Medieval and early modern writers were largely silent on women's employment outside the home, and where they are listed in city records, women are often referred to by their father's or husband's last name, with terms that refer to their relation to that male—i.e. *dona, femme, wench*—complicating research and data gathering about the labor these women were doing. While the building trades were male-dominated, women still worked making barrels, bed frames, tables, benches, armoires, doors, windows, carts, roofs, scaffolds, and clogs. City records in thirteenth to fifteenth-century Spain, France, Germany, and England show that women were even being hired as day laborers in stone and wood construction (Ellison, Craftswomen and the Guilds, 2016). In Europe's guild system woodcarving was a highly skilled and well-respected trade within woodworking. However, it was defined as a craft instead of a "fine art," even when complex and beautifully realized; this distinction between the fine and decorative arts dates to the Italian Renaissance and has echoes in the discourse about craft today. Like other forms of woodworking, most woodcarving was historically done by craftspeople who didn't sign their work and remained anonymous.

Medieval women also labored under Biblical constructions of their sex as dangerous and polluted. For example, one story in the fourteenth-century Holkham Bible goes that when the blacksmith was asked to make nails for Christ's crucifixion he refused, but his wife agreed to do it. Stories like this reinforced the idea that there was something intrinsically untrustworthy about women. In fact, women at the time worked in the blacksmith shop, contributing to the family income, and would have continued making nails to supplement that income into the nineteenth century (Ellison, Women in the Workshop, 2016).

Early modern Europe: Economic transitions and the changing meaning of work

Cyclical changes have allowed women to enter the woodshop only to see those doors close again, as women's opportunities for full participation in the public domain have been more limited in times of economic scarcity or uncertainty. In the early modern period, economic and cultural shifts—high inflation, the Protestant Reformation, the transition to a market-based economy, and changing social mores—destabilized the family workshop and

Figure 1.2: "The Four Conditions of Society: Work (Vellum), Jean Bourdichon, 1457–1521." Bibliotheque de l'Ecole des Beaux-Arts, Paris, France. (Bridgeman Images, OAD)

Figure 1.3: Carpenter's shop (a woman is using a bellows to keep coals under a glue pot warm), Balthasar Behem Codex, printed in 1505. (Codex: Carpenter's Shop Free copyright available as owned by Getty Institute, https://www.getty.edu/research/library/using/reproductions_permissions/index.html)

guild membership, displacing women from the woodshop. Gendered social constructs shaped the story that was told, and only in recent decades has a more complex history emerged. In *Women and Gender in Early Modern Europe*, scholar Merry Weisner argues that the actual work done by men and women in the early modern economy was very similar, much as it had been in the medieval period. However, the ways in which that labor was understood within society were quite different. A man's economic role and position were determined by age, class, and training; he moved through

Figure 1.4: Cooper's shop, Balthasar Behem Codex, printed in 1505. (Codex, free copyright available as owned by Getty Institute, https://www.getty.edu/research/library/using/reproductions_permissions/index.html)

levels of employment—transitions from apprentice to journeyman to master— systematically, and with male peers and ritualized transitional celebrations. A woman's role in the economy—though also shaped by age and class—was determined principally by biological and social markers like motherhood and marital status. Women might have little control over those events and—unlike their male counterparts—experienced shifts in their economic role as individuals rather than with a cohort of similarly trained peers. Women might also change occupations several times in their lifetimes, or practice more than one at a time, decreasing their identification with a single trade. Societal rituals reinforced males' affiliation with an occupation, while, with few exceptions, events in which women participated—births and funerals—reinforced familial and communal relationships over professional ones (Weisner, 1993).

In stark contrast to the later Victorian representation of the female as passionate hysteric, in the early modern period women were believed to have the benefit of coldness, which was said to cool their brains, prevent overheating, and lead to greater intelligence and a longer life. Men's warm blood was associated with their physical strength and shorter lifespans, since they "burned out" faster. Despite some advances in thinking about equality, characteristics attributed to the sexes were used as the foundation to exclude women from legal parity as well as educational and labor opportunities. With sexual determinism also came the increasingly deep divide between the private/home sphere (belonging to women) and the public/economic sphere (the terrain of men) (Ellison, From La Femme de Charpentier to the Lumberjill, 2016).

Capitalism

The early modern period was marked by a broad, transformative economic shift: The rise of capitalism. From a medieval concept of work, which included all the tasks that contributed to the family, work was then understood to mean participation in production for a market economy. This dramatic shift left out much of the labor that women did to support and sustain their families; the productive labor of women was "simply a part of her domestic role of being helpmate to her husband and an example for her children" (Weisner, 1993). Wiesner argues, however, that this economic explanation alone does not account for increasingly gender-biased conceptualizations of work. Many occupations were professionalized, and women rarely received formal training: The male medical practitioner was a *physician*, paid up to ten times as much and formally recognized, while his female counterpart who healed community members was not. Similarly, first Protestant and later Catholic clergy started to use the term *vocation* to describe work blessed by God; the only vocations open to women in this construction of labor were wife and mother. Wiesner notes that this delineation quickly permeated civil systems and laws so that tax records, guild laws, and occupational groups began to categorize the labors of women—even if it was the production or repair of goods for sale outside of the home—as domestic work. Increasingly, trades were also now understood to be skilled or unskilled; the gender of the workers, rather than the dexterity required to achieve the task, was the principal determinant in the categorization. For example, glass-cutting was understood to be skilled, while making lace or silk thread—commonly done by women—was not. Status and pay paralleled this delineation (Weisner, 1993).

Women in—and out of—the craft guilds

While women participated with gendered limitations in the craft guilds in the medieval period, in the transition from the late medieval to early modern periods women's participation in the guilds grew increasingly constrained. Societal and religious views of women's appropriate roles coincided with economic tumult, and guild regulations grew more and more restrictive, destroying what economic status women held. Ironically, those restrictions—the fines and warnings—and the associated complaints brought by widowed women, have helped researchers understand the contributions women were making to all the craft guilds. A widow's rights to continue to operate her late husband's shop were increasingly constrained, as was her ability to hire journeymen. A guild might only allow the widow to complete work unfinished at the time of death of the male master, and further limited women's economic participation by eliminating their daughters' ability to inherit shops. Guilds might also constrain the master's ability to employ his daughters and, in the most extreme cases, might restrict him from teaching daughters the craft at all (Ellison, Craftswomen and the Guilds, 2016).

Even before increasingly restrictive guild policies magnified their economic disenfranchisement, women were paid less than men for the same work and supplemented their income by making small items for sale, including pins, brooms, brushes, spoons, and bowls. Guilds refrained from regulating the sale of these goods out of the home unless a woman was successful enough that her products were outselling or preferable to those manufactured by (male) guild members. Then it was understood that she had overstepped and would be prohibited from selling those goods (Weisner, 1993).

The apprenticeship structure within the guild system lasted into the mid-nineteenth century when the rise of factory-based production and its attendant labor model transformed all forms of woodworking and "posed legitimate threats to most artisan livelihoods" (Mayer, 2003) in both Europe and, shortly thereafter, the United States. Well into the twentieth century, the exclusion of women from guild membership, the furniture shop, or tradesperson's union was customary—traditional, even—and believed to follow the natural order of things rather than being the result of systematic, exclusionary cultural and economic practices and assumptions. Historically, the social, educational, and institutional barriers to women becoming woodworkers were even more pronounced than those for entry into other applied arts, whether through exclusion from guilds or by assumptions about physical strength or gendered predilection.

Sexual determinism and women's economic participation

With their economic participation increasingly limited, women's lives were confined more and more to marriage and the home. Despite a shift toward a more secular society during the early modern period, sexual determinism persisted, albeit sometimes in the most surprising ways, further limiting women's participation in the public sphere and eroding her economic standing. Because of this erosion, records of women in woodworking-related crafts from the seventeenth and eighteenth centuries are even more scarce. Female apprentices were few—as were shop mistresses—and most of those were widows, as only the woodturning guild allowed women to be masters of their own accord. Still, there are records of a few named women woodcarvers in the Renaissance and Baroque periods who thrived, including Sevillian sculptor Louisa Roldán (1656–1704), Swedish carver Anna Maria [van] Schurman (1607–1678), Dutch carver Anna Tessala, and Bolognese sculptor Properzia di Rossi (1490–1530). There are also records of Swiss and German women carving and making wooden toys, plates, spoons, and ornamental figures (Mayer, 2003).

Among these documented women with significant connections to wood is Kenau Simonsdochter Hasselaer (1526–1588), a wood merchant from

Haarlem in the Netherlands, who has endured as a contemporary folk hero. Widowed in 1562, she continued in business, including owning a ship that made four to five trips to Norway each year carrying wood. Her ship's captain was taken hostage in 1588 and she went to Norway to recover her ship, where she disappeared, presumably at the hands of pirates.

From the Industrial Revolution to the Arts and Crafts movement

The Industrial Revolution began in mid-eighteenth-century England, toward the end of the early modern period, revolutionizing the production of goods—first textiles and later almost everything—and making England the capital of commercial manufacturing. The consequences were enormous, transforming virtually every sector of life at every scale, from the economic, social, environmental, and political landscapes globally, to the role of home and family in the production of goods. Industrialization transformed our collective understanding of labor and value, quickly expanding wage labor and the consumption of fossil fuels to power factory production while also increasing the availability of consumer goods to sectors of society that saw a growth in their disposable income. The centrality of England and, to a lesser extent, its European neighbors in global manufacturing helped usher in a rapid expansion of colonial rule, so that by the early twentieth century European nations controlled more than eighty percent of the globe.

Sarah Tabitha Babbitt

An inquisitive and enterprising weaver in early nineteenth-century United States advanced women's contributions to woodworking in the middle of the Industrial Revolution. Sarah Tabitha Babbitt (1779–1853) grew up in the Shaker community in Harvard, Massachusetts. Sometime between 1810 and 1813 Sister Babbitt watched the workers at the local sawmill using the hand-held **whipsaw** to resaw logs. A whipsaw has a handle at either end of a long blade and requires two workers laboring in rhythmic unison. The blades of the period only cut going forward, meaning that every other pull was just returning the blade to its starting position. Drawing on her knowledge of weaving, Babbitt prototyped a circular blade to improve efficiency (Barrett, 2020). The spinning wheel uses drive wheel, table, treadle, and legs. Babbitt's

Figure 1.5: Isaac Tirion; "Engraving of Haarlem Heroine Kenau Simons Hasselaer in 'Hedendaagse Historie' 1760." (https://upload.wikimedia.org/wikipedia/commons/a/a7/Kenau_Simonsdochter_ Hasselaer.jpg)

design is based on the continuous movement of the drive wheel; the circular sawblade cuts as it spins, and no energy is wasted. After modeling her saw blade with a pedal-powered spinning wheel, the blade was then attached to waterpower, cutting through wood with far less human effort.

The Shaker ethos of sharing intellectual advances—what we think of as intellectual property rights—freely with the whole community precluded Babbitt from filing for a patent, leaving her invention subject to competing claims of being the first. However, Babbitt's circular saw was both distinct enough from its peers to merit a patent of its own and was the one which became popularized in American sawmills (Barrett, 2020). She is credited with later improving on the spinning wheel and was working on false teeth at the time of her death.

Industrial capital and the home

As in medieval Europe, the home and household were the center of production in pre-industrial America. Families worked together to produce what they needed to survive and sold or bartered goods beyond those that met immediate needs. Men were heads of household, but both men and women contributed value to the wellbeing of the family. With much the same impact that the rise of capitalism in early modern Europe had on redefining the labor of men and women, the rise of industrial capitalism in the United States shifted the locations in which men and women labored, and consequently changed how that labor was understood and valued. While on the one hand many women found work in factories, they were fewer in number and worked at a significantly lower wage than their male peers. Men dominated factory work, making goods in the workplace and bringing home their wages. Women's labor at home was unpaid, and their emphasis shifted to making the home a haven for their husbands when they returned from work (Tsongas Industrial History Center/Boott Cotton Mills Museum, n.d.). In 1841 Catherine Esther Beecher, sister of abolitionist Harriet Beecher Stowe, published *A Treatise on Domestic Economy*, a lengthy guide for young women on how to perform domestic duties, with chapters such as "On Clothing" and "On the Care of Parlors." Though a reform-minded advocate for girls' education, Beecher was opposed to suffrage for women, believing women could best contribute as mothers and teachers. These complex—and seemingly contradictory—positions on sex and gender are a useful lens through which to view the many women who believed that girls and young women should focus on their roles in the domestic sphere.

A cyclopaedia of woman's work: Decorative goods in the age of industry

As early as the 1840s steam-powered machines could rip and plane wood, and by 1850 the Industrial Revolution had already made possible mass-produced versions of items that were considered decorative household goods. Despite those technological advancements, artisans from Europe who immigrated to the United States mid-century could still find jobs in their fields. Even furniture factories that had purchased the steam-powered carving machines might nonetheless employ woodworkers and carvers to do detailed, high end work.

In the latter half of the nineteenth and even into the early twentieth centuries, turning and carving were the two arenas within woodworking that remained more generally acceptable for women, who carved or turned individual elements that were often then added to furniture pieces fabricated by men. A couple of woodcarving companies even marketed their tools to women as well as male clientele. In 1863 Virginia Penny published *The Employments of Women: A Cyclopaedia of Woman's Work*, intended

Figure 1.6: Tabitha Babbitt's circular saw, invented 1813. Babbitt's first is in Albany, New York; a larger version of it was then used in the local sawmill. (Alchetron.com)

to educate women about the value of their labor in the years during and after the Civil War, when, as with subsequent wars, more women had to work outside the home. Carving is number 306/516 in the encyclopedia and includes the observation that, "In wood sculpture, all that belongs to its simple ornament might receive a special grace from the inspiration of women" (Penny, 1863).

Philadelphia Centennial International Exhibition

In May 1876 the Philadelphia Centennial International Exhibition (officially the International Exhibition of Arts, Manufactures, and Products of the Soil and Mine)—part celebration of the American Centennial and part international exposition—opened in Fairmount Park in the city most closely associated with American independence. Every state and thirty-seven nations were represented in this event that was both domestic celebration

Figure 1.7: 1876 Centennial Exhibition, Women's Pavilion, interior. (National Gallery of Victoria, Melbourne, The Dr Robert Wilson Collection. Gift of Dr Robert Wilson, 2014, https://www.ngv.vic.gov.au/explore/collection/work/105234/)

and international exposition. The exhibition—positioned at the cusp of the turn of the twentieth century—played a significant role in the history of woodworking and furniture in the US and internationally, in many respects reflecting both the tensions and possibilities of the transition from hand labor to machine production, and from manual to vocational education. The exhibition included examples of machine carving alongside more traditional methods, illuminating the promise that factory production held in replacing hand labor even in tasks most closely associated with craft. Russia, still governed by the tzars, attended, and was represented by a large exhibit, including a display of machine tools made by the students from the Moscow Imperial Technical School. Closer to home, the Grand Rapids Regional furniture movement exhibited an array of furniture works. And perhaps most significantly, the women-dominated Cincinnati Art Carvers displayed more than 200 pieces in the Women's Pavilion, as no women artists were represented in the Memorial Hall Art Exhibit.

The Aesthetic movement and the Cincinnati Art Carvers

> It is a new era for women—that has been opened by women—placing all on an equality, the equality of art; dignifying labor, the labor of love; clearing the path, and elevating and ennobling the labor by which they might earn their daily bread.
>
> (Mayer, 2003, 132; William Fry, 1876, in a
> letter to his father)

In the middle of the nineteenth century, an art-for-art's-sake endeavor emerged in England that drew on John Ruskin's writings and articulated a vision of beautifying the home that was built on regional art idioms rooted in local plant and animal life. Though relatively short-lived in England and supplanted by Arts and Crafts, the Aesthetic movement took shape across the pond in Cincinnati, Ohio, a middle American city that, with its adoption of steam-powered machinery around 1844, had become a hub for the manufacture of wood furniture and a center for decorative arts (Schwarz, 2012). Like Grand Rapids, Michigan, to the north, Cincinnati had an abundance of nearby forests with cherry, oak, maple, poplar, and walnut—hardwoods which were used to make chairs, tables, cabinets, and

CARVED BEDSTEAD.

Figure 1.8: Bedstead carved by Hattie and Mary Johnson and exhibited at the Philadelphia Centennial International Exhibition of 1876. (Wilcox, J. (1878, March). Fret-Sawing and Wood-Carving. *Harper's New Monthly Magazine*, (56), pp. 537. Collection of the Public Library of Cincinnati and Hamilton County)

bed frames. The Cincinnati Art Carvers started in the early 1870s and lasted more than fifty years. About 1,100 students and artisans participated, 851 of whom were women. Altogether, the carvers, best known for carving natural elements in relief, produced between 5,000 and 10,000 objects.

The movement was catalyzed by the arrival in Cincinnati of three British émigré carvers; by the early 1870s Henry Lindley Fry (1807–1895), his son William Henry Fry (1830–1929), and Benn Pitman (1822–1895) were offering private carving classes in what seems to have been a friendly competition among the instructors. Women outnumbered their male peers by about eight to one in the carving classes. According to scholar Roberta Mayer, it was very unusual to have such an enduring movement of hundreds of women publicly and successfully pursuing woodcarving in courses in which they so dramatically outnumbered their male counterparts. Many—though by no means all—of the women students were well-to-do, with time to devote to the craft as well as the ability to bring attention to their work through their social status.

In addition to the private classes, Pitman also launched the wood-carving department at Cincinnati's McMicken School of Design in the 1873–74 academic year, offering equally popular courses. Twenty years later when he resigned from that teaching post (McMicken became Art Academy of Cincinnati in 1887) William Fry took the job (Mayer, 2003). While the three instructors may have seen their wealthier students as potential patrons, all three men also came from a European guild tradition in which women were carvers, and they professed no misgivings about teaching women the craft. Though they believed that furniture fabrication was the province of men, all shared a belief that women had some advantages over their male counterparts in carving, whether through attention to detail or willingness to "labor for love."

> For some women, the carving of items ranging from bread plates to beds to mantelpieces truly did represent a personal desire to create a beautiful home as an emblem of familial harmony and domestic bliss; these women accepted the Ruskinian goals established by their male mentors. For others, carving was a public performance that provided a shared experience of sisterhood. What has not been sufficiently emphasized in the past, however, is that some women also pursued woodcarving as a path to viable employment as independent artists and teachers.
>
> (Mayer, 2003)

In a letter to his father written in 1876, William Fry suggested that women—freed of commercial and economic interests—could carry on the artisan traditions threatened by industrialization (Mayer, 2003). Their beliefs about gender and carving had a complex relationship to tradition: Though the Frys and Pitman all understood that some of their students were interested in professional pursuits, they adhered to and spoke publicly about

A CLASS IN CARVING, CINCINNATI.

Figure 1.9: "A Class in Carving, Cincinnati," Cosmopolitan 18 (November 1894): 28. (Collection of the Public Library of Cincinnati and Hamilton County)

Ruskin's call to "beautify the useful," reinforcing traditional ideas that the home was the domain of women, where they were guardians of harmony and good taste—a role with moral implications. "A house was not only an individual's castle but a moral foundation, a sanctuary from the social ills associated with the industrial city" (Vitz, 2003).

In 1982 scholar Kenneth R. Trapp likened the first year McMicken enrollment roster to the Cincinnati social register. Because the last names of the wealthier students can be cross-referenced with the social register as a historical record, they are easier to track, whereas the other students' names were recorded but harder to trace. At the same time, however, Trapp also noted the five-decades-long duration of the art carvers' movement, which, Mayer argues, has been mostly overlooked by writers citing Trapp's scholarship. The sustained endurance of the movement and many students' long commitment to the study of the craft suggests that there are other histories to uncover. Mary Alice Heekin and Amy L. Miller compiled extensive data that tracks enrollments and gender distribution across the nearly fifty years of wood carving students at McMicken/Art Academy. While more than half of the women studied carving for only a year, nearly one quarter took carving for three or more years, clearly indicating that they sought a higher level of skill and professionalism. More than one hundred of the women carvers participated in large public projects, including the screen for the Cincinnati Music Hall organ. Approximately ten percent became studio artists, nearly four dozen became art or carving teachers, and nine became professional woodcarvers. Only one, Janet Scudder, is known to have entered the male-dominated world of furniture manufacturing. These data don't include those who took private lessons.

Although the carvers regularly showed their work at regional expositions and attracted national and international attention, they were often their own consumers; few pieces were sold relative to the large number of works created. Some of those who tried to sell their work were met with resistance. When a few women carvers attached price tags to their work at the Philadelphia Centennial, they attracted the attention of men in the field who were quick to predicate the future success of these carvers on the generosity of male architects to employ them. There is, however, evidence that some women found paid carving oppor-tunities privately, and suggestions that still others may have sold their work through the Cincinnati Women's Exchange, which provided low-income women a marketplace for homemade wares while preserving their privacy.

~

One of the more extraordinary members was Adina White (ca. 1861–1930), the only known African American woman carver in Cincinnati, who started out with ambitions that extended beyond the beautification of her home, church, or community. Born into an abolitionist community in New Richmond, Ohio, White began carving as a child. "I used to cut figures on everything that came in my way when I was a very small child," she relayed to novelist and editor Pauline Hopkins, who wrote an article about White for the *Boston Globe* in 1900 and featured her in the series "Famous Women of the Negro Race" for *The Colored American Magazine*. "It always seemed natural for me to do this since I used to

Figure 1.10: Catherine Peachey, writing desk, 1870. (https://commons.wikimedia.org/wiki/
File:Writing_Desk_by_Catherine_Peachey,_1870s,_American_black_walnut,_mahogany,_black_cherry,_
yellow_poplar,_brass_-_Cincinnati_Art_Museum_-_DSC03041.JPG)

make toy teacups and miniature baskets out of peach stones" (Hopkins, 1902). White's interest in and skill at drawing led to her studying under Pitman at both McMicken School of Design and the Cincinnati Art Academy.

A dressing bureau and picture frame that White carved were part of a large collection of Pitman's students' work sent to the Women's Pavilion at the

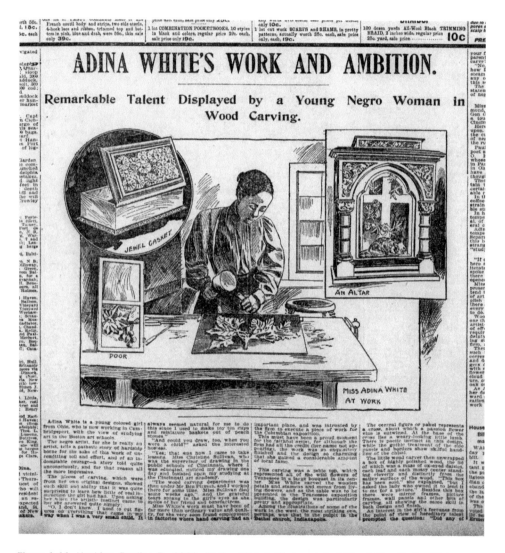

Figure 1.11: Hopkins, Pauline E., 1900, "Adina White's Work and Ambition." *The Boston Globe*, February 4, p. 24. (Newspapers.com)

Philadelphia Centennial International Exhibition, and White was one of more than 100 women who carved the elaborate organ screen for the Cincinnati Music Hall. By the end of the decade, White was at least partially supporting herself from the sale of her work. In the early 1890s, she was one of three women—and the only African American woman—in the city directory listed as an independent woodcarver (Mayer, 2003). She did hand carving in a factory where she made a tabletop that included a large, central, carved bouquet of Tennessee wildflowers, which was exhibited in the Tennessee Exposition Building at the World's Columbian Exposition in Chicago in 1893. White also carved the pulpit at the AME Bethel Church in Indianapolis: "The central figure or panel represents a cross, about which a passionflower vine is entwined. At the base of the cross lies a weary-looking lamb. There is poetic instinct in the design, while the gothic treatment of the side panels and borders show skilful [sic] handling" (Friends of Mount Auburn, 2020).

White later moved to St. Louis, where she taught drawing, and eventually went on to Massachusetts, where, as both a property owner and business owner around 1900, she continued her art study and worked as a woodcarver.

~

Despite being rooted in Aesthetic values of clear design and material integrity, the style of woodcarving taught by Pitman and the Frys became associated with Victorian excess and waned in popularity after the turn of the century. Between 1910 and 1920 diminished interest in hand-wrought carving coincided with the rapid growth of mass-produced goods for the home, fueled by the electrification of factory motors. Fewer craftsmen were employed in the factories, and men felt the threat of competition more acutely. Most of the women carvers moved on to other creative media, including china painting, ceramics, or metal work (Vitz, 2003). The movement died in 1926 when William Fry taught his last class.

The art and craft of resistance

Though the Aesthetic movement was a response to the perceived ugliness of the Industrial Age, it was not accompanied by the kind of philosophical and political critique that was more fully articulated in the Arts and Crafts movement, which overlapped with and eventually supplanted Aestheticism. Taking the rejection of industrialization a step further, the Arts and Crafts movement was a call to resist and reform factory production—for the laborer and the material goods created. Machine production, it was said, "crushed [the art instinct] out of the laborer," (Addams, 1902) while adherents of the movement also reacted against the perceived "shoddiness" of factory-made furniture, pursuing instead idealistic concepts of honesty in construction and the worth of the individual in the making process.

A network of guilds, organizations, and clubs, the Arts and Crafts movement called for design reform, the unity of arts and crafts, and railed against the classical art education model that rigidly distinguished between the fine and decorative arts. In particular, English designer, writer, activist, and theorist William Morris advocated for hand-made alternatives to the cheaply made goods he saw fabricated in factory assembly lines, where the wage laborer had no control over the design of goods and worked without a relationship to the whole production cycle. He pointed to this as a contradiction intrinsic to modern life and especially at odds with the American narrative: A culture that celebrated the individual had produced an economic model in which the individual had no control (Adamson, 2021). However, the economic challenges and contradictions of the handmade model were intrinsic from the outset. Handicrafts necessarily mean higher labor costs; since the beginning of the Arts and Crafts movement, makers have struggled with reconciling the call for social reform with the aesthetic dimensions and their attendant costs, seeking to provide quality designed and crafted goods to consumers of limited economic means.

The Arts and Crafts movement was in many ways an idealistic or romantic movement that celebrated "real" over imitation, "essence" over superficiality. Designer and maker should be one and the same in creating objects that were less about perfection as an end in itself, and more about the role of objects and the process of making in the creation of a meaningful life. Popular culture rooted in Arts and Crafts romanticism invites us to imagine the singular craftsperson hunched over their bench with an almost spiritual relationship to their tools and the wood, which they make conform to their imagination. While historians have already deconstructed the problems of this romantic narrative and linked it to the Western European colonial pursuit, the story still pervades our collective imaginary, standing in for a better, purer past of integrity through workmanship. This nostalgic narrative valorizes the individual, who—through the flow state of concentration and labor—enters a place outside of themselves. This is a meditation of busy hands and a mind cleared through engagement with a task.

American and English versions of the Arts and Crafts movement diverged in their relationships to technology in ways that can be linked to larger cultural and economic imperatives. Believing that art should be for and by ordinary thinking people engaged in handicraft, English designers working with Morris's ideas most often rejected the inhuman machine and created works that showed conspicuous labor, sometimes in the extreme. A deeper faith in technology and a stronger value on commercialism prevailed in the United States, where Arts and Crafts adherents instead argued for the wise use of technology rather than its outright rejection.

Morris's solution to the capitalist conundrum of higher labor costs resulting in higher costs of goods was straightforward: He advocated dismantling capitalism. Most American Arts and Crafts movement members did not go as far as Morris in their anti-capitalist sentiments; many embraced the moral and aesthetic dimensions over the call for social and economic reform. That said, some adhered to the economic theories of the American political economist and journalist Henry George, who observed that the growing wealth inequality that accompanied technological and industrial advances was related to land ownership. George railed against the fact that private profit was being earned from restricting access to natural resources; he advocated a land tax in place of taxing profits from one's own labor.

Though informed by Morris' and Ruskin's deeply philosophical tenets about the integrity of labor and honesty of materials, the Arts and Crafts movement in the US brought comparatively few social reforms; the settlement house movement is the most prominent of them. Settlement houses took shape first in England, before spreading throughout much of the United States after social worker and reformist Jane Addams visited London's settlement house Toynbee Hall. By 1913 there were more than 413 settlement houses across thirty-two states, including Hull House in Chicago, which Addams cofounded. They were fueled by a social and economic critique of industrial labor conditions and the concomitant growth in urban immigrant communities living in substandard tenements. Settlement houses, often led by women, were designed to bring communities together across class and culture, support immigrants to retain their cultural heritage, and promote reciprocal relationships across class, economic mobility, and participation in democratic processes. Working within the settlement house movement allowed women some measure of autonomy to engage with architecture, design, and housing because it happened under the framework of philanthropy (LaFarge, 2019).

Addams spoke specifically to the relationship between Arts and Crafts and the settlement house movement: "Ruskin has said that labor without art brutalizes. The man who labors without knowing why he does it, without any refreshment or solace from his labor, grows more or less dehumanized" (Addams, 1902). At Hull House—as at many settlement houses—community members participated in arts and crafts, linking the material and cultural traditions of their country of origin to the experience of their new home, passing skills down generations, and experiencing the solace of making (Addams, 1902).

While Arts and Crafts as a design philosophy may have been supplanted by machine-age Modernism in the 1920s, and the settlement house movement became a thread in a complex web of non-profit services and urban programming, the aesthetic and moral values articulated within Arts and Crafts continue to shape our cultural conception of the individual maker. Echoes of the movement are evident in our image of craft or handiwork as a value intrinsically related to the expression of the self in the world. Beyond its monetary rewards or the utility of a product, we often understand *meaningful work*—taking an object from design to completion—to be both beneficial to the worker and an expression of our humanity.

American industry

Furniture City: Grand Rapids, Michigan

By the middle of the nineteenth century, Grand Rapids, Michigan, had emerged in the US as "Furniture City," so much so that a furniture manufacturer in Grand Rapids, Minnesota, failed to mention Minnesota in its advertisements, hoping to capitalize on the other's renown (Lewis, 2008). As late as 1836 it was still a trading post on the frontier, but as the century wore on and northeastern forests were increasingly depleted,

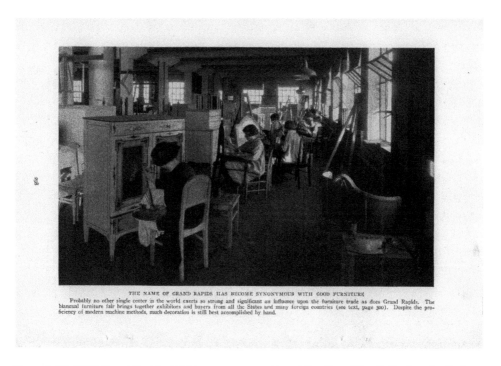

THE NAME OF GRAND RAPIDS HAS BECOME SYNONYMOUS WITH GOOD FURNITURE
Probably no other single center in the world exerts so strong and significant an influence upon the furniture trade as does Grand Rapids. The biannual furniture fair brings together exhibitors and buyers from all the States and many foreign countries (see text, page 300). Despite the proficiency of modern machine methods, much decoration is still best accomplished by hand.

Figure 1.12: 1928 Grand Rapids, Michigan, women working at Furniture City. (Author's collection)

immigrants moved west. They were both labor force and consumer base for growing markets in the Midwest and Great Lakes region. The pine and hardwood forests outside Grand Rapids yielded valuable lumber for harvest, and sawmills and woodworking—particularly furniture making—businesses began to flourish. Felled logs were floated down the Grand River and milled in the city. Both milled lumber and manufactured goods could be shipped out via the Great Lakes or the growing rail system, solidifying the city's reputation as a furniture capital for the country, which attracted buyers from around the world (Schaetzl, n.d.).

Margaret E. Page (1888–unknown) was the first female furniture designer in Grand Rapids at a time when—though women were employed in factories doing detailing and finish work—few women entered the design field. Interested in drawing since she was nine years old, she decided to pursue the arts and then committed to furniture design, with the belief that since women were the primary decision makers about retail furniture, there was an important role for them in its design. Page began as an apprentice with freelance commercial designer Otto Jiranek, mastering working drawings and blueprints. She also took drawing classes, mechanical drafting, rod making, and furniture construction. Intent on mastering both the mechanical and design facets of furniture, but unsatisfied with the pace of her progress, she left Jiranek's office and accepted a job with John D. Raab, who encouraged her to open her own studio in 1912, running both the business and design ends. She designed pieces for factories across the country, going to them personally to stay on top of manufacturing techniques from construction methods to finishes. Page's gender perhaps gave her unique insight over the competition as she acutely understood women's roles in the factory as well as the household, remarking that "since it is generally conceded that ninety percent of the furniture retailed is selected by women, their enlightenment on this subject would greatly improve further conditions" (Margaret E. Page, City's First Woman Designer, n.d.).

High Point, North Carolina

By the late nineteenth century, High Point, North Carolina, and the Piedmont region in which it is located, had an emergent furniture industry. A factory opened there in 1889 and, as in the Midwest, the furniture industry grew, supported by abundant local forests, a new Southern Railway, and cheaper, non-unionized labor. Shortly after the turn of the century, a few dozen ambitious manufacturers decided to create a local furniture exposition that would compete with the more established and popular events in Chicago, New York, and Grand Rapids, which still held the title, "Furniture City of the United States." The first Southern Furniture Market was held in High Point in 1909. With the depletion of local forests and the start of World War I, Grand Rapids' manufacturing sector began to diversify and move into metals; ultimately, Grand Rapids lost its furniture crown to High Point. By the end of World War I, the southeastern city was holding large exhibitions twice-yearly (except for the years of the Second World War).

Seeing the direction in which things were moving, in 1932 Page relocated from Grand Rapids to Lenoir, North Carolina, not far from High Point (Margaret E. Page, City's First Woman Designer, n.d.). The scale of the North Carolina furniture manufacturing industry continued to grow through the rest of the twentieth century, eclipsing Grand Rapids in the 1960s and exploding further in the 1980s and 1990s with an enormous increase in square footage of showroom space. In 1989 the Southern Furniture Market became the International Home Furnishings Market, and by the mid-1990s had nearly 14,000,000 square feet of exhibition space (The Evolution of High Point Market, 2009).

Postcards and the popular imagination

In Europe—and particularly in France—the decades on either side of the turn of the twentieth century came to be known as the *Belle Époque*, or "Beautiful Epoch." Predating the devastation of the First World War, the period was marked by optimism and a flourishing cultural sector, economic prosperity and colonial expansion, and social progressivism, with a growing movement for sexual parity. The first generation of women emerging from universities with the expectation of moving into formerly male-dominated careers were met with cultural anxiety—and in some cases outright hostility—about what this shift in gender roles might mean. In this golden age of postcards, when they were broadly exchanged and kept in albums by the recipients, European publishers created series of postcards depicting "The Emancipated Woman," and "The Woman of the Future." Thousands of postcards were printed with a stark difference between the treatment of women moving into new professional terrain and those in working class jobs that had been previously deemed more acceptable.

In what from today's vantage point reads as a campy visual language, large-bosomed and bawdy women with mischievous, playful, or sexually suggestive expressions are dressed in military uniforms two sizes too small, or in sexually alluring clothing with a helmet perched atop their heads. A woman lawyer is depicted with a child in tow or unruly locks escaping the confines of her legal cap, suggesting that her more slatternly nature was incompatible with the formal rigor of the profession. Female doctors met with somewhat less derision, as it was a field linked to the care of others (a feminine trait), but nonetheless were also sometimes depicted in sexually provocative ways. Such postcards were novelties, confirming that these liberated women weren't suited to the demanding professional roles they sought. By contrast, in an analysis of 314 postcards from the period, scholar Juliette Rennes argues that working class women in factories, mines, or more traditional proletarian roles weren't subjected to this mockery. Instead, whether oyster gatherers or shepherdesses, they were portrayed on these postcards doing difficult work in challenging conditions (Rennes, 2013).

The importance of self-representation: Juliette Caron

> The lady carpenter works these days at the machine depot. Dad has seen her ... she works well, they say. She works hard and doesn't mind people watching her.
>
> (Unattributed)

Born in 1882, Juliette Caron was the first female *compagnon*—journeyman— in France. The daughter of a mason, Caron worked on the repair of the barracks of Montluçon, the commune where she resided, though she earned two to three francs per day compared to the six to ten earned by her male colleagues. The unattributed quote above suggests that she was something of a spectacle, which is reinforced by a series of at least five photographic postcards of her at work that were printed, distributed, and sold by Caron herself. She was posed in a manner that was consonant with the labor she was performing, dressed in attire that would have been likely the most pragmatic allowable for a woman at the time, and positioned with her tools as they would have been used, representing herself as competent and the labor she was performing as not intrinsically gendered. She was, as accurately as the medium allowed, just being herself.

Though certainly aware that her presence on the construction site was novel and thus potentially marketable, it is likely that Caron also saw these depictions as calling cards for more women to enter the trades. Published at the same time as "The Emancipated Woman" and "The Woman of the Future" postcards, Caron's contribution struck a decidedly more serious— and ultimately more enduring—cultural note.

~

At the same time, in the US a series of postcards from 1910 also reflect the growing popularity—albeit novelty—of women working in traditionally male domains. Published by F. Blum, the cards commonly depict a white woman dressed in haphazardly cutoff overalls, a puffy-sleeved crisp white blouse,

Figure 1.13: Juliette Caron postcard triptych. The caption notes that she was the only woman in France working in carpentry. Caron designed and distributed this series of postcards. (Public domain)

Figure 1.14: Series of postcards from F. Blum printed in 1910. (Author's collection)

stockings, and low-heeled dress shoes, wielding various tools associated with manual labor, including woodworking, masonry, or mechanical work.

Utilizing one of the images of the dark-haired model from the Blum card photo shoot (Figure 1.14) is a customized postcard with a stamp for Ranchester, Wyoming, a timber mill town. On the road between Billings, Montana, and Rapid City, South Dakota, Ranchester's local timber was milled for railroad ties. In 1908, the Big Horn Timber Company had only recently purchased the existing mill and log flume and was planning to expand, adding jobs and increasing business in the town. Civic boosters were working feverishly to get Ranchester incorporated, so it is not a coincidence that a postcard was selected featuring a woman holding a square to promote the town. With its smiling playfulness and straightforward message—"The girls are on the square in Ranchester, Wyoming/But wise just the same"— the card did at least two things: It let enterprising, independent women know that there were non-traditional labor opportunities awaiting them in Ranchester, and it also let eligible men know that there were women in this

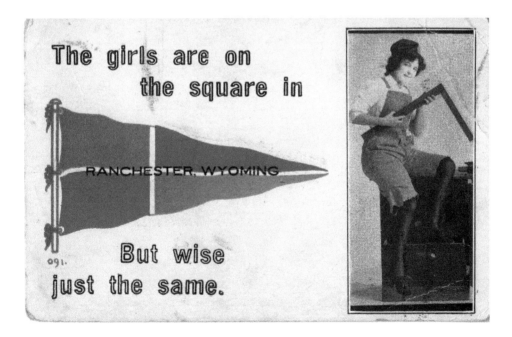

Figure 1.15: Early twentieth-century postcard customized for Ranchester, Wyoming (1920 pop. ~ 150; 2010 pop. <1000). (Author's collection)

tiny town in Wyoming who could more than hold their own, in both cases making Ranchester a desirable destination for putting down roots. Though the actual answers are surely varied, it can be reasonably understood that the intent—and the outcome—was to support boosterism, not hinder it.

The popular imagination plays an integral role in women's movement into non-traditional spaces, and these hundred-year-old material culture artifacts were an early indicator that there was more to the history of women in woodworking than is visible in familiar histories or arts-based narratives. With photographic *cartes-de-visite*, cabinet cards, and postcards sparking a collecting craze in the second half of the nineteenth century, such representations became prized possessions, denoting the holders' intellect, curiosity, and worldliness. According to photo historian Carla Williams, members of the middle and upper classes would have albums of photographs and postcards from around the world that they would share with visitors to their homes. It is easy, Williams (2020) notes, to imagine Caron's novel, progressive images, or the seriously silly Blum cards, in such private compendiums.

References

Adamson, G. (2021). *Craft, An American History.* New York, NY: Bloomsbury.

Addams, J. (1902, July 9). *Arts and Crafts and the Settlement.* Retrieved March 2021, from Jane Addams Digital Edition: https://digital.janead dams.ramapo.edu/items/show/1166

Barrett, P. (2020, July 2). *Tabitha Babbitt (1779–1853).* Retrieved March 31, 2021, from The Mills Archive: https://new.millsarchive. org/2020/07/02/tabitha-babbitt-1779-1853/

Britannica, T. E. (2011, February 8). *Spring and Autumn Period, Chinese History.* Retrieved December 30, 2020, from Brittanica: https://www. britannica.com/event/Spring-and-Autumn-Period

Ellison, S. (2016, April 18). *Craftswomen and the Guilds.* Retrieved June 2019, from Lost Art Press: blog.lostartpress.com/2016/04/18/crafts women-and-the-guilds

Ellison, S. (2016, April 24). *From La Femme de Charpentier to the Lumberjill.* Retrieved June 2019, from Lost Art Press: blog.lostartpress. com/2016/04/24/from-la-femme-de-charpentier-to-the-lumberjill

Ellison, S. (2016, April 14). *Women in the Workshop*. Retrieved May 2019, from Lost Art Press: blog.lostartpress.com/2016/04/14/women-in-the-workshop

Friends of Mount Auburn. (2020, May 1). *Adina E. White (1861?–1930)*. Retrieved June 19, 2021, from https://mountauburn.org/adina-e-white-1861-1930/

Hopkins, P. E. (1900, February 4). "Adina White's Work and Ambition". *The Boston Globe*, p. 24. Retrieved from Newspapers.com.

Hopkins, P. E. (1902, September). "Famous Women of the Negro Race: X: Artists". *The Colored American Magazine*, pp. 362–367. Retrieved 2021, from The Colored American: http://coloredamerican.org/wp-content/uploads/2017/02/CAM_5.5_1902.09.NS_.pdf

Johru Bahru Furniture Association. (2012). "Luban Comic Strips – (pp. 67–70)." Retrieved December 2020, from https://jbfurniture.com.my/jbfa/index.php/en/about-us/aboutluban/lubanxiaozhuan (last accessed 12/2020)

LaFarge, A. (2019). *Louise Brigham and the Early History of Sustainable Furniture Design*. Cham, Switzerland: Palgrave McMillan.

Lewis, N. (2008). *Grand Rapids: Furniture City*. Charleston, South Carolina: Arcadia.

Margaret E. Page, City's First Woman Designer. (n.d.). Retrieved May 2021, from Furniture City History: http://www.furniturecityhistory.org/article/4389/margaret-e-page-citys-first-wo

Mayer, R. A. (2003). "Against the Grain"? Perspectives on Women and Woodcarving in Cincinnati, 1873–1925. In E. J. Howe, *Cincinnati Art-Carved Furniture and Interiors* (pp. 121–147). Athens: Ohio University Press.

National Gallery of Victoria, Melbourne (2014). The Dr Robert Wilson Collection. Gift of Dr Robert Wilson. Retrieved from https://www.ngv.vic.gov.au/explore/collection/work/105234/

Penny, V. (1863). *The Employments of Women: A Cyclopaedia of Woman's Work*. Boston: Walker, Wise, and Company.

Rennes, J. (2013). *Femmes en métier d'hommes, cartes postales 1890–1930*. Saint-Pourçain-sur-Sioule: Bleu Autour, pp. 72–83.

Ruitenbeek, K. (1993). *Carpentry and Building in Late Imperial China: A Study of the Fifteenth-century Carpenter's Manual, Lu Ban Jing*. Leiden, New York: EJ. Brill.

Schaetzl, D. R. (n.d.). *The Grand Rapids Furniture Industry*. Retrieved March 2021, from The Geography of Michigan and the Great Lakes Region: https://project.geo.msu.edu/geogmich/furniture_mfg.html

Schwarz, C. (2012, October 9). *Cincinnati's (Unvarnished) Woodworking History*. Retrieved June 2021, from Lost Art Press: https://blog.lostart-press.com/2012/10/09/cincinnatis-unvarnished-woodworking-history/

Taylor, K. (2009–2021). *Women Woodworking, Now & Then*. Retrieved June 2021, from Wooden-Box-Maker.com: https://www.wooden-box-maker.com/women-woodworking.html (last accessed 12/2020)

The Evolution of High Point Market. (2009, April 25). Retrieved March 2021, from Furniture Today: https://www.furnituretoday.com/business-news/the-evolution-of-the-high-point-market/

Tsongas Industrial History Center/Boott Cotton Mills Museum. (n.d.). *The Role of Women in the Industrial Revolution*. Retrieved April 2021, from Tsongas Industrial History Center: https://www.uml.edu/tsongas/barilla-taylor/women-industrial-revolution.aspx

Vitz, R. C. (2003). Cincinnati and the Decorative Arts: The Foundations. In J. Howe (Ed.), *Cincinnati Art-Carved Furniture and Interiors*. Athens, Ohio: Ohio University Press.

Weisner, M. (1993). *Women and Gender in Early Modern Europe*. Cambridge: Cambridge University Press.

Wilcox, J. (1878, March). Fret-Sawing and Wood-Carving. *Harper's New Monthly Magazine*, (56), pp. 537.

Williams, C. (2020, September 8). (D. Visser Interviewer).

Chapter Two

Changing educational models

From the 1890s to the 1910s, the Progressive Era in the United States was marked by an array of social movements that included organizing for women's suffrage, calls to end the power of political bosses, and a range of efforts to use science and rationalism to address the challenges brought on by industrialization, widespread urban poverty, and influxes of low-income European immigrants. Though the philosophical and ideological roots of what was understood as "progressive" varied, the changes advocated in the nation's educational system reflected a belief in using schools "as a vehicle of social reform and individual improvement" (Reese, 2003).

In this context, trade and craft skills—but most specifically woodworking—emerged in two competing models of shop class in American education. The Russian system of industrial arts and Educational Slöjd (Sloyd) both had European origins and were introduced in the United States at the 1876 Centennial International Exhibition in Philadelphia. Both were manual education models, and each sought to educate the "whole boy" with a shortened general education curriculum and an expanded and integrated program of manual skill development, but there were important differences. Educational Sloyd was a non-vocational pedagogy premised on the belief that learning manual skills—particularly woodworking—offered cognitive, emotional, and even moral benefits for student development, whether or not they pursued a manual career. The Russian system of industrial arts was more explicitly vocational, and intended to foster mechanical dexterity and train young people for future employment in industrial fields. It was presented in Philadelphia in an exhibit of student work which demonstrated its systematic sequencing of skill development. This captured the imagination of Dr. John

DOI: 10.4324/9780429345418-3

D. Runkle, then president of Massachusetts Institute of Technology (MIT). Runkle and his colleagues at MIT were struggling to balance the theoretical curriculum of engineering students with practical, hands-on mastery of tools and fabrication processes. His attention to the Russian System can arguably be credited with the growth of manual training in US schools; the curricular model was ultimately replicated in classroom shops across the country.

Pedagogy and culture

The underlying rationale for devising a distinctive curriculum for women was the same: women were to be trained to be effective wives and mothers. Men, on the other hand, were to be prepared for a variety of roles in the wage economy.

(Rury, 1984, 38)

Through most of the nineteenth century, school curricula and pedagogy were structured on classical studies taught in Greek and Latin, an increasingly outdated model as the century wore on. The degree to which this curriculum was detached from the reality of American life was reflected in low enrollment in secondary education. Fueled by demographic changes in cities and towns across the United States and an industrial sector that was transforming both labor practices and conceptions of work, the progressive vision of public education broadened to address the perceived needs of working- and middle-class students.

Implemented variously in public and private schools and at different levels of education, the vision and possibilities of manual education and its successor, vocational education, were limited by normative cultural values and assumptions. Since the antebellum period and the emergence of a vision for public education in the US, co-education had been a celebrated value understood as a measure of the nation's progressive vision. At the same time, it was widely accepted that men's and women's roles and economic opportunities were—and should be—different. The rise of vocationalism in education tied classroom curricula directly to future employment (or one's vocational destiny), resulting in sexually differentiated curricula at both the junior high and high school levels, running counter to the foundational value of co-education. By the early twentieth century American students spent increasing amounts of time in single-sex educational environments limited by gendered anxieties about the home and family.

The consequences of the manual and vocational education systems mirroring and reinforcing cultural norms are many, but in the context of this study, the educational route that opened up woodworking as a possibility to most young males was—through much of the last century—closed to young women. Instead, the arts have played a critical role in opening the door to women interested in woodworking and furniture.

Educational Sloyd, an introduction

Educational Sloyd, started by Finnish educator Uno Cignaeus in 1865 and further articulated in the 1870s by Otto Salomon in Sweden, was a principled pedagogy premised on the idea that craft and manual skill development has cognitive, emotional, and even moral dimensions; Sloyd became part of early education for both boys and girls in schools that adopted it. Salomon and his compatriot August Abrahamson began to promote the pedagogy around the world through the publication of Salomon's first book, *The Slöjd in the Service of the School*, and it was they who sent models to the Centennial Exhibition (Stowe, 2008).

Sloyd was first implemented in the US educational system in the late 1880s at the progressive North Bennet Street School, a private school founded in Boston's North End in 1879. It was subsequently introduced in New York and beyond as teacher trainees took the practice back to their districts and schools. While the term *Sloyd* translates to any manual skills, woodworking was believed to be most conducive to the development of the desired mental, moral, and physical characteristics in young children, as this quotation culled from an early treatise attests:

> The influence of slöjd is cultivating and educative ... certain faculties of true value for life reach a development which could not be attained otherwise, or, at least, not in the same degree ... it is usual to bring forward pleasure in bodily labour, and respect for it, habits of independence, increase of physical strength, development of the power of observation in the eye, and of execution in the hand.
>
> (Salomon, 1892)

Between 1880 and 1907, 5,500 teachers from more than forty countries were trained as Sloyd educators. At North Bennet Street School, it is estimated that from 1890 to shortly after the turn of the century the school trained hundreds of teachers, both men and women, who in turn taught about 34,000 students (Stowe, 2004). The legacy of Sloyd is visible in the pedagogies of schools—often private—who have embraced the values of "head, heart, and hands." This system of educating the whole student also seems to have philosophical and pedagogical parallels with Rudolph Steiner and the Waldorf program, which emerged close to forty-five years later and continues into the present. Though it doesn't place woodworking at its center, Waldorf does value handicrafts for pedagogical and philosophical rather than vocational reasons. Still mandatory in Finland, Denmark, Sweden, and Norway, Educational Sloyd continues to inform local woodworking clubs and groups across the United States but is no longer formalized in any school system in the US despite its undeniable early influence.

The woodworking classes offered at North Bennet beg further questions. What happened to the women who were trained at North Bennet to teach children woodworking? Did any of them pursue further training? Miguel Gómez-Ibáñez, former President of North Bennet Street, could point to no record of them pursuing woodworking on their own (Gómez-Ibáñez, 2018), however, it is difficult to believe that not one of them pursued the imaginative possibilities.

Historically Black colleges and universities: Industrial education
and the Arts and Crafts movement

> Slavery presented a problem of destruction; freedom presents a problem of construction.
>
> (Washington, 1903)

In post-Reconstruction United States—what historian Rayford Logan termed the "nadir of the Negro's status in American society"—many Black scholars, writers, and artists navigated a complex relationship to white cultural ideals, of which the Arts and Crafts movement was at the forefront. Historically Black colleges and universities (HBCUs) were established primarily in the segregated South following the Civil War with the assistance of Northern white missionaries to educate formerly enslaved people and their descendants to foster self-sufficiency. At most HBCUs in the nineteenth and well into the twentieth centuries, the administrators and faculty were all white, so it is unsurprising that the tenets of the Arts and Crafts movement would seem perfectly adaptable to a population so newly out of bondage.

As such, Ruskin's philosophies of labor and art had a formidable influence on college-educated Black art and culture of the period. Elaine Pinson's 2012 thesis, "'The Dignity of Labor:' African-American Connections to the Arts and Crafts Movement, 1868–1915," elaborates on this overlapping history, citing shared tenets for "moral education," and social reform rooted in honoring labor. If the Arts and Crafts movement sought to reclaim the dignity of labor in the face of the diminishing effects of factory work and mechanization, manual or industrial education for African Americans sought to redeem labor in the wake of the dehumanizing degradation of enslavement (Pinson, 2012). While too often manual and vocational education—"shop class"—has reinforced racialized and gendered ideas about what students can and should pursue in the world, manual education in some HBCUs at the turn of the twentieth century disrupted normative gender assumptions while explicitly and critically addressing the history of slavery and its impacts on one's conception of self and opportunities in the labor market.

Educator Booker T. Washington was an internationally recognized proponent of industrial education. He built Tuskegee Normal and Industrial Institute (now Tuskegee University) in Alabama consonant with Ruskin's ideal integration of morality, labor, nature, and art in a design language of pastoralism (Bieze, 2005). In a comprehensive essay on the advantages of industrial education at Tuskegee published in *The Atlantic* magazine in 1903, Washington explored both the pragmatic and philosophical arguments. He began by establishing the cultural and political context for discourse in the post-Reconstruction era, a time in which he described deep and bitter divisions between Black and white and North and South, with little landscape of shared ground. He saw in industrial education for African Americans "the first basis for anything like sympathetic interest and action between the two races in the South and between whites in the North and those in the South." In fact, he went on, industrial education "furnished a basis for mutual faith and cooperation" (Washington, 1903).

Washington describes what we understand today to be the deeply racist premises on which much of the white support for industrial education was predicated, while also heralding the possibilities of finding shared interest that would support the economic development of the South at a time when the vast majority of immigration and investment was occurring in the North. For example, in 1892, of the one million immigrants to the US, only 2,278 moved into southern states. While manual training was growing in the North, it wasn't until it proved so successful for African Americans that southern white schools began to adopt it. Washington concludes his essay by arguing that opposition to manual education lessened with time, as it allowed students to gain an economic foundation from which to succeed. "It is now seen that the result of such education will be to help the black man to make for himself an independent place in our great American life" (Washington, 1903).

Washington had worked his way through college as a janitor at Hampton Normal and Industrial Institute in Virginia, an experience that shaped his educational philosophy and belief in "the dignity of labor," a phrase attributed to Ruskin in the mid-1870s. Hampton Institute, which survives today as Hampton University, was founded three years after the end of the Civil War in 1868 by General Samuel Chapman Armstrong with the support of pro-abolitionist missionaries. Armstrong had been raised in Hawaii by missionary parents and exposed to a school for native Hawaiians in which the students were required to perform manual labor. That experience informed his belief that the newly emancipated African Americans should be equipped with practical, manual skills. And not only African Americans: Between 1878 and 1923, more than 1,400 Native Americans representing sixty-six tribal groups traveled to Hampton to participate in a program that would become the forerunner of the US government's late nineteenth-century boarding school system.

Like Educational Sloyd, the object of manual education at Hampton was to shape the mental, moral, and physical characteristics of a person. "A rounded character rather than mere technical skills is our point" (Talbot, 1904). The curricula at both Hampton and Tuskegee reflected a balance of academics and trade skills; a 1910 catalog at Hampton—which fifteen years earlier already included thirteen subject areas, from carpentry to printing, and from wheelwrighting to tailoring—clearly indicated that students must pass the academic courses to enroll in trade skills classes. As early as 1886 carpentry classes at Hampton were co-educational. "All are taught the use of the hammer, the plane, the saw, and the chisel, also the simple principles

Figure 2.1: Young African American women training in Educational Sloyd at Hampton Institute, Hampton, Virginia. While there were many industrial schools for African American students in this time, Hampton and Tuskegee were the most influential and enduring. Note that the instructor in the foreground is a white woman, likely a former student of the Sloyd method. (Frances Benjamin Johnston Collection, LOC, LC USZ62–121908, https://www.loc.gov/resource/cph.3c21908/)

of house building and hoe to make useful articles for school use" (Pinson, 2012). As with the students trained in Sloyd at North Bennet, there appears to be no extant record of if or how the women trained in these shop settings at Hampton pursued woodworking after school.

Some African Americans opposed Washington's philosophy in part because of its white proponents. Others feared that it meant compromising political power since classical education was still the norm, particularly for wealthier whites. And yet others believed it would limit the development of the student, "smothering ... his spiritual and aesthetic nature" (Washington, 1903).

W.E.B. Du Bois, co-founder of the National Association for the Advancement of Colored People (NAACP), was among those who believed that given the state of industrialization, manual education was already obsolete, and "that industrial education would relegate blacks to continued second-class citizenship" (Pinson, 2012). However, to the contemporary eye there is less distinction between Du Bois' and Washington's positions than history has maintained. The Paris Exposition of 1900 (*Exposition universelle internationale de 1900*) included an exhibition on what it termed "social economy," for which Du Bois and journalist and educator Thomas J. Calloway assembled for the US exhibition a collection of 500 photographs, thirty-two charts, and additional maps and plans illustrating the advancements African Americans had made since the Emancipation Proclamation. As Calloway described it:

> It was decided in advance to try to show ten things concerning the negroes in America since their emancipation: (1) Something of the negro's history; (2) education of the race; (3) effects of education upon illiteracy; (4) effects of education upon occupation; (5) effects of education upon property; (6) the negro's mental development as shown by the books, high class pamphlets, newspapers, and other periodicals written or edited by members of the race; (7) his mechanical genius as shown by patents granted to American negroes; (8) business and industrial development in general; (9) what the negro is doing for himself [through] his own separate church organizations, particularly in the work of education; (10) a general sociological study of the racial conditions in the United States.
>
> (Terrell, 2015)

Du Bois believed that photographic representation of the breadth and richness of African American experience and culture would challenge and undermine the racist social and scientific claims of the period. The photographic exhibition included a broad range of images, including African American home and business ownership, military regiments and religious orders, and HBCU classrooms from sewing to the sciences to the woodshop. Pinson's analysis links the accomplishments of African American industrial education to the respectable homes and solid institutions pictured in the exhibition (Pinson, 2012).

~

Figure 2.2: Co-educational manual training shop at Claflin University, Orangeburg, SC, 1899. Exhibited at the 1900 Paris Exposition. (LOC LC-USZ62–107846, https://www.loc.gov/resource/cph.3c07846/)

Louise Brigham and the possibilities of the box

While HBCU students were trained in self-sufficiency, self-reliance, and careful use of resources as a matter of survival, thirty-one-year-old Bostonian Louise Brigham created a broader model for sustainability decades before it became a widely addressed social, economic, and ecological question. In 1906, Brigham spent several summer months as the guest of family friends who managed a coal mining camp on Spitsbergen, a Norwegian island more than 750 miles north of the Arctic circle. The nearest supplies—which only arrived in the summertime—came from 535 miles to the south and east. Much of the year the camp was cut off by snow and ice. What did arrive came in cheaply made wooden crates from companies like Proctor and Gamble who were newly trying to systematize their packaging. Brigham had been exposed to Sloyd training while traveling in Europe in college and spent some time experimenting with making things from scrap wood. When she arrived in Spitsbergen to find a sparsely furnished cabin, she turned to the packing crates around her, deconstructing them to first build a sideboard and then a hall table. In a landscape that wouldn't have electricity for a few more years, she used only hand tools, including a carpenter's plane, brace and bit, file, and hacksaw.

Brigham came back the following summer and spent the long days refining a systematic method and design vocabulary for functional, modular furniture that presaged flat-pack, open-source design, IKEA, mid-century modernism, the language of upcycling, and the DIY movement by many decades. Her designs and material choice preempted the more well-known Gerrit Reitveld's Depression-era Crate Chair by nearly thirty years. Writing about the experience a few years later when she published *Box Furniture: How to make a Hundred Useful Articles for the Home*, a compendium of furniture designs built from these crates, Brigham recalled, "Two summers on the island of Spitsbergen taught me, more than all previous experiments, the latent possibilities of a box" (Dickinson, 2020).

In *Louise Brigham and the Early History of Sustainable Furniture Design*, scholar Antoinette LaFarge points out that through the second half of the nineteenth century scattered concepts for furniture made from packing materials had appeared. Often built from packing barrels, these designs typically tried to hide the materials' utilitarian origins. A few companies through those decades suggested ways their crates could be reused, but LaFarge argues that these amounted to little more than public relations ploys. Before gas heating, in fact, the crates were often burned. Brigham's systematic, thorough study of the possibilities of turning packing crates into furniture was, by contrast, a project that integrated materials reuse and a social philosophy into a serious argument for upcycling (LaFarge, 2019).

A product of the Progressive Era values of utility, simplicity, frugality, efficiency, and self-education, Brigham didn't want to be known for charity but rather reciprocity. She believed her life's work should address the growing social inequality, made particularly palpable in a time when millions

Figure 2.3: Drawing of Brigham's dining room furnished with box furniture, from the third installment of Brigham's article, "How I Furnished My Entire Flat with Boxes," in *Ladies' Home Journal*, November 1, 1910. (Uncredited drawing, possibly by George A. Newman)

of immigrants were arriving in US cities. Like William Morris, she believed in bridging the beautiful and the practical; good, multifunctional design makes life better, and good design should be freely available and able to be replicated by anyone. To this end, when Brigham returned to New York, she wrote and spoke about the potential of box furniture, publishing articles in *Ladies' Home Journal*, traveling around the country speaking about this work, and designing and exhibiting rooms of box furniture for model homes—scaled to the size of urban apartments. Her own home—which she called Box Corner First—was decorated exclusively with her furniture pieces, and Brigham sewed her own linen and curtains.

The worker who would pay a week's wages for a single piece of new furniture could—on the same budget—afford to furnish their whole apartment or small house with Brigham designs. While contemporary critics of industrial production were decrying the impacts of standardization on laborers and the quality of goods, LaFarge argues that Brigham was championing standardization and the use of low-cost available materials as a way to support individual rather than mass production (LaFarge, 2019). Influenced by both her own work in wood and her exposure to Sloyd, when Brigham returned to the States she began offering woodworking for boys from low-income homes. In 1912 she founded the Home Thrift Association which trained 600 young people in New York in the first year. Boys took woodworking but ironically, despite her own interests, girls took classes in more traditional areas, learning to make mattresses and tablecloths. Three years later Brigham started Home Arts Masters, a mail-order catalog from which one could purchase ready-to-assemble furniture, and in 1918 she founded a school and a store dedicated to training young women in carpentry skills. Information about this phase of her life and work is sparse, though it is known that she continued to grow the audience for her work and the social and design values it represented. By 1919, *Box Furniture* was in its third edition (Dickinson, 2020).

Brigham's modular designs share some aesthetics with European Modernism, the work of her mentor and friend, Josef Hoffman, and the values that would manifest in De Stijl or Bauhaus furniture a decade later. LaFarge describes Brigham's designs in *Box Furniture* as "recipes rather than blueprints." While her contemporaries who wrote how-to articles included detailed drawings and cross-sections, Brigham offered proportions rather than exact measurements. The shipping crates that were the centerpiece of her designs weren't made to exact specifications, and the range of wooden crates available to her intended audience was wide. Basing her designs on dimensions of common and standard crates so that they were readily accessible to her intended audience, her recipes had to account for the variability in sizing.

The Russian system of industrial arts

More visible than Educational Sloyd in most trades or vocational education in the US today is the legacy of its contemporary and competitor in the schools: The Russian system of industrial arts. While sharing with Sloyd some common processes like model making, the Russian system of manual training was a task-based pedagogy oriented toward the goal of moving young people from agriculture into industrial jobs. At the 1876 Centennial Exhibition in Philadelphia—which included a display of tools and machinery parts built by Russian students learning woodturning, joinery, and black-smithing—MIT's Dr. Runkle saw the Russian method as offering the answer to balancing the theoretical and practical needs of his students through its four distinct teaching methods: Construction shops were divided from instructional classrooms; each kind of work was completed in a distinct shop; each shop was outfitted with enough tools for the number of students that could be instructed in the space; and assignments or sample projects to be replicated were scaffolded and sequenced by increasing levels of difficulty.

Dr. Runkle spoke and wrote extensively about the application of the Russian System at MIT, garnering publicity which helped manual training take root across the United States, from St. Paul to New Orleans. The two best known examples were the Chicago Manual Training School and Washington University's Manual Training School in St. Louis.

Manual training schools in Chicago and St. Louis

Reverend William Eliot, founder of Washington University in St. Louis, spoke passionately to trustees about the importance of manual education as early as 1854—only two years after the school received state charter:

> To elevate mechanical, agricultural, and mercantile pursuits, into learned professions. It would annihilate that absurd distinction, by which the three pursuits of Law, Medicine, and Theology, are called professions, and everything else, labor or trade.
>
> (Schenck, 1995)

By 1870 the manual training program had already begun to fade, only to be renewed and expanded by Dr. Calvin Woodward, a math professor who sought to teach applied mechanics and found his students bereft of manual skills. He, too, had also seen the Russian exhibit in Philadelphia, and found the systematized, sequenced approach to learning mechanical skills was a pedagogical breakthrough. He quickly saw the possibility of teaching all boys manual skills. It wasn't expected that all students would become mechanics or engineers; rather he anticipated a growing interest in mechanical careers, and also saw it as valuable training that would cultivate better lawyers, skillful doctors, and useful citizens (Schenck, 1995). This training model was so successful that it became part of the public domain; by 1915 the St. Louis public school system had integrated manual training into its curriculum and the program known as the Manual Training School closed.

~

The Chicago Manual Training School was a private institution founded in 1884 by members of the Chicago Commercial Club as vocational training for boys. Based principally on the Russian System, the Chicago Manual Training School was also influenced by the philosophy of Sloyd in the ways the school's founders sought to bridge the divide between book learning and shop work. Students were given a high school education in mathematics, science, and literature as well as training in drawing, carpentry, and mechanics. This was both a pedagogical principle and a political one. Believing that "a republic should have no proletariat," (*Special Collections Research Centre*, 2010) Founding Director H.H. Belfield and the school's trustees rejected both traditional secondary school instruction and the apprenticeship model for trades. In its first ten years the Chicago Manual Training School more than tripled its admissions and added business and college preparatory courses to its program. At the turn of the twentieth century, financial troubles led the trustees to transfer ownership of the school to the University of Chicago, where it became one of the University's Laboratory Schools. That program offered woodworking and furniture making to young men, and courses in domestic economy—the practices understood to be part of managing a household—to young women.

Chicago's program inspired the founding of many others, including the Toledo Manual Training School, which did include woodworking in their "Domestic Economy" curriculum for first year female students. An excerpt from their 1893 course of study includes "Light Carpentry, Wood Carving," and "Care and use of tools."

~

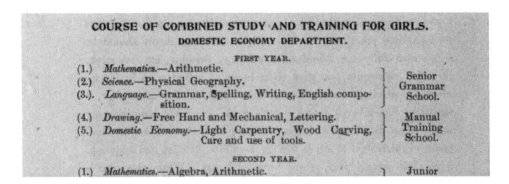

Figure 2.4: The Toledo Manual Training School, World's Fair Edition, 1893

Manual training as an educational paradigm was at odds with the ideas of traditional educators who adhered to the mainstream pedagogical theory of the time, "faculty psychology," which asserts that the brain is made up of faculties that can be strengthened with mental exercises. For example, the faculty for reasoning could be strengthened by memorization of Latin. Manual skills were ascribed to lower faculties, and information was understood to be found in books rather than in the handle of a tool. Thus, manual training took off in private schools first before its educational value was embraced by public secondary schools. Ultimately manual skills training was supplanted by vocational education, a model seemingly demanded by the need for skilled labor in a burgeoning industrial sector. Though sharing with manual skills training a task-based approach and a value placed in preparing students with mechanical skills, vocational education reflected a more outcomes-based pedagogy, employing factory methods that might even include using factory record keeping and having a student take a foreman role over groups of students (Schenck, 1995).

Vocationalism and women

At the turn of the twentieth century, US cities were growing rapidly. Drawn by a burgeoning industrial economy, rural Americans were moving away from farms and into urban centers, and millions of immigrants were arriving in northeastern cities each year, creating rich cultural and ethnic enclaves and transforming the nation from a largely agricultural society to an increasingly diverse, industrial, and urban one. Without the legal and material infrastructure to support this rapid growth, health and sanitation problems, growing economic inequality, poverty, and terrible labor conditions beset urban neighborhoods. This was the social and economic context that spawned the Progressive Era, a time in which reformers sought to create change across a wide range of issues.

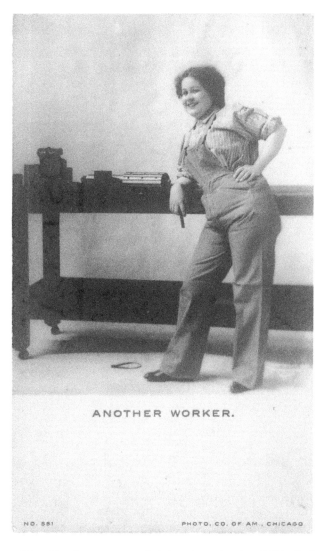

ANOTHER WORKER.

NO. 551   PHOTO. CO. OF AM., CHICAGO

Figure 2.5: Woman pictured leaning on a carpenter's bench, postcard, c. 1910. (Author's collection)

Women's participation in the labor force—as typists, clerks, teachers, telephone operators, domestic servants, and industrial seamstresses— was growing apace, raising alarms for conservative social reformers who anticipated dire consequences for the nation's social order. Some explicitly correlated women's economic independence with the destruction of the home (Bernard-Powers, 2012). More often discourse and policy reflected a deeply held ambivalence about women and labor, and a cultural assumption that women would only work for four to five years before marriage. The new educational experiences for girls and young women designed and implemented at this time to prepare them for changing economic and social roles were somewhat piecemeal, reflecting this cultural ambivalence.

Even though the content of trade education which was generally needlework was not new, the notion of an educational program that would train young women for industrial employment was both new and controversial in the Progressive Era. ... The issue of trade education for young women emerged at a time when women's participation in the labor force was widely debated. Specific issues such as the effects of women's competition on men's wages and the effects of particular industries on women's physical and moral health were argued along with broader concerns about the role of women.

(Bernard-Powers, 2012)

Figure 2.6: Unattributed photographs found in the Pacific Northwest; women working in a box factory, c. 1915. (Author's collection)

For boys, the values of dexterity and mechanical knowledge taught in manual education gave way to the vocationalism of industrial education, training boys to participate in industry; for young women, vocationalism meant home economics or domestic science. When applied to young women, "vocation" was meant to convey a sense of women's true calling. Homemaking and child-rearing were vocations for which only women were suited and were a cornerstone of the nation's self-perception. Middle-class white women educators, like their male colleagues, often saw home economics as a means of ameliorating the conditions of urban poverty, improving living conditions, and strengthening the community. Absent a clear analysis of labor relations or the impacts and causes of growing wealth disparities, they linked poor living conditions in the cities to failure of the family and a decline of national morality. Home economics as a subject area in education elevated homemaking to a respectable—albeit exclusively female and unpaid—occupation. The rhetoric of vocationalism, however, presented a challenge: It was difficult to make the argument that women needed training to do unpaid housework. Advocates made complex associations between teenage labor and missing out on training at home on the one hand, and the complexity of the modern household on the other. By 1928 virtually all young women took Home Economics at some point in their high school education. This curriculum, like trade skills for young men, was funded by the federal government as vocational education, part of a major federal education reform effort of the period.

The curriculum was least popular in dense urban settings in the Northeast where the problems it was meant to ameliorate were most prevalent. The key difference between housekeeping and other types of work was one which advocates of home economics failed to emphasize, but which in the last analysis was probably most important to many working-class families: Women were never paid for keeping their own homes. It is small wonder, then, that women from these urban neighborhoods showed little interest in home economics. Homemaking was one career that offered no financial return on the time invested in secondary schooling. Conceptualizing industrial education for young women was also hampered by the limited opportunities available to women in industry. Most positions in the Northeast were in sewing factories and most often there was little advantage to being "skilled"

Figure 2.7: Young woman in the woodshop, Massachusetts Normal, c. 1918. "Normal" schools trained high school graduates to become teachers. "Normal" was used to refer to social norms. (Unattributed, Author's collection)

or trained as the jobs available were for unskilled workers, laborers who were regularly laid off (Rury, 1984).

"Commercial education" was another arm of vocationalism that grew exponentially more popular at the turn of the century. Included in this

Figure 2.8: Unattributed photograph taken in 1914 at Camp Anawan for Girls, located on Lake Winnipeasukee in Meredith, NH. (Author's collection)

curriculum were courses like bookkeeping and principles of business for boys, and stenography and typing for girls, addressing emergent technologies and offering training for those jobs open to women in the labor market.

References

Bernard-Powers, J. (2012). *The 'Girl Question' in Education (RLE Edu F): Vocational Education for Young Women in the Progressive Era.* London: Taylor & Francis.

Bieze, M. (2005, Summer). Ruskin in the Black Belt: Booker T. Washington, Arts and Crafts, and the New Negro. *Notes in the History of Art, 24*(4), 24–34.

Brigham, L. (1910, 1 November). "How I Furnished My Entire Flat with Boxes". *Ladies' Home Journal*, part III.

Dickinson, E. E. (2020, May 6). *The Radical Possibilities of a Box.* Retrieved January 2021, from Curbed.com: https://archive.curbed.com/2020/5/6/21248660/sustainable-furniture-louise-brigham-history

Gómez-Ibáñez, M. (2018, June 15). President, North Bennett Street School (D. Visser, Interviewer).

LaFarge, A. (2019). *Louise Brigham and the Early History of Sustainable Furniture Design.* Cham, Switzerland: Palgrave McMillan.

Pinson, E. F. (2012). "'The Dignity Of Labor:' African-American Connections To The Arts And Crafts Movement, 1868–1915." Washington, D.C.: The Smithsonian Associates and Corcoran College of Art + Design.

Reese, W. J. (2003). American Education in the Twentieth Century: Progressive Legacies. *Paedagogica Historica*, *39*(4), 415–416. doi:10.1080/0030 9230307478.

Rury, J. L. (1984). Vocationalism for Home and Work: Women's Education in the United States, 1880–1930. *History of Education Quarterly*, *24*(1), 21–44.

Salomon, O. (1892). *The Teacher's Handbook of Slöjd.* Boston: Silver, Burdett & Co.

Schenck, J. P. (1995). *ERIC.ed.gov.* Retrieved March 2021, from Manual Training Schools in America: https://files.eric.ed.gov/fulltext/ED391039.pdf

Special Collections Research Center. (2010). Guide to the Chicago Manual Training School Records 1882–1913. Retrieved November 2020, from University of Chicago Library: https://www.lib.uchicago.edu/e/scrc/findin-gaids/view.php?eadid=ICU.SPCL.CMTS

Stowe, D. (2004). *Educational Sloyd: The Early Roots of Manual Training.* Retrieved January 2021, from www.dougstowe.com: http://www.dougstowe.com/educator_resources/w88sloyd.pdf

Stowe, D. (2008, October). *Nääs: Placing the Hands at the Center of Education.* Retrieved April 2021, from DougStowe.com: http://www.dougstowe.com/educator_resources/113naas-jkjl.pdf

Talbot, E. A. (1904). *Samuel Chapman Armstrong: A Biographical Study.* New York: Doubleday, Page and Company.

Terrell, E. (2015, February 24). *Du Bois in Paris – Exposition Universelle, 1900.* Retrieved June 2021, from Library of Congress Blog: https://blogs.loc.gov/inside_adams/2015/02/du-bois-in-paris-exposition-universelle-1900/

Washington, B. T. (1903, October). *The Fruits of Industrial Training.* Retrieved January 2021, from The Atlantic: https://www.theatlantic.com/magazine/archive/1903/10/the-fruits-of-industrial-training/531030/

Chapter Three

Shifting economies

World War I: British women enter manual fields

> The war changed life for women, and it changed the women themselves.
> When men returned from war, they inevitably tried to reassert their
> dominance in family and society. But their own broken conditions and
> circumstances at home challenged these attempts.
>
> (Davis, 2014)

In the years before World War I certain industries and types of manufacturing
like textiles were still considered women's work. Working-class women were
already employed in various industries, but the higher paid fields like metal
forges and machine factories were considered men's domain. The economic
and social pressures of the war forced open these doors and women moved into
traditionally male jobs; in fact, the introduction of conscription by the British
government in 1916 made hiring women urgent, and the number of women
employed in industry grew from 3.3 million in 1914 to 4.9 million in 1918
(Welner, 1942).

~

One of the avenues that opened up for young British women in wood-
related fields was timber harvesting. The foundations of timber-cutting
work were laid in 1916 with the formation of the Women's Forestry Corps,
which became part of Britain's Women's Land Army (WLA), created to fill

DOI: 10.4324/9780429345418-4

Figure 3.1: "Willing and skilled workers in a women's carpentry shop in France." *Weekly Magazine*, 1917. (Author's collection)

agricultural positions vacated by men headed to the front. Among the many jobs performed by members of the WLA was forestry, and by January 1918, 400 women worked as foresters, clearing hillsides and sawing up timbers for railway sleepers. In the US, women's colleges and universities, suffrage groups, garden clubs, and the Young Women's Christian Association (YWCA) came together to form the Women's Land Army of America (WLAA), which similarly trained women for agricultural work.

World War I marked the first measurable wave of British and American women moving into woodworking-related fields. They were not initially recruited into the building trades but when they were allowed into construction it came with a caveat: They were to be paid less than men, kept in semi-skilled work, and considered "dilutees," a pejorative term suggesting their presence had a deleterious effect on the field (Ellison, 2016).

Figure 3.2: Women at work in lumber yards. YWCA, Photographer. February 5, 1919. (National Archives, NWDNS-86-G-6S(7), https://catalog.archives.gov/id/522867)

But for all the restrictions on where they could work and how they should be considered, women in building-related trades in England grew in number from 7,000 to 31,400 during the war years (1914–18) (Clarke and Wall, 2006). At the close of WWI, women in the US constituted twenty percent of

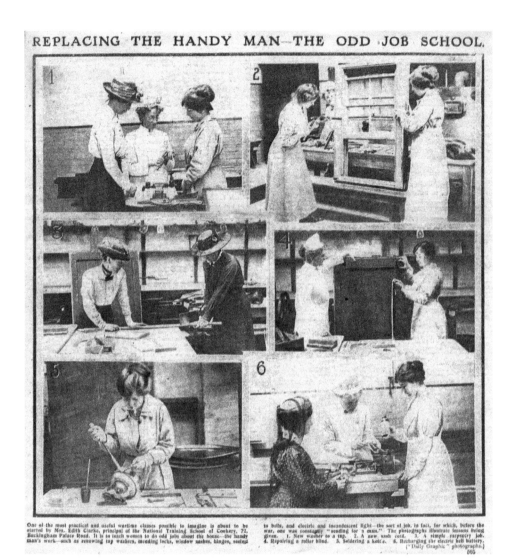

REPLACING THE HANDY MAN—THE ODD JOB SCHOOL.

One of the most practical and useful wartime classes possible to imagine is about to be started by Mrs. Edith Clarke, principal of the National Training School of Cookery, 72, Buckingham Palace Road. It is to teach women to do odd jobs about the house—the handy man's work—such as renewing tap washers, mending locks, window sashes, hinges, seeing to bolts, and electric and incandescent light—the sort of job, in fact, for which, before the war, one was constantly "sending for a man." The photographs illustrate lessons being given. 1. New washer to a tap. 2. A new sash cord. 3. A simple carpentry job. 4. Repairing a roller blind. 5. Soldering a kettle. 6. Recharging the electric bell battery.
("Daily Graphic" photographs.)

Figure 3.3: "Replacing the Handyman: The Odd Job School." Clipping from the *Daily Graphic*, 1917. Women learning odd jobs, carpentry, and soldering on Buckingham Palace Road at a school founded by Mrs. Edith Clarke. (Author's collection)

the manufacturing workforce (Welner, 1942). In 1919 demobilized soldiers and unions that claimed to represent them urged employers to lay off the female workforce; in fact, many factories returned to peacetime production and refused to rehire the women who had been employed during the war.

Figure 3.4: British women carpenters near front, 1917, Bain News. (Author's collection)

Despite a suggestion that wartime employment didn't radically change women's workforce participation in subsequent years, most historians argue that the social landscape was dramatically altered. Women in most countries got the right to vote in the few years after the First World War (France excepted, where women waited until the early 1940s for voting rights), and expectations for autonomy and participation in social, economic, and political life were forever changed (Davis, 2014).

Figure 3.5: Women in a construction class, c. 1920. (Unattributed. Superior View Photographic Collection, Marquette, Michigan. Author's collection)

Nancy Cook and Val-Kill Industries

Following WWI the US turned inward, insular and isolationist, part of a reactionary nationalist anxiety about increasing immigration, urbanism, and modernism. A burgeoning petroleum-based economy fueled the roaring twenties before the Great Depression struck in 1929. Out of economic hardship many people turned back toward the handwork and craft skills of their parents and grandparents (Fenton, 2007).

In 1926 Nancy Cook (1884–1962)—entrepreneur, suffragist, political organizer, and skilled woodworker—collaborated with her partner, Marion Dickerman (1890–1983), and future First Lady Eleanor Roosevelt

Figure 3.6: Eleanor Roosevelt, Marion Dickerman, and Nancy Cook in Campobello, July 1926; Collection FDR-PHOCO: Franklin D. Roosevelt Library, 1882–1962. (https://commons.wikimedia.org/wiki/File:Eleanor_Roosevelt,_Marian_Dickerman,_and_Nancy_Cook_in_Campobello_-_NARA_-_195627.jpg)

(1884–1962) to create Val-Kill Industries. Together they built a small, shared cottage and envisioned and then built an accompanying factory in Hyde Park, New York, on land once part of the Roosevelt estate. The Arts and Crafts style—which privilege simplicity, utility, the beauty of the material, and nature as inspiration—was waning in popularity while Colonial Revival, which romanticized early American design, was ascendant. For their stylistic differences, the two movements shared a reverence for a pre-industrial past and placed a high value on honesty to materials and the integrity of labor. Val-Kill both embraced the cultural values of Arts and Crafts and responded to the demand for reproductions of colonial-style furniture. They promoted furniture making as a small industry for immigrants and out of season farmers with the intention of creating a viable business model; they later added a pewter forge and homespun textiles (Wilson, 2017).

Cook designed and built the cottage furniture, and designed the furniture for, taught in, and managed the daily operations of the woodshop and business until it closed in 1936, a casualty of the Great Depression. Though itself perhaps not a viable cottage industry in the long-term, it served as a model for larger-scale initiatives from the Roosevelt administration.

Between the wars

In the bleakest years of the Depression, the entrepreneurial and training model explored by Val-Kill Industries helped inform the Works Progress Administration (WPA), the ambitious employment and infrastructure program started in 1935 as part of Franklin Roosevelt's New Deal. By creating federally funded jobs, the US government was trying to ameliorate the devastating impacts of the Depression and the high burden that unemployment placed on states, counties, and cities. While many women found employment in traditionally female realms like sewing, many thousands of others across the country participated in crafts and trade-skills related programs, from building toys to making and repairing furniture. The WPA organized more than 3,000 craft projects and the FSA (Farm Securities Administration), which succeeded it, also embraced and advanced cottage industries in response to the crushing economic and social impacts of the Depression (Futral, 2009).

Figure 3.7: Educational toys, Milwaukee Handicraft Project, c. 1930s–40s. (From the Archives Department, University of Wisconsin-Milwaukee Libraries)

Milwaukee Handicraft Project

In Milwaukee, Wisconsin, Harriet Clinton, head of the Women's Division of Wisconsin's WPA, was tasked with creating jobs for 2,600 Milwaukee County women who applied for employment as heads of household but had never worked outside the home (Prigge, 2020). Clinton's initial concept was a handicraft program in which she imagined the participants making scrapbooks with wallpaper clippings. She reached out to Elsa Ulbricht (1885–1980), a member of the art education faculty of Milwaukee State Teacher's College (now the University of Wisconsin, Milwaukee), who was intrigued by Clinton's idea but disgusted by what she saw as a "make work" idea. Ulbricht was herself a craftsperson and educator and was certain

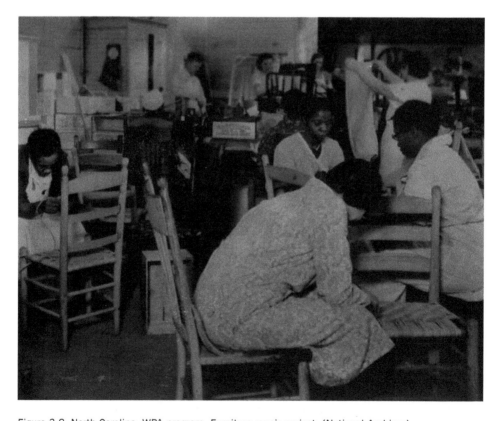

Figure 3.8: North Carolina, WPA program: Furniture repair project. (National Archives)

the women could be trained to make products both practical and artistic, weaving together economic, social, and creative values. Ulbricht worked with Anne Feldman and Mary June Kellogg, both former students, to develop the Milwaukee Handicraft Project (MHP).

The four women's proposal was to produce household goods from wood, paper, yarn, and cloth. Participants created an array of creative and practical goods from block prints to furniture, woven and hooked rugs, draperies to furnish offices and dormitories, as well as durable soft and wooden toys. Unlike many WPA programs, the Milwaukee Handicraft Project was racially integrated, and ninety percent of the participants were able to support themselves on the wages they earned (Powers, 2020). In keeping with WPA

Figure 3.9: Furniture, Women's Division, WPA, New Mexico. (National Archives, 69-MP-40–2, https://catalog.archives.gov/id/176251186)

program guidelines, the products couldn't compete against those of private industry, so products were instead sold to libraries, schools, and other publicly funded institutions. The wooden toys were so durable that many could still be found in local schools as late as the 1970s. Over the seven years of the program, more than 5,000 women and people of color were employed in the county (Women's Work: The WPA Milwaukee Handicraft Project, n.d.).

Building and repairing furniture from New Mexico to North Carolina

Other WPA programs from Ohio to Mississippi to North Carolina employed women to build, reupholster, and repair furniture; participants were then able to improve either their own homes or the homes of neighbors and community members. Describing a WPA housekeeping aide project in 1939, an Ohio journalist wrote about creative use of scrap material in the repair process: "When the dilapidated furniture came to the aides, they took the clean burlap sacking, bought 50 cents worth of dyes, created their own upholstering material and, with sack padding, turned out creditably upholstered and certainly attractive and colorful furniture" (New Deal of the Day, 2018).

From 1935 to 1939 the National Youth Administration (NYA), a vocational training program for young people aged sixteen to twenty-five, was run by the WPA. In New Mexico both young men and women learned Spanish Colonial handcrafts, including furniture making—a style that typically used the local Ponderosa pine and was characterized by **mortise and tenon** joinery, quarter round edges and carved embellishments (Wood For Wood, 2020). Because Ponderosa pine tends to be brittle and cracks along the **grain**, lines were often simple, unlike their more baroque Spanish predecessors (Morelli, n.d.).

The New Deal WPA projects form a bridge between the women who entered traditionally male fields in the First and Second World Wars. The children's toys made in WPA woodshops in Milwaukee are a touchstone that can inform toy making endeavors today, such as the rattles Sarah Marriage (Profile pp. 262–272) made as a small business venture before launching A Workshop of Our Own. These are just a few examples of a more complex and interlocking web of women throughout Western Europe and North America in the last century engaged in the utilitarian, domestic, material, and social possibilities of woodworking and furniture making.

Figure 3.10: San Augustine, Texas. Girls with chairs they made in woodworking shop under the NYA (National Youth Administration) war training program, 1943. (National Youth Administration Library of Congress, 2017852252)

The Second World War: Lumberjills

We're the girls who fell for victory
We're the girls who chop the trees
Every time we swing our axes
It's a stroke for victory.

(Law, 2019)

During the Second World War, timber was again critical to the British war effort, a resource upon which all other industries relied, from coal mines to ammunition production. By 1939 England was almost entirely reliant on timber imports and had only seven months of supplies stockpiled. Despite the urgent need for wood and the dramatically reduced number of men available for domestic forestry work, the suggestion that once again women could be called upon to work in forestry, as they had in the First World War, was met with reluctance and even hostility. Cognizant of the urgency to re-establish the Women's Land Army and the forestry corps, Lady Gertrude "Trudie" Denman took on a propaganda campaign. By 1942 the program would be formally called the Women's Timber Corps, the members informally known as "Lumberjills."

The program recruited close to 15,000 women as young as fourteen from all over England, Scotland, and Wales. Denman was particularly conscious of recruiting urban women, as it became another form of evacuation from the threat of wartime bombing. Forestry was regarded as a more desirable station than farming and still promised countryside and fresh air. The Lumberjills downed trees with fourteen-pound axes, drove tractors, and ran sawmills, sometimes suffering horrible injuries. Despite their invaluable contribution, Women's Land Army and Women's Timber Corps members received no recognition after the war and were excluded from Remembrance Day events. They were first acknowledged with veterans' medals in 2008, more than sixty years after the war ended, when most were no longer alive (Foat, 2019).

Comfort craft

When the US entered World War II in 1941, the mobilization of American men for military service once again opened new opportunities for women in the workforce. From 1940 to 1945 the percentage of employed women in the United States grew from twenty-seven to thirty-seven percent of the workforce, an increase of 6 million women (Rosie the Riveter, 2021).

Largely unheralded from this period is the woodworking associated with a darker chapter in American history, though individuals emerged to defy

Figure 3.11: "They Learn to Be Lumber Jills: Women's Land Army Forestry Training, Culford, Suffolk, 1943." (Ministry of Information Second World War official collection. IWM D 14098, 2021)

their forced disappearance. Spokane, Washington-born George Nakashima (1905–1990) was trained as an architect but decided to make his life as a furniture maker. He was teaching woodworking to boys with the Maryknoll Mission in Seattle when Executive Order 9066 came down and the family

Figure 3.12: Ann Moffat sitting around a smoky campfire with other Lumberjills on the Isle of Wight, United Kingdom, Second World War. (Foat, Joanna, *Lumberjills: Britain's Forgotten Army* (The History Press, 2019), p. 93. Courtesy of Joanna Foat)

was moved with 120,000 other Japanese Americans to remote concentration camps in California and the interior western states. Thus confined, Nakashima was among the artisans in camp who married ingenuity with necessity, making wood furniture reminiscent of Brigham's turn-of-the-century box furniture from whatever resources they could find—remnants of old building materials, packing crates, and little bits of bitterbrush—to create "spaces of survival" during their imprisonment by the US government in the barrack-like shelters.

Furniture making was a primary concern for many detainees upon arrival, as crafting their own tables, chairs, beds, shelves, desks, benches, partitions, and closets was one of the only means of creating comfort under such unimaginable circumstances. At the same time, the precious commodity of wood was used for traditional woodcarving techniques such as *bon-kei*,

Figure 3.13: Heart Mountain Relocation Center, Heart Mountain, Wyoming. A class of early teenage students, 1/11/1943. (National Archives and Records Administration Ctr, NWDNS-210-G-E671; NARA ARC: 539228)

taught in one camp by Mrs. Ninomiya, who at one point had ninety-two students in her *bon-kei* class; *kobu*; and the carved wood jewelry of Kiyoka and Yoneguma Takahashi (Dusselier, 2015).

Though the furnishings were largely built by men, women did participate, and their efforts were noted. At the Manzanar Internment Camp in central California, Fumi Marumoto crossed gender lines and made

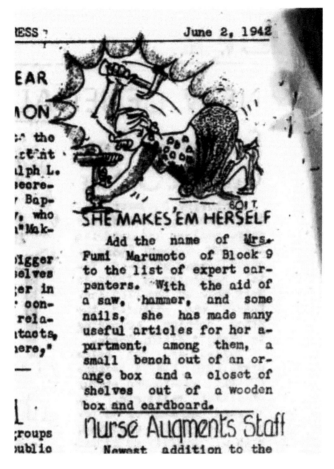

Figure 3.14: Clipping from *Manzanar Free Press*, June 2, 1942. (LOC 84025948. https://www.loc.gov/resource/sn84025948/1942-06-02/ed-1/?sp=4&st=text&r=0.491,0.038,0.655,0.648,0)

furniture with the available scrap materials. A brief writeup in the *Manzanar Free Press* read:

> Add the name of Mrs. Fumi Marumoto of Block-9 to the list of expert carpenters. With the aid of a saw, hammer, and some nails, she has made many useful articles for her apartment, among them, a small bench out of an orange box and a closet of shelves out of a wooden box and cardboard.
>
> (Dusselier, 2015)

Though nothing further is recorded about Marumoto's pre- or post-internment circumstances—for example, did she previously work outside of the home in a carpentry role?—Nakashima went on to become one of the most celebrated and respected American woodworkers of the twentieth century. In the camp he worked alongside a Japanese carpenter who taught him a lot about the use of tools, joinery, and a way of working with wood that starts with a focus on the internal logic of the material. Following internment, Nakashima relocated his family to Pennsylvania. The lesson he learned from that carpenter in the camp is one that continues to inform the work of George Nakashima Woodworkers, significant for being headed since his death in 1990 by his daughter, Mira Nakashima.

The GI Bill and the institutionalization of art education

As World War II drew to a close, Congressional representatives anticipated the return to civilian life of more than ten million servicemen and 350,000 women in a dramatic shift away from a wartime economy. After fifteen years of combined Depression and US combat in World War II, the act popularly known as the GI Bill of Rights was intended to head off risk of further economic depression that awaited the returning servicemembers. Though the passage of the Servicemen's Readjustment Act of 1944 went largely unheralded at the time of signing, it would help propel a post-war expansion in higher education that grew only more dramatic in the 1960s and ensuing decades. This cultural shift has been seen around the world in the more than half-century since; it has both mirrored and reinforced economic trends, transformed the labor market, and reinforced the production of a global professional class. In the craft and arts fields, the GI Bill was instrumental in moving woodworking and furniture education into the university woodshop.

Before World War II only twenty-five percent of Americans had a high school diploma and only six percent had a college education. In 1940 about 1.5 million students were enrolled in colleges and universities, though fewer than 200,000 earned degrees. With the educational provisions of the GI Bill, in the years following the war, 2.2 million veterans attended two- and four-year universities, and another 3.5 million attended vocational schools. Upwards of two million more used the benefits for on-the-job or farm training (Greenberg, 2004).

To take advantage of the Veteran's Administration benefits, service-members needed only to show proof of military service for at least ninety days, with an honorable discharge. With minimal red tape they would be afforded unemployment payments, loan guarantees, and tuition, fees, books, and living stipends for college, vocational school, or job-related apprentice-ships for up to forty-eight months, depending on how long they had served. While the implementation and consequences of the GI Bill reflected the systemic racial biases and structural disenfranchisement of people of color in the United States, particularly denying African American veterans equal access to those benefits, the legislation also altered the landscape of higher education.

Craft scholar Glenn Adamson describes the subsequent explosion of craft courses in universities as an "unintended consequence" of the GI Bill. Many veterans were the first in their families to attend college and were inclined toward practical courses. To accommodate this impulse universities added craft offerings, including ceramics, woodworking, metalwork, and textiles, dramatically expanding the presence of craft in college curricula. This began a model in which successful artists in craft traditions didn't have to rely on their craft to make a living but could instead pursue their craft and teach. Freed from economic imperatives, they could pursue their work in more experimental and artistic ways, rather than market-driven or more utilitarian pursuits (Adamson, 2021).

Aileen Osborne Webb I founder, American Craft Council

Aileen Webb (1892–1979) was a contemporary of Eleanor Roosevelt and a member of the same social circles, with a shared and sustained belief in doing good in the world. Watching the palpable human struggle around her during the Depression, she sought ways to impact change and—like Roosevelt and Cook—turned to the possibilities of economic autonomy through the sale of handicrafts, at first directing her efforts toward rural makers. Toward the end of WWII Webb turned her attention to education. Her resourcefulness and commitment to the possibilities of craft—she herself pursued both poetry and ceramics—were foundational in the creation of the American Craft Council in 1943 (originally called the American Craftsmen's Educational Council) and the School for American Craftsmen the following year, which was first housed at Dartmouth College and then Alfred University, before finding its current home at Rochester Institute of Technology. Webb was also involved in the 1956 founding of the Museum of Contemporary Crafts in New York (later the American Craft Museum and later still the Museum of Art and Design), and then the World Crafts Council in 1964. These institutions are the most visible and prominent of many projects Webb guided and catalyzed that have shaped the world of craft in America today (Lovelace, 2011).

Post-war: Black Mountain College

The history of craft and fabrication since industrialization has been an ongoing dialogue with the technologies and materials, as well as organizational structures and systems of industrial production. In the early 1920s, Modernism's embrace of technology's promise displaced the romantic values of the Arts and Crafts and Aesthetic movements: The centrality of the maker's hands and their engagement with the entire arc of the creative process, the essential integrity of natural materials, and a relationship to the local. The years that followed World War II saw a return to a truth-to-materials ethic in crafts, from ceramics to woodworking. Newly rooted in academia and its language of professional development, there was a growing emphasis in craft on concept, craft theory, and personal expression. Taking cues from the art world, woodworkers were changing how they viewed the possibilities and trajectories of their careers and were understanding the approach and content of their work through a more conceptual lens.

The years leading up to and during the Second World War had brought to the US an influx of émigré artists and progressive cultural theorists escaping the rise of fascist regimes across Europe. They arrived in New York and helped make it the center of Abstract Expressionism, a modern art movement that encompassed action and color field painting, both informed by an emphasis on emotional expression and the unconscious. Many of the artists arriving in the US had been involved in and even helped shape the Bauhaus, a German architecture and design school that sought to unify art with craft, individual expression with industrial production, and beauty with function. Founded by architect Walter Gropius, the school was only in operation for fourteen years before closing in the wake of Nazi pressure.

Especially given its short lifespan, the Bauhaus was enormously influential in architecture, industrial and graphic design, and art and craft.

Artists who spent time at the Bauhaus exported those ideas around the world; the formative tenure of German émigrés Anni and Josef Albers shaped Black Mountain College in Lake Eden, North Carolina, which was founded on John Dewey's progressive vision of education and a belief that art and craft should be integrated into the education of all students, regardless of the area of study. Black Mountain provided a safe haven and a two-year visa to many artists leaving Europe, so while most contemporary craft schools in the Appalachian region taught indigenous and traditional methods, Black Mountain became home to a Modernist avant-garde. The Albers brought to the college a Bauhaus-infused attention to bridging theory and practice. Students participated in the day-to-day operations of the site, working both on the farm and in the kitchen, and building the furniture for the dormitories while also studying for rigorous courses.

Mary (Molly) Gregory | builder, designer, architect, woodworker

Up until this point in the twentieth century few individual woodworkers had emerged to distinguish themselves as named makers. The notion of a singular named maker had, with few exceptions, not yet begun to take hold among women woodworkers in the US—even Nancy Cook's handiwork was marketed under the Val-Kill label and not, for example, as a "Nancy Cook" piece.

Massachusetts-born Mary Gregory (known also as Molly) (1914–2006) pursued woodworking and a life as a builder, designer, architect, and furniture maker. She grew up on the family farm and in 1932 was part of the first class enrolled in the newly formed Bennington College in Vermont, which was founded as a women's college. After graduating in 1936 Gregory took her first job teaching sculpture to middle and high school students at the Cambridge School outside Boston. Gregory became aware of Black Mountain College while she was a student at Bennington. In 1941, with five years at Cambridge School under her belt, Gregory was offered an opportunity to come to Black Mountain to study with Albers and teach, first as an Apprentice in Plastics, then full instructor in Crafts and eventually Woodworking.

Figure 3.15: Mary Gregory at Black Mountain College, carrying the lumber. (North Carolina Department of Natural and Cultural Resources)

The Black Mountain College Project, dedicated to preserving the legacy of the innovative and now defunct school, describes Gregory as a polymath deeply immersed in the life of the school who held multiple roles. Shortly after she arrived many of the male students and faculty were drafted into the military, and so her skills were needed in the woodshop, where she took the lead in meeting the school's practical needs. Gregory built both furniture and signage for the college and oversaw students who were tasked with building the tables, chairs, and bookshelves for their dorms and classrooms. Describing the furniture Gregory designed and fabricated at Black Mountain, curator Lydia See speaks of the alignment between her work and Morris' conception of marrying the values of beauty and utility. Resources during the war were scarce, and Gregory was using accessible materials most often sourced from the campus grounds. In addition to directing the work program, Gregory kept the books, managed the farm when the farmer left unexpectedly, and renovated the farmhouse to fit two families. On top of all that, while at the school she also took on private design and construction projects in wood and metal. When she left in 1947, the school hired two farming couples to fill the space left by her departure (Black Mountain College Project, n.d.).

After Black Mountain, Gregory became the designer and manager at Woodstock Enterprises in Vermont, producing custom furniture and cabinetry,

Figure 3.16: Mary Gregory, *Lazy-J* chair and stool, Black Mountain College. (North Carolina Department of Natural and Cultural Resources)

and six years later she started her own woodworking business, where for more than thirty years she did custom interior woodworking, furniture design and fabrication, and church furnishings. She also continued to design, renovate, and build homes in a style that reflected her New England roots: Well-made, clean-lined, and functional work influenced by Shaker furniture and English Arts and Crafts.

Leadership changes and challenges during WWII, during which time many of the male students were drafted for military service, were followed by an infusion of federal funds and students in the wake of the GI Bill. Enrollment grew and many of the best-known US-based artists of the twentieth century studied at Black Mountain, including Ruth Asawa and Robert Rauschenberg. By the early 1950s, the school was attracting an emerging post-war generation of artisans who heralded a return to making unique, handcrafted objects for use in an industrial society. The dynamic intersections of all these sensibilities helped fuel the emergence of the studio craft movement (Fenton, 2007).

Joyce Rinehart Anderson I fine woodworker

> We were both exploring, in a way, I think. He started with a lot more knowledge of what he was doing, but I'm a quick study and we worked things out together.
>
> (Anderson, 2002)

In some ways not unlike the women who worked alongside their spouses in the medieval woodshop, Joyce Rinehart Anderson (1925–2014) entered the field through her husband, Edgar Anderson, whom she married in 1946. While living in Chicago so that Edgar could study construction, Anderson found herself intrigued by her husband's work (she had studied economics). She joined him in the shop, initially as a helper, doing finishing and then turning on the lathe—which would become one of her specialties—before they began to design and build together. In 1950 the Andersons bought fifteen acres in her hometown of Morristown, New Jersey, and, sharing the labor, built a house and woodshop with stone and wood from the property, with Joyce running the bulldozer. As emerging furniture makers the Andersons did plenty of refinishing and repair, bringing in work to pay the bills while they learned techniques and considered how they might do things a little differently.

Proponents of Scandinavian design—the early twentieth-century design movement characterized by spare, clean lines, simple accents, and an emphasis on functionality—the Andersons would eventually develop their own aesthetic which merged elements of furniture and sculpture. As their skills developed and they got more opportunities for design and fabrication, they mixed furniture commissions with small works, jewelry, and turned ware. The latter two types of work were principally Joyce's domain, but their collaboration was such that soon it was hard to distinguish one's contributions from the other. Thus began a sixty-plus-year collaboration and integration of the home environment, a committed stewardship of the land, art, and craft.

As their work progressed and visibility grew, the Andersons met their contemporaries, including George Nakashima and Wharton Esherick. Joyce was the only woman among this small group of makers in the nascent American studio furniture movement. The woodworkers who identified with the concerns of this emergent movement were few and scattered across the country; they barely knew of each other's existence until they all eventually showed their work at the Museum of Contemporary Crafts in New York. The Andersons and their peers were conscious of being part of a new and modern language in the world of craft that eschewed both the reproduction of antiques and the growing presence of plastics and **veneers** in contemporary furniture. In 1950 Joyce and Edgar Anderson were among the founding members of the New Jersey Designer-Craftsmen (incorporated as a non-profit in 1967) (*The Star Ledger*, 2015), with whom they had regular exhibits, which allowed them not only to see their work juxtaposed with that of their peers working in other materials but invited a growing audience for this new idiom.

The Andersons received significant publicity early on, including a feature in the *New York Times* in May 1956 that helped the couple garner attention. As their creative work developed and grew in visibility, the Andersons' works were widely collected by both private collectors and museums that included the Newark, Montclair, and New Jersey State Museums. Some of their most celebrated pieces include "Chest of Drawers," a curvy female torso comprised of a stack of shallow drawers with carved fronts; and "Time

Piece," which similarly uses a verbal pun to describe a six-foot-high carved hand and forearm with a working wristwatch (Kimmel, 2010).

Post-war USA: A suburban dream

> The only new science made available to female students in the years immediately following the war embodied patriarchal mandates and a fulfillment of women's sex role: domestic science.
>
> (Swaine, 1983)

With cyclical predictability, the Women's Bureau of the Department of Labor found in the post-war years that, "Women are likely to suffer unemployment to a disproportionate extent and to find difficulty in regaining jobs, particularly those characterized by better pay and better working conditions" (Pidgeon, 1947). Protectionism and gender discrimination marked the post-war labor market; employers sought to fill jobs with returning servicemen. Despite these labor conditions, many women stayed in the workforce after the war both by choice and necessity, and by 1945 one in four women in the United States was working outside the home, though opportunities in non-traditional industries shrank and were replaced by administrative jobs.

Nonetheless, mainstream media depicted women—particularly middle-class, heterosexual, married white women—operating primarily in the domestic sphere. The nationally expanded television marketplace was a powerful driver of this cultural narrative; advertisers selling appliances understood their ideal viewers to be homemakers who were meant to understand their power as rooted in consumption. Women were the decision makers in a domestic landscape of consumer capitalism that supplanted eleven years of economic depression and four years of wartime scarcity and deprivation (Bernstein, 1996). Wages for middle-class men were growing amidst a booming manufacturing sector that sought new markets and consumer products to replace wartime production. And the construction sector was growing apace, opening up suburban housing markets to growing middle-class families sold on a single-family home and a new car.

These market-driven narratives required that women understand themselves to be better suited to work inside the home, and that their power was heightened by effectively and strategically manipulating market power.

Figures 3.17 and 3.18: Joyce and Edgar Anderson, chest of drawers, 1975. (Courtesy of browngrotta arts)

This paralleled a long-held American ideal that the strength of the family hinged on women identifying primarily as wives and mothers.

Doing-it-yourself: *Family Togetherness and the Suburban Ideal*

In *Family Togetherness and the Suburban Ideal*, scholar Laura J. Miller examines the social and spatial design of suburbs, and the central

preoccupation with familial togetherness, a goal which she ultimately argues is undermined by the heightened strain it places on that very social structure, the family. However, the suburban dream arguably reached its apotheosis in the 1950s, dovetailing with this media-driven narrative of women's powerful role in the home. Suburbs—free of both the distractions and complex mix of classes and ethnic groups that characterize urban centers—were marketed to be the ideal location for white middle-class families, undergirded and incentivized by government policy and private banking practices. Though the do-it-yourself ethic had roots far earlier, this home-centered lifestyle predicated on a single-family suburban home

Figure 3.19: *Workbench*, magazine cover, May–June 1957. (Reprinted with permission, Active Interest Media, Holdco, Inc)

Figure 3.20: *Workbench*, magazine cover, March–April, 1957. (Reprinted with permission, Active Interest Media, Holdco, Inc)

was full of opportunities for do-it-yourself projects, both for pleasure and maintenance, that family members could often do together. The ranch-style home with picture windows and sliding glass doors to bring nature into the living room was an investment, and large amounts of family time were spent preserving and growing the value of one's property (Miller, 1995).

In print: Publications and media representation of woodworking

Mainstream media helped shape and reinforce the do-it-yourself movement, in the process shaping the roles in which each family member would see themselves inside this landscape of home. In 1957 *Workbench* magazine launched with a vision to capitalize on this growing marketplace. While they didn't have a "Women's Page" until the March/April issue of 1962, several early issues did depict women—always white and posing in what could be read as single-family detached homes—prominently displayed on the covers, most often to make visible the beauty, utility, and simplicity of the featured project. While just such an image appears on its cover, the interior pages of the March–April 1957 issue, for example, show only one woman, who uses a scroll saw to cut out pattern pieces for lawn ornaments (see Figure 3.21). Children of any age pictured with tools in their hands are typically boys. Even in woodworking publications targeting an audience of women, to this day many if not most projects are designed to be simple decorative elements that can either be quickly completed to beautify the home or done with children.

As the American public in the 1960s and 1970s was increasingly drawn to the countercultural allure of craft and the growing availability of tools suited for the home workshop, publishers reflexively responded to the burgeoning interest. Paul Roman dropped out of corporate life to start *Fine Woodworking* in 1975. Ten years later it had a quarter of a million readers. Printed on heavy coated paper and in unusual large format, the magazine had a stately typeface and a seductive blend of dignity and documentary grittiness. Roman sought to conjure the timelessness of the craft and "somebody who demonstrably had touched the hand. Who had been taught by master-to-apprentice, father-to-son [sic] and as far back into the mists as you could see" (Binzen, 2000/2001). In the twenty-fifth anniversary issue in 2000, the editors claimed that there were productive tensions between

MRS. MOODY'S CUTOUTS sometimes serve a utilitarian as well as a decorative purpose. This advertising sign is suspended between two wooden deer.

WOODEN FIGURES
that brighten lawns

HOWARD E. MOODY

The woman of this family makes use of a jig saw to earn $1,000 a year through sale of cutouts to decorate yards.

MRS. NELLIE MOODY saws out one of her lawn cutouts on the jig saw she bought to enable her to keep up with a growing demand for the figures.

BOX UPON box of small lumber and plywood scraps plus the desire to create with wood, started my wife, Mrs. Nellie Moody of Upper Jay, New York, on a very successful home enterprise.

It all started five years ago when I started bringing home boxes of pine lumber and exterior plywood scraps from a wooden toy factory where I was shop foreman. But let Mrs. Moody tell it: "My husband thought that the scrap wood, as he called it, being very dry, would make excellent kindling wood. But I had other ideas on this. I have always had a secret desire to create with wood. Now I felt that certainly this was the opportune time to start. But what could I make from this kind of scrap lumber?"

Mrs. Moody decided that she would try to make some lawn cutouts, something that she had wanted for some time but that had not been available in her locality.

She purchased several sets of lawn cutout patterns from advertisers in a magazine. These sets cost $1 each and each set contains from twenty to 110 different patterns, depending on size and quality.

"My first cutouts were hardly worthy of display on the lawn," recalls Mrs. Moody, "but they did prove one thing—that with patience

24 & WORKBENCH

Figure 3.21: *Workbench*, page 24, March/April 1957. (Reprinted with permission, Active Interest Media, Holdco, Inc)

Figure 3.22: "While I'm not sure the shoes are entirely appropriate, it's impressive that in the photo she is using the panel saw, not looking on while someone else does the work (and nowhere does it say 'so easy your wife can do it.')" (Kate Taylor, 2009–2021, *Workbench* magazine, cover, July–August 1970. Reprinted with permission, Active Interest Media, Holdco, Inc, last accessed 12/2020)

"older and younger readers, experts and beginners, power-tool junkies and hand-tool absolutists, makers of period and contemporary furniture, professionals and amateurs, art furniture makers and devotees of pure function." But the magazine's gravitas and consistently high production values ultimately grew into a conservatism that has struggled to respond to a changing field; its most glaring shortcoming was predictable. "When I first started doing my woodworking classes [*in the mid-80s*], I wrote to Fine Woodworking," recalls Debey Zito. "I wanted to start a group called Women Furniture Makers Connecting with Women Furniture Makers. They wouldn't put it in. They said, what do you mean connecting? The heading for the section in the magazine was called 'Connecting.'"

Yet for those who wanted it, *Fine Woodworking* was also a valuable resource for technical information. Sarah McCollum, founder of the Furniture Society, recalls that it was "the total education" for her in the late 1970s and early 1980s. She had graduated as an architect and worked in a construction company but wanted to learn furniture techniques and skills. McCollum believes *Fine Woodworking* "influenced our whole profession profoundly. And especially with the indexes, because you could go back and reference" (McCollum, 2016).

The high production values and technical rigor helped make *Fine Woodworking* the industry standard. For whatever diversity there was in publishing models and content, woodworking publications have been consistently and overwhelmingly male and white. They are also rooted in a concept of home and furnishing that reflects the suburban American dream.

Forty-five years after its debut, *Fine Woodworking* featured Nancy Hiller (Profile pp. 197–206) on its April 2020 cover. Between spring 2008 and summer 2021 (the limits represented on their website) she is the only woman to appear with her work on a cover. In a Women's History Month series of blog posts in 2021, Hiller points out that while the magazine should be called out for the dearth of diversity in representation, it's also incumbent on readers to submit proposals to an overextended staff, and reflecting on her own efforts to submit proposals, she invites readers to be both patient and persistent (Hiller, 2021).

Art and Craft: The freewheeling '60s

The 1960s were a tumultuous, revolutionary cultural period around the world. The US witnessed a nationwide anti-war movement on college campuses and in cities, the flowering and suppression of Black Power, the

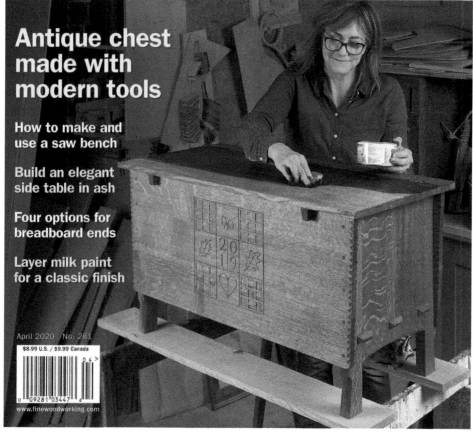

Figure 3.23: *Fine Woodworking*, cover, Nancy Hiller, April 2020

Chicano Movement, newly emergent second-wave feminism, the first moon landing, and Woodstock. In *The Maker's Hand,* Edward Cooke, Gerald Ward, and Kelly L'Ecuyer describe woodworking in this period as a dynamic tension between the purity and reverence for wood embodied by mid-century makers like Nakashima, Krenov, or Maloof, and "a counterculture-based emphasis on the artistic qualities of wood in the exciting 1960s" (Edward Cooke, 2003). Because training in furniture and woodworking in the United States had shallower roots in tradition and the legacy of the apprentice model than in much of the world, the woodworkers emerging in the 1960s were more likely self-taught or educated in university art programs. Though the philosophical roots in the Arts and Crafts movement remained visible in the self-concept of the maker and their relationship to authorship, the culture of experimentation was growing, and the work that emerged in the sixties was often playful, sculptural, and narrative.

The experimental relationship to wood wasn't accompanied by a parallel social progressivism; the gendered conception of woodworking went largely unquestioned through the decade, from exhibitions that purported to represent woodcraft in the United States to the high school woodshop. Woodturner Virginia Dotson (b. 1943) was in high school in the late 1950s. After taking a battery of standardized tests she was told she scored, "too well in areas considered male expertise, such as depth perception and manual dexterity." A few years earlier, woodturner Merryll Saylan (b. 1936), who also scored highly in both aesthetics and mechanical interest, was told these traits "could not go together, especially in a girl" (Saylan, 1998). Likewise, Rosanne Somerson (b. 1954) and Wendy Maruyama (b. 1952), both profiled in this book (Profiles pp. 322–332 and pp. 273–287), were among many girls and young women who, even into the late 1960s, were turned away from shop class.

Pamela Weir-Quiton I "That girl woodworker"

Pamela Weir-Quiton (b. 1944) has been working with wood since 1964. Initially in love with fashion, Weir-Quiton—then Weir—wanted to go to Parsons School of Design to study clothing design. As luck and the roving lifestyle of military families would have it, she instead went to California State University, Northridge, and ended up in their craft department majoring in ceramics and photography. One day her advisor and woodworking instructor suggested that instead of ending her day covered in clay dust, she could try out the woodshop and get covered in sawdust. She did and fell in love almost from the first. The class took a fieldtrip to a lumber yard, a place called Rare Woods run by Louie Rigglesberger, and she felt an immediate connection to the "vibrations of the exotic hardwoods." She hung out there often enough that she was sometimes mistaken for Rigglesberger's granddaughter.

One of Weir-Quiton's first assignments in the class was to laminate pieces of hardwood to create a doll or toy. She did. Responding to another assignment shortly thereafter, she scaled the doll to life-size, catalyzing an exploration she's been ensconced in ever since. Not long after college, she was pictured on the cover of *Home* magazine, valuable affirmation for an emerging maker. Like George Nakashima and Sam Maloof, she says, she found her style early and has been exploring it deeply ever since.

Wood sculpture

Weir-Quiton's work shared a language with Parisian-born Venezuelan sculptor Marisol (1930–2016), who was creating large figurative and narrative sculptures that combined wood carving and assemblage. Marisol was one among a small cohort of women artists working with wood as a purely sculptural medium whose work was growing in visibility from the mid-century onward. *Revolution in the Making: Abstract Sculpture by Women 1947–2016*, which opened in 2016 at Hauser Wirth & Schimmel, included work by thirty-four artists, at least four of whom work or worked primarily in wood: Louise Nevelson (1899–1988), Louise Bourgeois (1911–2010), Jackie Winsor (b. 1941), and Ursula von Rydingsvard (b. 1942). Another, Jessica Stockholder (b. 1959), worked with found furniture as her primary medium. Not unlike more traditional women woodworkers, these mid-twentieth-century women artists encountered twin biases: Difficulty acquiring technical knowledge, and a presumption that sculpture was a male domain. They were also either subtly or overtly excluded from studio spaces where large-scale works could be fabricated.

> ... it is important to recall that for many women artists of this period, particularly sculptors, there were considerable impediments to working in the studio—the artist's space was synonymous with what Virginal

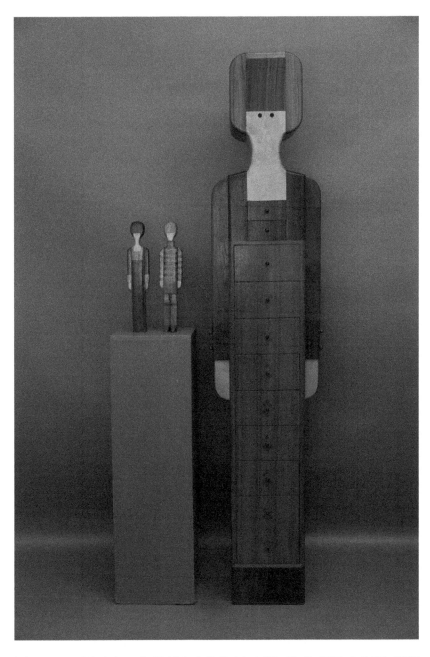

Figure 3.24: Pamela Weir-Quiton, (L–R) *Little Dolls* (Original #1), *Phyllis* (Little Doll #2), 1965; *Sloopy Doll Chest of Drawers*, 1967. (Courtesy of the artist)

Figure 3.25: Pamela Weir-Quiton, cover of *LA Times'* *Home* magazine, July 1968, with *Georgie Girls*. (Courtesy of the artist)

Woolf famously termed "a room of one's own" in her 1929 essay of the same title. The studio was largely gendered as "male." This ideal was exemplified by the image of the lone male artist performing angst in an urban loft or a rural barn—a trope that persisted ...

(Rothwell, Sorkin, and Schimmel, 2016)

In the foreword to the exhibition catalog Jenni Sorkin and Paul Schimmel describe the importance of the studio, a space of both isolation and intimacy that invites the "rawness of experimentation," and the "development of new forms." And yet art critic and curator Lucy Lippard wrote,

In the winter of 1970, I went to a great many women's studios and my preconceptions were jolted daily. I thought serious artists had to have big,

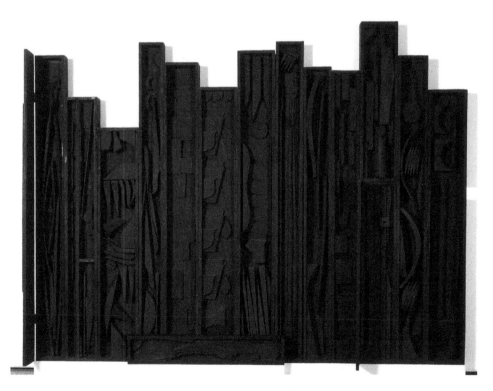

Figure 3.26: Louise Nevelson, *Tropical Garden II*, 1957. (Purchased permission from Art Resource, NY, and Artists Rights Society)

professional-looking spaces. I found women in corners of men's studios, in bedrooms and children's rooms, even in kitchens, working away.
(Rothwell, Sorkin, and Schimmel, 2016)

Because of spatial constraints, the work of these women sculptors tended to be modular and accretive, easier both to make in smaller spaces and to manipulate before assembly—to lift and work the pieces as separate entities. Despite its overall dimensions of 90 1/5" × 114 3/5" × 12 1/5" (229 × 291 × 31 cm), *Tropical Garden, II* was created, as most of Nevelson's work, from small bits of wood often found in the street. Bridging collage and Cubism in Joseph Cornell-inspired boxes, Nevelson "stacked boxes against a wall and filled each compartment with found wooden scraps including moldings, dowels, spindles, and furniture parts" (*Louise Nevelson, Big Black, 1963*, 2017). Similarly, Von Rydingsvard's long-time favorite material, 4" × 4" cedar posts, were cut into chunks and carved, then assembled in layers and then in blocks, with the completed works scaled to public spaces but only fully assembled on site into their final, geologically stratified, and towering forms.

~

Throughout the 1960s women in woodworking—as in the arts—continued to be underrepresented in exhibitions, and the decade ended with a rather spectacular omission. In October 1969 *Objects: USA* opened at the Smithsonian National Collection of Fine Arts in Washington, DC, before it went on to tour the United States and Europe. New York gallery owner Lee Nordness conceived and organized the show "to expose ... the objects being created today by artists in materials which have been traditionally called 'craft media,' such as clay, glass, fiber, wood" (Metcalf and Koplos, 2010). Working with Paul J. Smith—then director of New York's Museum of Contemporary Crafts (today the Museum of Arts and Design)—they selected 308 works across every craft discipline, intending to capture the diversity of makers, media, and aesthetic concerns of craft practice. Contemporaries thought of it as a watershed exhibition, capturing the moment and pointing to the ways that the lines between craft and art were blurring. The exhibition drew crowds wherever it was on view, whether Birmingham, England, or

Warsaw, Poland. Today the Museum of Arts and Design holds 123 works from the show and many of the other works were donated to the museums across the country that had exhibited the collection.

In the wood category there were twelve artists; none were women, making wood the only material category in the exhibition without any representation of female makers. The same glaring oversight would repeat in craft survey shows throughout the next decade: 1972's *Woodenworks: Furniture Objects by Five Contemporary Craftsmen* and *Craft Multiples* in 1975 included no women. In 1979, *New Handmade Furniture: American Furniture Makers Working in Hardwood*, organized by the American Crafts Museum (formerly the Museum of Contemporary Crafts and today the Museum of Arts and Design) in New York, featured thirty-seven woodworkers, including two women: Joyce Anderson and Judy Kensley McKie.

Woodworking as a woman in the 1970s: Building blocks

Once suffrage became law in 1920, first-wave feminism began to fragment and didn't coalesce again until the early 1960s, catalyzed in part by the 1963 publication of Betty Friedan's *The Feminine Mystique*, which sold three million copies in three years. Friedan decried a culture that denied women the right to fully realize their intellectual and creative potential, that limited their power to the management and decoration of the domestic sphere. The broad reach of her book into the hands of middle-class house-wives across the country was transformative, giving voice to anger that fueled a series of legislative victories addressing questions as diverse as domestic violence and women's right to hold credit cards in their own names. Under the rallying cry of "the personal is political," the movement was a call for social transformation, for a change in the way society viewed women and the way women viewed themselves (Grady, 2018). While first- and second-wave feminism are rightfully critiqued for the absence of a strong class and race analysis and for failing to recognize the transformative and intersectional voices of women of color, the movements also catalyzed substantive changes—legal and cultural—that have had an enormous impact on generations of young women and men emerging into adulthood since.

The late 1960s and 1970s were a time of burgeoning resistance to the conformity and consumerism of the 1950s and early 1960s. Among many types of resistance, women entered fields from which they had been tradi-tionally excluded. In the San Francisco Bay Area, then a hotbed of progressive ideals, women were starting to break new ground in the building trades. Priscilla Rice went to construction school in an airplane hangar at the edge of the city, finishing up in 1971, the year before Title IX anti-discriminatory legislation passed. Though her school experience was positive, when it came time to move into paid work the opportunities for women didn't materialize. Lacking formal support mechanisms for employment, a group of women came together, called themselves Tabitha Babbitt Builders in honor of the Shaker inventor, posted an ad in the local paper, and got to work.

A couple of years later, Rice (then Priscilla Danzig) was among the first women to join the state carpenters' union; facing plenty of gender discrimination, a group of women again came together in mutual support and incorporated as Seven Sisters Construction Company, named for the Pleiades cluster of stars. Ruth Ann Crawford (b. 1943) first met Rice and her friend Jean Malley in a café on the Mendocino Coast in 1973 when Malley and Rice were building an octagonal barn in the area. A few years later when Crawford, who had been working as a handywoman on the north coast, moved down to the Bay Area she joined up with Seven Sisters. The group, whose number varied between six and nine, found jobs together and were committed to the ideals of cooperative leadership and equal pay. Rice recalls that female clients wanted to hire women, and when they could, the Seven Sisters subcontracted to other women working in the electrical and plumbing trades, fostering a network of mutual support. Crawford remembers it as a "flowering time. We were in Berkeley! Everyone was on board with this; they were really excited to have women doing the projects." The East Bay was awash with women's spaces like bookstores and coffee shops, and the staff in the two lumber yards they frequented knew them and welcomed them.

Throughout the late sixties and early seventies, groups of women along Northern California's Mendocino County coastline were creating "back to the land" cooperative communities. County average income was three-quarters of the state's average, land was affordable, and county infrastructure was spare, as were building code requirements. Similar enclaves formed up and down the west coast in places where land was available and building codes relaxed. Rooted in communal living, non-hierarchical leadership, and women's ownership of land, they formed communities and raised vegetables, animals, and children. By 1970 there were enough women's land communities in the Mendocino area that *Rolling Stone* magazine did a feature on them in December of that year (Perry, 1970).

Some of the county's new residents began publishing *Country Women* magazine, which, "typewritten and hand-illustrated, was both agricultural and consciousness-raising, with DIY-minded articles on farming and building houses. 'For a while,' said publisher Carmen Goodyear, *'Country Women* had more subscribers than *Ms.'*" Most of the communes folded, but many of the residents remained. "'Women taught each other, empowered each other,' (Goodyear's partner) Laurie York says. 'It's a dandelion effect. That early consciousness-raising was a time of planting seeds. They blew into the wind and spread everywhere'" (Bengal, 2017).

The cooperative model served the Seven Sisters for more than seven years. When they closed the company it was amicable, a decision about economics and changing lives as they got older. Looking back, Crawford wonders if they heralded the change they anticipated:

> I don't know if this speaks for all of Seven Sisters, but I thought we were in the vanguard, that we were setting the stage for women to come after us, take up their hammers and get going. That didn't happen. I think it was because it was the middle eighties and computers were taking hold of everybody's psyches. Women weren't drawn to that [*trades work*] so much anymore.
>
> (Personal interview, 2021)

Self-help and DIY

In 1973, Florence Adams published *I Took a Hammer in My Hand, The Woman's Build It and Fix It Handbook*, intending to be a resource for women, demonstrating that home repairs were easier than they looked, and encouraging her audience to be doers rather than helpers or onlookers. A few years later, Dale McCormick published *Against the Grain: A Carpentry Manual for Women* with Iowa City Women's Press. When McCormick graduated with her teaching credential in 1971 there were no jobs in education, so when she saw a posting for apprentice applications for the local carpenters' union,

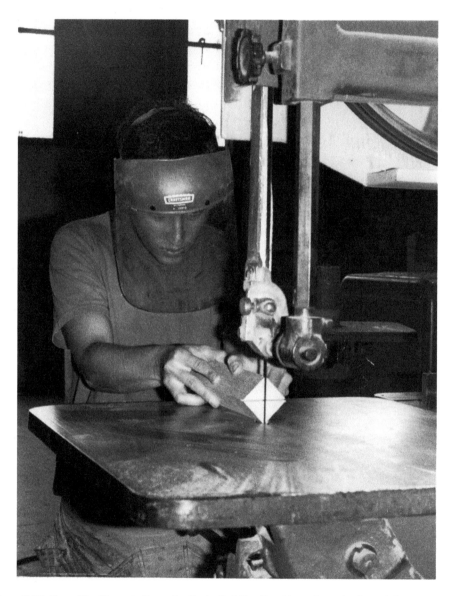

Figure 3.27: From *The Woman's Carpentry Book: Building Your Home from the Ground Up.* (Photograph by Carol Osmer Newhouse, 1978–79)

she applied. She'd grown up around tools, attended an elementary school that offered shop for both girls and boys in the second and third grades, and measured her life by what she'd been building at a given time, whether forts, theatre sets, or sheep pens. Evident in both writing style and the structure of *Against the Grain* is that McCormick had insight into the field's subtle and not-so-subtle barriers to entry; she begins with the basics, not—as carpentry books are often structured—starting at the foundation and moving upwards, but rather starting with philosophy and moving through tools, fasteners, and joints, before coming to the construction of a wall. The comb bound book that sold in 1977 for $6 is generously illustrated with hand-done drawings that are accessible, clear, warm, and attentive to representing a diversity of bodies and skin tones. The illustrations are both philosophical and pedagogical, demystifying tasks, like carrying a full sheet of plywood by most effectively using one's body for leverage rather than relying solely on upper body strength. As important, she addresses—and anticipates—the mistakes we will all make as our mechanical skills develop, inviting readers to see themselves with patience, empathy, and humor. The book found its audience and was reproduced in a second edition only a year later. McCormick followed this a decade later with a book titled *Housemending: Home Repair for the Rest of Us*, that similarly balanced accessibility and technical clarity.

Jeanne Tetrault (1944–2004), one of the founders of *Country Women* magazine, discovered a love of woodworking and a passion for educating women about construction. She moved from Mendocino County down to the Bay Area, joined Seven Sisters, and edited *The Woman's Carpentry Book: Building Your Home from the Ground Up*, a thorough how-to guide taking readers page by page from layout to foundation and all the way to roofing for multiple kinds of houses. Published in 1980, one of the book's early sections, "What Did We Miss in High School Shop?" begins with Tetrault's reflection:

Like most women I know of various ages, backgrounds, and present lifestyles and persuasions, I grew up within a culture and an educational system that quite clearly delineated the 'natural' spheres of women and men. In the realm of carpentry and building, this delineation took its usual gross and subtle forms. Although I was accepted as somewhat of a "tomboy," ... I was never given the hammer I yearned after, or the tool set to practice with.

(Tetrault, 1980)

Throughout, the book depicts "Women's Work": A broad selection of black and white photographs of women in action, wielding hammers and circular saws, working both alone and together to build homes. Far from the images that filled the pages of popular magazines like *Workbench*, the women that animate the pages of *The Woman's Carpentry Book* are working with other women to imagine and literally build their home environments from the ground up. More than a series of how-to drawings or diagrams, the pages are filled with explanations that demystify construction, providing—as Brigham had—recipes rather than blueprints, that a community of makers can adapt to context and design idiom.

Women in shop class

I took woodworking and it saved my life, just saved my life.

(Debey Zito)

In 1972, the 92nd US Congress passed Title IX as part of the Education Amendments Act, prohibiting gender discrimination in "any education program or activity receiving Federal financial assistance." Although the work of educational equity is far from complete, it would be hard to overstate the importance of Title IX in changing the legal framework for the US educational system, which in turn materially shifted expectations and opportunities for girls and young women to imagine their futures. Sonoma County furniture maker Debey Zito grew up in the Sherman Oaks/Van Nuys area of Los Angeles and entered her senior year of high school in fall 1972, months after the passage of Title IX. She hated her sewing teacher, so her boyfriend suggested she try woodworking.

It was my senior year. I walked into the class and Ben Halpern [the instructor] said, 'I knew with this women's lib stuff we were going to get a girl in here eventually.' So, I was the first girl—luckily, I was the

Figure 3.28: Photograph by Carol Osmer Newhouse, 1978–79

senior and they were the young kids—so then I didn't feel as intimi-
dated by being in a group of all guys.

That fall Zito took woodworking and in her final semester took the class
two hours a day. At graduation Halpern gave her an award that provided a
little financial help for college. The summer after she graduated, Zito pulled
out the phone book and cold-called every cabinet shop in Los Angeles.
"They laughed at me, asked me if I was calling for my husband. Only one
person was willing to see me, and he looked at me and he said, let me see
those fingernails." She held out her hands, to which he responded, "I see
you're not wearing nail polish, but if you were, you were going to sand those
fingers to the bone." Discouraged, she moved to Northern California where
she enrolled at Sonoma State University. To stay involved in fabrication she
built stage sets and turned her attention to botany, her other love. Her first-
year biology professor saw Zito's passion for wood and told her, "'No way! If
you really want to be doing woodworking, do not give this up; go for it!' She
was encouraging me, absolutely."

The women who emerged in the field of woodworking in the 1970s were
not all seeking the same thing. Susan Working (b. 1953) was motivated by
political passion. Dropping out of the University of California, Berkeley in
1972 to do anti-war work, she wove her way through non-violent activism,
anti-prison groups, and queer politics before landing firmly in labor and
non-traditional work for women. Working drove a truck, got her steamfitters
and operating engineer qualifications, and learned to drive a bulldozer, but
at each turn and with a growing list of qualifications, she was never offered
a union job. It was her next-door neighbor, Lynette Breton, who helped her
get her first job in woodworking, building chairs at Pacific Atlas in San
Francisco's Mission District, which she describes as something akin to
diving into the deep end of a pool.

Working labored alongside "an old guy named Charlie" at that first
shop, whom she remembers appreciatively, "He could be really mean, but
he knew a lot of stuff." The year and a half she spent there at the cusp
of the eighties she likens to dog years. "There were a lot of conflicts with
the men, you know, because they didn't really like having women in the
shop." In a production shop with hard divisions of labor, her task might
be to make the parts for fifty chairs for Gump's, the San Francisco-based

luxury retailer founded in 1861. "And so I'd have all these back rails and I would get to the end and if I'm supposed to make fifty chairs, there would be forty-nine back rails. Like what happened to that one? Somebody would just trash it, you know?" When the shop hired a male woodworker and asked Working to train him, she found out that he was making $8.50 to her $7.50 per hour. Furious, she was talking about it outside the shop, not realizing that the bathroom window was open, and the shop owner happened to be using the restroom; she was laid off the following week.

Working stayed in furniture and eventually became shop mates with John and Carolyn Grew-Sheridan (1947–1996). Carolyn came to woodworking after studying architectural history, and—switching career paths—completed eighteen months of training and apprenticeship at Peters Valley Crafts Center (now Peters Valley School of Craft) in New Jersey, where Joyce Anderson was her first woodworking instructor and later a friend and mentor with whom she became close (Noll, 1997). When the Grew-Sheridans moved to California in 1974 they settled in San Francisco; together they made commissioned and speculative furniture and taught woodworking. They gathered around them a group of mutually supportive woodworkers, many of them women, including Working. Their circle was driven less by a desire to make more technically challenging pieces than to build community and camaraderie.

Still others were driven by the desire to challenge themselves. Rosanne Somerson (b. 1954) (Profile pp. 322–332) entered Rhode Island School of Design (RISD) in 1972. An A student all her life, she got into design, drawing, and woodworking at the school. Though woodworking didn't come easily, she was inspired by both the challenge and the possibilities. "I was just interested in seeing how things would look and coming up with ideas for furniture that was different from everything I'd seen. I had ideas that didn't exist, and I wanted to see what they would look like. That kept me trying more than anything." In the mix, she says, was some part female empowerment. "It was the fact that people were surprised that I wanted to do it, and I wanted to just prove that women could do anything that they wanted to, so there was bit of political proving in there. It wasn't that I was doing it for that, it was just that I was making sure that I wasn't stopped because of that."

Figure 3.29: Susan Working, (L–R) *Coatrack/Self-portrait*, 1997. (Mark Johnston); *Little Mister*, 2009. (Howard Freeman)

Figure 3.30: Carolyn Grew-Sheridan, *The Difference Between Art and Craft is a Matter of Degree*, 1996. (Carolyn Grew-Sheridan)

Studio craft programs

In the wake of the liberatory social movements for civil rights of the late 1960s and 1970s, the number of female students entering studio craft programs at colleges and universities began to grow. Numbers for women in trade skills settings remain remarkably low even today, and most women interviewed for this book entered the woodshop through a college or university art department. In "This is My Work: The Rise of Women in Woodworking," Anne Carlisle points out that since the early 1980s women have been earning more college degrees than their male counterparts, with especially strong presence in art schools (Carlisle, 2018). In 2015 women made up sixty-four percent of the student body at art schools, a number which is slightly higher still at schools like RISD (Lem, 2015). The number and percentages of women in college woodshops is growing too, and while that doesn't equate with gender equity in the shop classroom, it has been an important driver of change in the field.

Several of the women who were educated through studio craft programs in the 1970s and 1980s started to move into positions of leadership, both in their work as makers and in the worlds of academia and craft education, having a formative impact on subsequent generations of makers. These woodworkers include Rosanne Somerson (Profile pp. 322–332) at Rhode Island School of Design, Wendy Maruyama (Profile pp. 273–287) at San Diego State University, and Gail Fredell and Susan Working at Anderson Ranch.

~

Craft schools

Removed from the shops and studios of university art departments, craft schools have played—and continue to play—an important role in the development of woodworking as a field of practice, offering a combination of courses open to practitioners across the full range of experience, and residency opportunities for experienced makers who also often serve as teaching faculty. In the 1970s, as leisure time increased for more Americans, the number and course offerings in craft schools grew. Typically craft schools run short courses of one or two weeks through an extended summer season, commonly with a single technique or material focus for a short-run course. Often located in beautiful locations, they bridge vacation with vocation, and—as much as if not more than career development—promise life enhancement. With primarily visiting rather than permanent faculty, the craft schools serve as meeting places for teachers, a place to make connections that are difficult to make either when ensconced in the studio or absorbed by professional demands. They are immersive and intensive: Students and teachers eat, sleep, learn, and mingle on one compound or campus. Other than the cost of tuition, there are no barriers to entry; as a result, students today are commonly older and better resourced, able to choose life-long, elective learning.

The concept of summer school for craft dates to the 1890s, though Penland School of Craft—founded in 1929—was the first to earn an international reputation and became the model for other programs throughout the twentieth century. Based in Penland, North Carolina, the school was founded by Lucy Morgan (1889–1991), who trained as a weaver at Berea College in Kentucky before returning to Penland in 1923. Craft was seen as a way of improving community life and supporting the economic empowerment of local women, and Morgan started the Penland Weavers, "a cottage industry which provided local women with looms and materials and then marketed their handwoven goods" (A Very Short History of Penland School of Craft, 2021).

In 1928, Morgan brought Edward F. Worst, Chicago-based educator and weaving expert, to visit Penland and work with the weavers. He returned the following summer and every summer after until his death in the late 1940s. That second summer Worst brought with him several out-of-state students to join the Penland Weavers for a one-week class; with that, Penland School was born. During the next few years Morgan began to fundraise and construct buildings on the site to house the growing craft center. Sculptor, designer, and educator Bill Brown took over after Morgan retired in 1962, enlarging the curriculum to include wood and glass blowing, and creating the residency model that Penland sustains today. Their present-day course offerings in wood are intentionally expansive, covering content from hand-cut **dovetails** to timber frame construction. Makers at all levels of experience and interest are welcomed into a deeply cross-disciplinary learning environment.

Arrowmont School of Arts and Crafts in Gatlinburg, Tennessee, is, like Penland, also in the Appalachian Mountains. Arrowmont dates to the 1912 establishment of the Pi Beta Phi Settlement School, founded by alumnae of the national sorority. This was the first national philanthropic endeavor by a Greek letter organization, members of which would have been aware of the settlement house movement as well as the proliferation of settlement and vocational schools in the Appalachian region and throughout the rural south. These schools nourished vernacular crafts as a means to build the local economies (Davis, 2007). In 1926 a shop was opened at what is now Arrowmont to sell local Appalachian crafts, and in 1945 summer craft workshops were begun under the auspices of the University of Tennessee. The school took its current form and name in 1967.

In 1950 Haystack Mountain School of Crafts was founded in Deer Isle, Maine, and a decade and a half later Anderson Ranch Arts Center started in Snowmass, Colorado, with a foundational belief that as an art center it could—and should—do something distinct from a college or university setting. Peters Valley School of Craft, in the Delaware Water Gap National Recreation Area of New Jersey, was incorporated as a non-profit in 1971, and The Center for Furniture Craftsmanship (CFC) in Maine was started in 1993 by furniture maker Peter Korn when he left Anderson Ranch. Unlike the other schools, its program focuses exclusively on woodworking, and they offer programs suited to both the beginning and the experienced professional, and anywhere from two weeks to nine months long.

Over time women have attended, taught, been in residence at, and directed all these centers. Gail Fredell (b. 1951) took over as program director of Woodworking and Furniture Design at Anderson Ranch in 1993. Fredell had fallen in love with woodworking as a child hanging out in the garage, making skim boards and skateboards with her dad. "I was like Velcro. Anytime he was out there I was there." When she went to college, he gave her a toolbox, and when she returned to the shop while studying architecture, she already had a spatial sensibility and confidence with tools. "He always welcomed me into the shop and taught me how to do stuff." Fredell and Wendy Maruyama (Profile pp. 273–287) became the first women in the country to earn MFAs in woodworking and furniture design. Her design language has always been the most important facet of the work, Fredell says. "All the technical stuff is purely a means to an end. It's just the way

I have to put things together in order to create the piece." Intricate joinery, Fredell adds, "just doesn't have that much of a place in the aesthetic of my work. I use wood, but I also use stone and metal ... a lot of people would do exposed dovetails, but I would hide them. I'll do a hidden dovetail corner tenon inside of a miter."

When Fredell arrived at Anderson Ranch, she had a vision to honor the tradition she'd inherited from Maloof and Korn while introducing the energy and vocabulary of the studio furniture movement with which she identified. Bringing in these new values and ideas was a way to both expand the audience for the program and still balance the budget. "There's room for everyone," Fredell notes. In a 1997 interview she reported that over the preceding decade she'd witnessed a substantial increase in the number of women attending classes; by the time of that interview women numbered about fifty percent. Although Fredell invited Maruyama, Madsen, and Grew-Sheridan to teach from the outset, with relatively few women in the

Figure 3.31: Gail Fredell, tansu in blue, 2014. (Gail Fredell)

field and only some of those having pursued teaching, the percentage of women faculty members had remained comparatively low (Sprenger, 1997).

~

While the representation of women or gender non-conforming makers in craft schools hasn't kept pace with their growing numbers in art schools, there are anecdotal reports that women's enrollment in woodworking within continuing education and craft schools is growing as well. For example, enrollment at North Bennet Street School is around fifteen percent women in their furniture program, but much higher in their continuing education courses. Numbers at the College of the Redwoods/The Krenov School, which, although not a trades program, also falls on the craft rather than art end of the spectrum, has also seen an incremental if unsteady growth in numbers of female students. In the eighties, its first decade, there was an average of two women, or about ten percent, in each nine-month cohort of twenty-two. Through the nineties and first decade of the new century the number crept up to around four students, or seventeen percent, and between 2014 and 2020, it has averaged about twenty percent. While numbers as a percentage of the enrollment have doubled, there remains work to do to get to parity.

Historically there has been a tendency at many of the craft schools for women instructors to be offered either beginning courses or courses that are adjacent to furniture: Turning, carving, or finishing, rather than construction and joinery classes. While that has been—and often remains—true, the teaching and residency opportunities and the chance to build community with other makers have been important in the professional and creative lives of many of the makers interviewed for this book.

Craft exhibitions

Between 1969 and 1977, Nancy Hanks—chairperson of the National Endowment for the Arts (NEA)—oversaw a fourteen-fold increase in the agency's budget, from $8 million to $114 million. While most of this money was allocated to projects that fall under the fine arts, some was directed to crafts fellowships, workshops, and apprenticeships, to "folk and traditional arts," and design, including in 1972 the Federal Design Improvement

Program (Bauerlein and Grantham, 2008). The American Craft Council had been organizing annual regional craft fairs since the mid-1960s, first in New England and then across the country. Ceramics and jewelry typically had the greatest number of booths, but there were nine woodworking booths at the first San Francisco fair in 1976, which included one woman, Carolyn Grew-Sheridan, who exhibited with her husband John. Craft shows and exhibitions at local galleries continued apace through the 1970s, featuring the work of makers creating speculative pieces for sale. Unfortunately, widely accessible documentation is non-existent. The absence of an ephemeral record of these regional or local exhibition and market spaces privileges those makers whose work was sold by high-end galleries on the East Coast, which are replete with archives and catalogs.

References

A Very Short History of Penland School of Craft. (2021). Retrieved March 2021, from Penland School of Craft: https://penland.org/about/history/

Adamson, G. (2021). *Craft, An American History.* New York, NY: Bloomsbury.

Anderson, J. (2002, September 18–19). *Oral history interview with Joyce Anderson, 2002 September 18–19*. (D. Gold, Interviewer).

Bauerlein, M. and Grantham, E. (2008). *National Endowment for the Arts: A History 1965–2008.* Retrieved May 2021, from arts.gov: https://www.arts.gov/sites/default/files/nea-history-1965-2008.pdf

Bengal, R. (2017, June 25). *VOGUE: Country Women.* Retrieved December 1, 2020, from https://www.vogue.com/projects/13532936/pride-2017-lesbians-on-the-land-essay

Bernstein, A. K. (1996, Fall). "Woman Speaks": Representations of Working Women in Postwar America. *Journal of Film and Video*, *48*(3), 30–45.

Binzen, J. (2000/2001, Winter). The First Years of Fine Woodworking. *Fine Woodworking* (146), 49.

Black Mountain College Project. (n.d.). *Mary Gregory*. Retrieved January 2021, from Black Mountain College Project: http://blackmountaincollegeproject.org/Biographies/GregoryMary/GregoryMaryBIO.htm

Carlisle, A. (2018, September 11). This Is My Work: The Rise of Women in Woodworking.

American Craft Inquiry, 2(1). Retrieved January 2021, from American Craft Council, https://www.craftcouncil.org/post/my-work-rise-women-woodworking

Clarke, L. and Wall, C. (2006). Omitted from History: Women in the Building Trades. *Proceedings of the Second International Congress on Construction History*, *1*, 35–59. Retrieved from University of Cambridge, Department of Architecture: https://www.arct.cam.ac.uk/Downloads/ichs/vol-1-35-60-clarke.pdf

Crawford, R. A. (2021, January 3). D. Visser, Interviewer.

Davis, B. (2014, July 2). *The Mighty Women of World War I*. Retrieved December 1, 2020, from https://www.cnn.com/2014/07/01/opinion/davis-world-war-i-women/index.html

Davis, S. (2007, July 10). *University of Tennessee, Knoxville.* Retrieved March 2021, from Libraries: https://databases.lib.utk.edu/arrowmont/Steve/The%20Founding%20of%20Pi%20Beta%20Phi%20Settlement%20School.pdf

Dusselier, J. E. (2015, June 13). *Arts and Crafts in Camp*. Retrieved January 2021, from Densho Encyclopedia: https://encyclopedia.densho.org/Arts_and_crafts_in_camp/#cite_note-ftnt_ref3-3

Edward Cooke, K. L. (2003). *The Maker's Hand: American Studio Furniture, 1940–1990.* Boston: MFA Publications.

Ellison, S. (2016, April 24). *From La Femme de Charpentier to the Lumberjill.* Retrieved June 2019, from Lost Art Press: blog.lostartpress.com/2016/04/24/from-la-femme-de-charpentier-to-the-lumberjill

Fenton, J. L. (2007). *Craft in America: Celebrating Two Centuries of Artists and Objects.* New York: Clarkson Potter Publishers.

Foat, J. (2019). *Lumberjills; Britain's Forgotten Army.* Gloucestershire: The History Press.

Futral, F. (2009). *The Hudson River Valley Review.* Retrieved January 2021, from HudsonRiverValley.org: https://www.hudsonrivervalley.org/documents/401021/1102522/HRVR+26.1+full/538855e0-0d48-4ae8-9887-90c1f31c9210

Grady, C. (2018, March 20). *The Waves of Feminism, and Why People Keep Fighting Over Them, Explained*. Retrieved December 2020, from Vox: https://www.vox.com/2018/3/20/16955588/feminism-waves-explained-first-second-third-fourth

Greenberg, M. (2004, June 18). *How the GI Bill Changed Higher Education*. Retrieved January 2021, from Chronicle of Higher Education: https://www.chronicle.com/article/how-the-gi-bill-changed-higher-education/

Hiller, N. (2021, March 18). *Fine Woodworking and Women's History Month, Part Two: Increasing the Visibility of Women in Fine Woodworking*. Retrieved June 2021, from Making Things Work: Tales from a Cabinetmaker's Life: https://nrhiller.wordpress.com/2021/03/18/fine-woodworking-and-womens-history-month-part-two/

The Star Ledger. (2015, April 12). Joyce and Edgar Anderson. Retrieved January 2021, from The Star Ledger: https://obits.nj.com/obituaries/starledger/obituary.aspx?pid=174617151

Kimmel, S. (2010, April 1). *Rooted in Art*. Retrieved April 2021, from Dickinson College: https://www.dickinson.edu/news/article/1662/

Law, S. (2019, April 8). *The Women Who Chopped Wood for Churchill: Fascinating Photos Show the Lumberjills Who Braved Horrific Injuries and Condescending Prejudice to Keep Britain's Military Supplied in World War Two*. Retrieved April 2021, from The Daily Mail: https://www.dailymail.co.uk/news/article-6897941/The-Womans-Timber-Corps-kept-Britain-supplied-wood-World-War-Two.html

Lem, P. (2015, June 9). *Big Gender Gap Persists in Arts Schools, and Math and Science Schools. Why?* Retrieved April 2021, from http://school-stories.org/2015/06/gender-disparities-found-in-many-of-new-york-citys-science-math-schools-and-arts-communication-schools/

Louise Nevelson, Big Black, 1963. (2017). Retrieved June 2021, from https://www.moma.org/collection/works/81177

Lovelace, J. (2011, July 25) *Who was Aileen Osborne Webb?* Retrieved June 2021, from American Craft Council: https://www.craftcouncil.org/magazine/article/who-was-aileen-osborn-webb

Manzanar Free Press. (1942, June 2). LOC 84025948. Retrieved from https://www.loc.gov/resource/sn84025948/1942-06-02/ed-1/?sp=4&st=text&r=0.491,0.038,0.655,0.648,0)

McCollum, S. (2016, June 23). Interview with Sarah McCollum, Building Community: An Oral History of the Furniture Society. (G. Adamson, Interviewer) American Craft Council.

Metcalf, B. and Koplos, J. (2010). *Makers: A History of American Studio Craft*. Chapel Hill: University of North Carolina Press.

Miller, L. J. (1995). Family Togetherness and the Suburban Ideal. *Sociological Forum, 10*(3), 393–418.

Morelli, L. (n.d.). *Spanish Colonial Furniture of the American Southwest.* Retrieved March 2021, from Laura Morelli: https://lauramorelli.com/how-to-collect-authentic-spanish-colonial-furniture/

National Archives. (February 5, 1919). Women at work in lumber yards. NWDNS-86-G-6S(7). YWCA, Photographer. Retrieved from https://catalog.archives.gov/id/522867

National Archives. (n.d.) Furniture, Women's Division, WPA, New Mexico. 69-MP-40–2. Retrieved from https://catalog.archives.gov/id/176251186

National Archives and Records Administration Ctr. (January 11, 1943). Heart Mountain Relocation Center, Heart Mountain, Wyoming. A class of early teenage students. NWDNS-210-G-E671; NARA ARC: 539228)

New Deal of the Day. (2018, March 19). Retrieved March 2021, from Remembering the WPA during Women's History Month: Furniture repair: https://nddaily.blogspot.com/2018/03/remembering-wpa-during-womens-history_19.html

Noll, T. (1997, Spring). Honoring a Life: Woodworker Carolyn Grew-Sheridan. *Tradeswomen*, pp. 14–16.

Perry, C. (1970, December 24). *Mendocino: Tryin' to Make a Dime in the Big Woods.* Retrieved January 2021, from Rolling Stone.com: https://www.rollingstone.com/culture/culture-news/mendocino-82730/

Pidgeon, M. E. (1947). *Women Workers and Recent Economic Change.* Department of Labor, Women's Bureau, Economic Studies. US Gov.

Powers, J. (2020, November 18). *WUWM 89.7 Milwaukee's NPR.* Retrieved April 23, 2021, from https://www.wuwm.com/podcast/lake-effect-segments/2020-11-18/milwaukee-handicrafts-project-gave-women-work-during-the-great-depression#stream/0

Prigge, M. (2020, November 18). *How Milwaukee Women Got to Work During the Great Depression.* Retrieved December 2020, from Milwaukee Magazine: https://www.milwaukeemag.com/how-milwaukee-women-got-to-work-during-the-great-depression/

Rosie the Riveter. (2021, February 9). Retrieved March 2021, from History.com: https://www.history.com/topics/world-war-ii/rosie-the-riveter

Rothrum, E., Sorkin, J., and Schimmel, P. (2016). *Revolution in the Making: Abstract Sculpture by Women 1947–2016.* Los Angeles: Hauser & Wirth.

Saylan, M. (1998, June). Women's Role in Woodworking. *Woodwork*, (51), p. 65.

Sprenger, P. (1997, June). Meanwhile, Back at the Ranch... . *Woodwork*, (45), pp. 70–75.

Swaine, M. H. (1983, August). Review: The Home Front and Beyond: American Women in the 1940s. *The History Teacher*, *16*(4), 615–617.

Taylor, K. (2009–2021). Women Woodworking, Now & Then, 2009–2021. Retrieved June 2021, from https://www.wooden-box-maker.com/women-woodworking.html (last accessed 12/2020).

Tetrault, J. (1980). *The Women's Carpentry Book: Building Your Home from the Ground Up.* Garden City, New York: Anchor Press; Doubleday.

Welner, M. A. (1942, July). *Employment of Women in War Production.* Retrieved November 14, 2020, from https://www.ssa.gov/policy/docs/ssb/v5n7/v5n7p4.pdf

Wilson, E. H. (2017). *The Three Graces of Val-Kill.* Chapel Hill, North Carolina: University of North Carolina Press.

Women's Work: The WPA Milwaukee Handicraft Project. (n.d.). Retrieved March 2021, from Milwaukee Public Museum: http://www.mpm.edu/research-collections/history/online-collections-research/wpa-milwaukee-handicraft-project/

Wood For Wood. (2020, September 9). Retrieved March 2021, from Las Cruces Bulletin: https://www.lascrucesbulletin.com/stories/wood-for-wood, 4740

Chapter Four

The American studio furniture movement

Technology and tradition: From virtuosic technique to exuberant whimsy

With fine woodworking and furniture making increasingly housed in academic environments, the emphasis placed on technical complexity and virtuosic skill grew. These values were sometimes at odds with the notion of craft that mid-century woodworkers like Nakashima and Krenov heralded, bound up in attention to the material characteristics and qualities of each piece of wood, but makers emerging from these academic settings might use a wide range of techniques to push the material to the limits, whether through bending, lamination, complex joinery, or other strategies.

In 1980 Martha Rising Rosson (b. 1954) created her signature work, the "Delight Rocking Chair," using compound **bent laminations** in maple with various exotic woods (purpleheart and Andaman padauk) as "racing stripes." The result is a gorgeous and expressive, dynamic and sinuous, virtuosic rocking chair which retains roots in function. Rosson majored in "Design in Wood," earning both a BA and an MFA in the 1970s and early 1980s at Cal State Northridge. She then apprenticed with the sculptor Michael Jean Cooper. Whereas Cooper's pieces tended to be objects with wheels, Rosson applied his techniques and aesthetics to the function of a rocking chair, extending the focus on unusual and complicated technique to the domestic sphere.

Delight Rocking Chair has very expressive line quality and Rossen used a beautiful combination of woods in the creation of a work that is techni-cally extremely complex, pushing the wood's material limits. It's important

DOI: 10.4324/9780429345418-5

Figure 4.1: Martha Rising Rossen, *Delight Rocking Chair*, 1980. (Photograph © 2021 Museum of Fine Arts, Boston)

to both distinguish among expressiveness of the line, inclusion of narrative, and the integration of quite technically complex methods in the making process; all three can be present in the same works. With each of these elements, emphasis on the hand and voice of the maker remained. In the ensuing decade, with a conscious embrace of craft by some leading galleries in the New York and Washington, DC, areas, conditions were ripe for the emergence of the studio craft movement.

Judy Kensley McKie | painter, carver, furniture maker

Judy Kensley McKie (b. 1944) is best known for the zoomorphic, narrative carving that characterizes her furniture works and promises to animate our domestic spaces. McKie studied painting as an undergraduate at RISD in the mid-1960s but says that in some ways she was working against her own

Figure 4.2: Judy Kensley McKie, (L) chest with birds, 1980; (R) table with dogs, 1980. (Judy Kensley McKie)

natural abilities, unable to translate a three-dimensional space or object to a two-dimensional canvas. Her partner Todd McKie was also a painting student at Rhode Island, and after graduation they scraped by together, taking small jobs and creating sewn wall hangings for sale. The first piece of furniture she made was a gift to Todd, a pine table from lengths cut at the lumberyard. They kept that rough-hewn table for more than thirty-five years, most often using it in the kitchen. When the wall hangings started to get some attention—too much attention, growing beyond the scale that Judy and Todd had imagined or hoped for—they pulled back from that to focus again on developing their own artwork.

Driven to build furnishings for a bare apartment, McKie started doing more woodwork, and almost by accident furniture grew to be an ever-larger part of her life and work. From simple, unadorned pieces inspired by Scandinavian design to cabinetry and built-ins, she kept building; shy of a decade into woodworking, McKie decided to teach herself to carve, adding decorative elements to her work that were inspired by African, Inuit, South American, and pre-Columbian traditions. These references have continued to inspire her work through time as the carving became increasingly three-dimensional, moving in some cases from relief carving to the form of the furniture itself, as in the "Table with Dogs" (Figure 4.2).

Dolly Spragins I furniture maker

Before Dolly Spragins (b. 1952) was a furniture maker she was a coloratura soprano opera singer in New York. Her first pregnancy changed her abdominal musculature and lung capacity and after her second child, Spragins went back to doing auditions before her body—and her voice— were ready. She left music, uncertain what to do next. Passing by the East Side YWCA on her way home one afternoon, she went in hoping to sign up for wood sculpture; however, the only course still open was a six-week class on sharpening chisels. She took it. And then she took another, this time a beginning woodworking class at the local junior college with a young Frank Pollaro. They became good friends, and she quickly came to share his love of veneers. It wasn't long after that first class that she knew woodworking was it:

> It seemed a great replacement for singing. It was creative and there wasn't any performance anxiety … you could just keep it in the shop until you were happy with it. And I started getting commissions, so … I was more successful within a year and a half in woodworking than I was in all of my singing. I was pretty successful singing, but there weren't jobs!

Spragins' growing enchantment with woodworking coincided with the emergence of the studio furniture movement, but she was largely unaware of both the movement and the group of women who came to prominence within it. Raising two kids at home, she started by making things that were driven by need; her first piece was a crib for her older child, "I wanted to make things we couldn't just go buy." Working out of the basement in her New Jersey home, with an old table saw and a bench-top **band saw**, she went to work. Scaling to what she understood as her skill set, she was drawn to Biedermeier and to curves, incorporating "as many as I could technically accomplish."

In the more than thirty years since, Spragins has taken just three or four courses at well-known craft schools, one at Anderson Ranch, another at Center for Furniture Craftsmanship, and a more recent class at Mark Adams School focused on the handheld, computer-controlled Shaper Origin.

Figure 4.3: Dolly Spragins, desk, 2012. (Dolly Spragins)

Mostly—she says with self-deprecating humor—she's reinvented the wheel over and over. With bookshelves chock full of woodworking guides and magazines, she articulated her style and taught herself what she needed to know. When needed, she sought technical support in the pages of wood magazines or in conversation with other makers.

Spragins forged her own path, quietly and without fanfare flying under the radar while pursuing her craft with intention and passion. Her husband's career allowed her to focus on her work without financial pressure; this is a complex manifestation of middle-class gender and economic norms that allowed her to pursue professional standards in a largely male-dominated field. Her furniture paid for itself, affording her a good set of tools. As the family moved around the country, making a life with their children and nurturing community with their neighbors, she'd fix up their houses, putting in countless hours in the painstaking work of repair and resurfacing, and adding value to their homes. Then this family with a restless impulse would move to a new place where they'd begin again. In what was probably her most intensely active period as a woodworker, Spragins had a large shop in Chicago that she sublet to other makers, creating a community with "a bunch of old guys." With her children then in college, she spent sixty to seventy hours a week building commissions through word of mouth. It was during this time, too, that she took on a leadership role in the Chicago Furniture Designers Association, which was responsible for the well-traveled *Rising from Ashes* furniture exhibition. The show, which included two other women—Laura Drake and Lisa Elkins—featured work made from lumber salvaged from trees killed by the emerald ash borer.

The studio in studio furniture

The language of the studio—what it afforded the maker and how the concept of the studio shaped both the maker's self-conception and the outside perception of their practice—became pivotal in the emergence of the studio furniture movement. It blurred the lines between the worlds of art and craft and placed furniture makers in the creative, critical, and economic landscape of the arts. In *The Maker's Hand*, authors Cooke, Ward, and L'Ecuyer discuss the word "studio" and what it evokes. Tossing aside "art furniture," "handcrafted furniture," "modern and postmodern furniture," and even "pluralistic furniture," the authors turn to "studio furniture." The makers of this work, they argue, are connected in "their interest in linking concept, materials, and technique; and the small shops in which they work." They didn't learn their skills as apprentices; they learned them in college woodshops or are self-taught, in either case a "less constrained learning process." And the word studio, they continue, evokes just this type of exploratory learning over time. If "shop" suggests production or manufacture, "studio" is associated with the arts, conjuring a setting where output isn't measured in quantity. "Studios" are smaller, more intimate and individual settings, part of a "decentralized (yet networked) social and economic culture." The maker in a studio is an artist whose approach to materials and ideas—and their name recognition and economic prospects—operate in the sphere of the arts (2003).

Artisans who identified with studio craft made one-of-a-kind pieces they controlled from conception to completion. With the philosophical value placed on the voice, creativity, and integrity of the maker, and the idea that skill could be a source of invention and experimentation rather than simply refinement of the product, the creative practice of the craftsperson moved closer to that of the artist. The development of smaller scale fabrication technologies in the 1960s—which also helped fuel the resurgent interest in crafts and DIY across the US—also meant that more artists could afford access to tools that would aid their production work.

The 1980s saw a notable cohort of quite visible women emerge at the forefront of the studio furniture movement. Some of the most prominent among the makers whose names and work appeared often are Somerson, Maruyama, Madsen, Fredell, Working, McKie, Grew-Sheridan, Anderson, and Wendy Stayman, whose works have often conjured early twentieth-century Art Deco architecture, realized with rigorous technique in exotic hardwoods. She brought virtuosic attention to surface detail, perhaps fueled by early training in art conservation. These makers were in the vanguard of this movement that blurred the lines between art and craft, bridging the languages of utility and the body with those of cultural and material history. The work of these women was and is quite diverse in intent and visual and material vocabulary, and as a group they allowed their personal identities, cultural histories, and experiences as women to inform and sometimes become the subject matter of their work. The movement was expansive and iconoclastic, introducing narrative and exploring the many meanings furniture can hold. A remarkably productive cadre of makers, they were profoundly influential, particularly for their number.

Theorizing craft: Postmodernism

The studio furniture movement emerged in tandem with postmodernism, a conceptual and aesthetic response to the austere formalism of Modernism in architecture, design, and the visual and performing arts. In each medium and realm, postmodernism took on distinct visual characteristics, but across all these disparate fields of practice it celebrated experimentation, narrative, ornamentation, and pastiche—the fusion of multiple recognizable styles. This way of referencing historical styles and symbols—coincident with social movements that made visible the distinct histories of cultural and ethnic groups—undermined the long-held image of the individual genius working alone in the studio and brought attention to the subjective identities of both maker and audience members.

In architecture and furniture design, one of the most prominent and influential collectives in the 1980s was the Memphis Group. Their playful, bold, even cacophonous use of color and plastic laminates in the redesign of everyday goods was described by Bertrand Pellegrin as a "shotgun wedding between Bauhaus and Fisher-Price" (Pellegrin, 2012). Their iconoclastic approach disrupted the reverence for wood exhibited by the prominent woodworkers of the mid-century, and in the late 1980s and 1990s viewers started to see even more makers appropriating and referencing earlier movements, and experimenting with ideas and materials, from applying color that concealed the grain of the wood to making furniture that eschewed function to instead consider its cultural references.

The title of Julia T. Hood's thesis on postmodern woodworking, *Furniture that Winks*, suggests that maker and viewer share a knowledge of the work's context, of the established social and historical codes to which it refers (Hood, 2011). The rise of postmodernism in the arts and in the world of studio furniture carved out space to explore the identity and social location of both audience and makers in communicating meaning. Makers in the studio furniture movement often tossed aside function altogether in favor of furniture's sculptural possibilities or poked at the cultural assumptions about utility: Whose body, whose history, and for what use.

Cheryl R. Riley | furniture designer, artist

> When I was an infant, my mother went back to school to finish her degree in fine arts at Texas Southern University. The first thing I can remember smelling was her oil paint and her clays that she was working on in the living room, making sculptures and doing paintings and things and me getting into them.

Cheryl R. Riley (b. 1952) moved to San Francisco in 1977 to work in marketing. She'd grown up in Texas with a mother who was passionate about art and created space for her daughter to make it. When Riley got into her mother's expensive art supplies, instead of limiting her access, Riley's mother gave her daughter a wall in her bedroom to draw on, which every now and then she'd paint over to let her daughter begin again. In the home Gladys Mae Dubois mixed art and furniture from multiple traditions: Chinese, French, Italian; the furniture pieces in her daughter's bedroom were reproductions of Louis XV and XVI furniture, and on the wall were reproductions of Thomas Gainsborough's *Blue Boy* and Diego Velasquéz's *Las Meninas*.

A few years into her stay in San Francisco, Riley wanted to decorate her apartment. Her father had passed away, leaving her a little extra money. By then it was the middle of the 1980s and the Memphis Group had turned postmodern furniture design on its head. Enthralled by the concept that furniture could eschew function and be art—or be functional and playful— Riley made a drawing of some chairs with very tall backs. Her girlfriend, Pamela Pastrana, was a cabinetmaker who could "pretty much build anything that (Riley) could conceive." The chair she described was her take on the Mackintosh, "if a Mackintosh and an art deco had married and had a baby and one was black, one was white." Riley drew up designs and handed them to her partner who handed them right back, asking her to put dimensions on them. "I said, well, can't you tell that the back is three times as tall? Can't you just figure it out?" The answer to that was no, "so she got me a scale ruler and taught me how to use it. I drew it to scale, she built them, and then I did a dining table for myself."

Riley loved to entertain; her friends were photographers, art directors, stylists, account executives, and other creative staff who saw at her dinner parties unique pieces for upcoming shoots. "What is this? I'm doing a shoot next week for Macy's; I could really use this as a set piece, you know. I'll rent it from you." With this encouragement, Riley kept making new work until finally one afternoon a photographer convinced her to build him a custom console. He also announced that he'd started a portfolio for her and thought she should take it down to a gallery that was showing Memphis Group work. "And so I did. I called the guy, made an appointment, and brought my drawings, as well as pictures of the pieces that were done. They said they wanted to do a window and take pieces on consignment." A commission followed, as well as an invitation to be in a show of folding screens, for which Riley created a piece that is now in the permanent collection of the San Francisco Museum of Modern Art.

Pastrana worked in a big multi-disciplinary studio space in San Francisco's Bayview Hunters Point, and Riley spent time wandering through the other shops, talking with metal workers, carvers, and all kinds of fabricators. She sat watching for hours to see how they used their materials, gleaning knowledge in the process that was then incorporated into her work as commissions continued to grow.

I had to come up with ideas that could utilize their materials, skills, and equipment, so I came into their space to learn the limitations and scope of what they did. Like the guy who poured glass for instance:

Figure 4.4: Cheryl R. Riley, *Scheherazade Bed*, wood, glass, metal. (Cheryl R. Riley)

142

how big of a piece could he pour? What slurries could be put in it? How structurally strong, and could I put weight on it? It was me sitting and learning or asking questions or telling them my ideas.

As a designer rather than a builder, Riley would draw up three ideas to scale and take them around to shops to get material samples and brainstorm approaches. Though, at times, her ideas pushed them beyond what they had done before, they figured out a way to do it. Riley talks about a dance of control, taking and relinquishing.

I wanted perfection and all the people I worked with had worked at their skill—some of them for decades—to get to the level that I was

Figure 4.5: Cheryl R. Riley, *de'Medici Sideboard II*. Commissioned by Curator Kenneth Trapp for the Oakland Museum of CA, 1994. (Cheryl R. Riley)

working with them. I wanted to have access to anything my imagination could come up with and just find somebody who could make that. And what about the equipment? My glass blower is not the person who's my glass pourer. And my cabinetmaker is not in the same shop as the guy who carves. I didn't want to be limited in my materials or the skillset. And so that allowed me to have much more freedom; anything I could imagine I could have done.

Once in the door, Riley continued to build relationships with artisans. "They all always came to the shows and brought their whole families with them. They were all very proud and happy about working with me. Sometimes they were in museums, and they hadn't *had* work in museums."

In the second half of the nineties the Bay Area swung between a recession and a burgeoning technology economy. Rents increased, the number of clients declined, and a wave of craftspeople moved out of the city. Riley felt a shift in the open-minded culture she'd fallen in love with and decided to move to New York. Today she's as much visual artist as furniture designer, and still integrates in her work a deep love of history and anthropology. With an eye for the similarities between people and cultures, Riley plays with combining what might seem like opposites. "I'm also very enthralled by beauty. I think beauty has a connection with quality, functionality, and how humans feel. What informs beauty is also in things functioning the way that they were intended to be used, you know? I used to say, I make antiques of the twenty-second century."

Art furniture and the Gallery movement

With the growing self-conscious professionalism in the arts and crafts came a sense of a movement and a scene. Galleries and schools, friendships and mentoring relationships, nourished a sense of a community. These galleries were paying attention to this emerging group of women in the field of woodworking. In fact, two shows in New York City in the mid-1980s focused exclusively on women in the field: *Women Are Woodworking*, at Workbench Gallery in 1983, and *Pioneer & Pioneering Twentieth Century Women Furniture Designers & Furniture Designer/Makers* in 1988 at the Bernice Steinbaum Gallery in SoHo. The latter featured six contemporary

Figure 4.6: Cheryl R. Riley, sketchbook page while Scheherazade was in development. (Cheryl R. Riley)

makers: Fredell, Somerson, Madsen, McKie, Maruyama, and Stayman, alongside earlier twentieth-century designers represented through photographs (Slesin, 1988).

Steinbaum was one of a handful of women gallerists on both coasts who helped support this development. Another was Margery Goldberg (b. 1950), who in 1978 founded Zenith Gallery in Washington, DC, still in operation today. In addition to curator, Goldberg is also a lamination and carved wood sculptor who became a city arts commissioner and influential advocate for the arts, recognized in 2010 and again in 2018 for Excellence in Service to the Arts.

Pritam & Eames' Gallery of Original Furniture—from owners Bebe Pritam Johnson and Warren Eames Johnson—was another important supporter of the studio furniture movement, and enjoyed one of the longest tenures among the galleries devoted to high-end speculative work. Through the 1980s and 1990s they mounted four or five shows a year—solo, two-person, and group shows on a theme—with a stable of furniture makers. McKie, Maruyama, Stayman, Somerson, Madsen, and Lee Trench all showed there through the 1980s. The gallery promoted a deep camaraderie among the makers, with show openings and gallery anniversaries serving as opportunities for makers and collectors to meet and socialize. Their readily available and extensive online exhibition documentation highlights the ways the historical record is shaped by access to and quality of documentation.

Peter Joseph—prominent among this early group of East Coast gallery owners eager to embrace this emergent furniture movement—dubbed it "art furniture." Joseph helped cultivate a growing audience and client base, particularly younger venture capitalists in their thirties and forties. His choice of language was part of a concerted effort to nurture a marketplace for the work that paralleled the gallery economy of the arts. Though not the only gallerist in this period to attempt to apply the principles of the sale of art to furniture, Joseph took it to the furthest extreme. He believed that with the correct marketing and placement, "art furniture" could obtain prices on par with fine art (Iovine, 1993), and with this in mind emphasized beautifully designed and produced catalogs with excellent photography and essays by prominent critics, including Arthur Danto and Witold Rybczynski. He also ran ads in the *New York Times* and city periodicals. These strategies created an overall impression of gravitas and provenance, with the work contextualized both within the arc of the maker's career and the larger landscape

Figure 4.7: Margery Goldberg, Margery with Chainsaw, taken around 1990 as a promotional image. (Margery Goldberg)

of art furniture. Perhaps his greatest innovation was to provide a stipend to twenty selected makers to give them resources to undertake ambitious long-term bodies of work for a solo exhibition every eighteen months. Somerson characterized the Peter Joseph Gallery this way:

I felt very fortunate to be part of Peter's stable, because for the first time, somebody was actually investing in my career, rather than just kind of partnering. He was literally investing. He was giving us stipends to create new work against our sales, and so we had the ability to hire assistants, to buy the best materials, to do really grand-scale pieces. The most ambitious pieces of my career are the Peter Joseph pieces, because I was able to afford to build them.

(*Oral history interview with Rosanne Somerson*, 2006)

Workbench Gallery in New York City opened in 1980 as a non-profit exhibition space within the flagship store of the Workbench chain of retail furniture stores (unrelated to the magazine). Founded by Bernice Wollman and Warren Rubin, Workbench Gallery was in operation for eighteen years. Rubin was the chairman of the retail chain, and Wollman, his wife, became co-director of the gallery with Judy Coady and Patricia Pullman. Coady wrote an article in *Fine Woodworking* that illuminated the role of the gallerist and salesperson in helping prospective buyers develop a relationship to speculative wood furniture in a gallery setting. She closed the piece by imagining a scenario, "with the gallery owner and client standing in front of your sleek, well-crafted, $800 pearwood end-table" (Coady, 1983). Developing a relationship with the maker, real or narrative, helps the buyer shift from a purely utilitarian relationship to the pearwood table to one in which the piece is imbued with history and meaning, according to the gallerist. This can happen through a relationship to the history of the material itself or to investment in the vision and development of the maker.

In this era of heightened interest, in 1989 Tom Toldrian launched *Woodwork* magazine. Scrappier than *Fine Woodworking*, the bi-monthly *Woodwork* was ninety percent freelance written rather than employing a writing staff. Based in Novato, California, it had a broad audience of woodworkers, from the enthusiast to the professional, and articles ranged from intermediate to complex. The cover was always the same format: A person at work in their shop, at their bench. *Woodwork* featured women makers both on its pages and its covers far more than its contemporaries. One of the magazine's strengths was its in-depth and wide-ranging personal interviews. Terrie Noll—who served as editor from early 1990 to early 1991—wrote several articles for the magazine, including lengthy interviews with Carolyn Grew-Sheridan in 1997 and Kristina Madsen (Profile pp. 253–261) in 1998. Issue 51 in 1998, edited by John Lavine, focused entirely on women woodworkers and furniture designers, including Madsen, Grew-Sheridan, Riley, and Saylan. The editorial uses the metaphor of sitting around a table but, as was characteristic of the period, resolutely states that it will not "put 'women woodworkers' in a separate category from men in woodworking. Much better not to have a separate month, or show, or magazine issue" (Lavine, 1998). A quick glance across the same page reveals an all-male editorial group, with women represented in the administration of advertising and circulation.

The 1990s

Mira Nakashima I designer, George Nakashima Woodworkers

Prominent among the legacies that begin to emerge in the field of twentieth-century furniture making is Mira Nakashima (b. 1942), who inherited what is inarguably one of the deepest legacies in contemporary woodworking. The child of master woodworker George Nakashima, she describes her young self as a tomboy, a shop pest who loved to hang out in her father's woodshop, playing with the sawdust and later serving Kool-Aid to the men who worked with her dad. Many years later, with a degree in architecture and a couple of young children of her own, she moved into a home across the road from her father and his shop, and created a life increasingly interwoven with his business.

George Nakashima died in June 1990, shortly after a fifty-year retrospective of his work opened in New York at the American Crafts Museum. After his death there was a pile of lumber down in their Philadelphia shop. "For a while I thought, 'Well maybe I'll just sell it. I don't know what to do with it.' And then I thought, dad bought those logs, he milled them himself. He had an idea of what that wood wanted to be, and I can't let it go. The woodpile kept us going," Mira Nakashima recalls. "Plus, the men in the shop." She took over as the head of the business and has stewarded it—sustaining her father's potent legacy—for thirty years.

Mira Nakashima's training in architecture and experience in the shop give her a strong sense of proportion and the ability to visualize furniture in built environments. She knows what works and what doesn't. Many of the

Figure 4.8: Mira Nakashima, High, Medium, and Low Mira Chair, walnut. (Mira Nakashima)

proportions her father developed were perfect; there is no need to change them. Her father's mantra, she says, was "Get rid of your ego," a value echoed by his peers who, like Nakashima Sr., were influenced by the teachings of Indian philosopher, yogi, and poet Sri Aurobindo. They took from Aurobindo's teachings an understanding that sublimating the ego was essential to being an artist. "Being an artist is not something you create from within your own ego. It's something that comes to you from above. Your hands, your mind, and your eyes are just conduits for this force that comes from elsewhere." These values placed on humility, the intrinsic wisdom of the material, and sublimation of the ego are ones that Mira Nakashima holds today.

You're here to make something beautiful. You're here to translate the power that grew in this tree into something beautiful that will live with people in their home and mean something to them. And that it's not anyone's ego that made this tree, but it's been given to us, and we try to make this something as beautiful as possible out of it.

While George Nakashima Woodworkers is still honoring the unbroken thread of tradition with her father's work, the culture of the shop is not the same as it was under his leadership; it's much more collaborative now than it used to be. Though her father relied on the other woodworkers in the shop, he was in charge, and the work bore his name. There was a cost: When he died, everybody thought he had been doing all the work by himself.

When asked to describe the differences between her designs and those of her father, Nakashima returns to something her son once said, "Well, Mom, your stuff looks more like spaceships than Grandpa's did." Unsure whether that's a good or a bad thing, Nakashima suggests that her work may have stronger lines, more curves, or different angles. "Of course," she says, "no two people are going to see things the same way. You could think you're doing things the same way, but it always comes out different, with different people. That's the beauty of making stuff by hand."

~

The drive to position furniture within the world of the arts that had started in the 1980s become more focused and concrete in the 1990s, but recognition by art critics and curators was slower to materialize. According to Cooke, Ward, and L'Ecuyer, "As for acceptance of furniture as art, there is little evidence that critics and curators thought differently about the field in 2000 than they had in 1990" (2003). Paradoxically, alongside the aspiration for recognition and review through galleries and collectors, the 1990s brought a growing awareness of, and disillusionment with, the realities of making work for an elite group of wealthy customers. In *Pioneer & Pioneering Twentieth Century Women Furniture Designers & Furniture Designer/Makers*, the authors reflect on a gallery-driven pressure that many artists feel, the "immense pressure to develop a signature style that would attract attention." As is true in the arts, this leaves young makers with less time, creative freedom, and energy to refine their expertise, explore the breadth of their interests, and build confidence.

Once makers have established a reputation in the field, they may feel more freedom—and have more economic independence—to disrupt that expectation of a "signature" style. Well-established in their careers, Maruyama and Somerson moved away from the highly wrought, obsessively detailed and polished singular objects as the focus of their work, albeit in very different directions. Maruyama moved toward more overtly political content, realized in gallery installations, and Somerson later worked in collaboration with colleagues to design and have manufactured sustainable furniture for use in the RISD dorms.

'Nobody knew we existed': The Furniture Society

In the early 1990s, Sarah McCollum, a woodworker in Free Union, Virginia, realized that she and her husband, Bob Sonday, also a furniture maker, and their peers in the field, were all struggling separately with the business and marketing side of their work. Each was attempting to sort it out from scratch and on their own without the benefit of dialogue with—and the experience of—their colleagues. Between 1994 and 1996 McCollum embarked on a series of research conversations with makers, interior designers, and architects, attempting to understand their businesses. She found that she and her husband were not alone: "Nobody knew we [furniture makers] existed." She concluded that, "we needed our own organization—for other reasons too, obviously: community, because we were lone wolves. But we needed an organization to help us attract the funding and administer that funding for programming, to bring about a huge increase in public awareness and to guide that process."

Two earlier efforts by furniture makers and woodworkers to create a similar professional organization in the field had failed: The Society of American Woodworkers (SAW) in 1980 and the American Society of Furniture Artists (ASOFA) in 1991. But in 1996 McCollum founded The Furniture Society, with significant early support from the Windgate Foundation.

... there was a center for the organization, and it was studio furniture. And anyone, whether they were a student or a supplier or a maker or a gallery or show coordinator or historian or anyone who was interested, was so welcome. And the convergence of—or the mix of—all of those perspectives and sensibilities was just so important, so fundamental to the diversity and thus the success.

(McCollum, 2016)

To this day The Furniture Society fosters important conversations, both internally between makers and externally with the larger public; their projects include a yearly conference, publishing interviews with contemporary craftspeople, and honoring makers who have been pivotal to the field. At the time of writing, of the 25 recipients of the Society's Award of Distinction, five are women: McKie 2005; Maruyama 2008; Somerson 2012; Bebe Johnson (with husband Warren) 2014; and Madsen 2020/2021. Though most members through time have been woodworkers, the membership also includes designers, collectors, curators, gallerists, historians, students, and makers in other media such as metal and upholstery. The first conference and accompanying exhibition was in 1997 at SUNY Purchase, with 350 participants. At the next conference in San Francisco in 1998 there was a panel about women in woodworking; participant Alice Porembski recalls the discussion:

I do remember that panel, at the time thinking it would be a sea change in the field and the Furniture Society. In fact, it was probably the least attended session and the discussion among the panelists, although very interesting, I recall little audience participation (or even much of an audience) and even less of a blip on the Furniture Society radar.

There was not another panel specifically addressing women in furniture making and woodworking until 2016, eighteen years later (Mays, 2021). *#Craftswomen*, a panel at the Society's national conference in 2016, was facilitated by Emily Bunker, who in reflecting on both her personal and professional experience believes in the importance of creating space for women-identifying makers in what is still a male-dominated craft. Following the panel, which was more energized, better attended, and farther reaching than its 1998 predecessor, Bunker received a grant to do a series of tours of women-led workshops, funded by the Leeway Foundation. Bunker's own work bridges furniture making and woodworking, community-driven design and advocacy, and materials research.

References

Coady, J. (1983). Notes and Comments section, "One gallery tells what it can sell". *Fine Woodworking*, November/December (43), pp. 104–106.

Cooke, E. S., Ward, G. W. R., and L'Ecuyer, K. H. (2003). *The Maker's Hand: American Studio Furniture, 1940–1990.* Boston: MFA.

Hood, J. E. (2011, July 26). *Furniture that Winks: Wit and Conversation in Postmodern Studio Furniture, 1979–1989.* Retrieved December 2020, from Corcoran-Smithsonian History of Decorative Arts Theses: https://repository.si.edu/handle/10088/18633

Iovine, J. V. (1993, December 26). *A Man's Home is His Collection.* Retrieved August 2, 2020, from nytimes.com: https://www.nytimes.com/1993/12/26/magazine/a-man-s-home-is-his-collection.html

Lavine, J. (1998). Editor's Note. *Woodwork*, (51), 2.

Mays, L. (2021, June 20). Conversation (D. Visser, Interviewer).

McCollum, S. (2016, June 23). Building Community: An Oral History of the Furniture Society (G. Adamson, Interviewer). American Craft Council.

Oral history interview with Rosanne Somerson. (2006, August 7). Retrieved August 8, 2020, from Smithsonian Archives of American Art: https://www.aaa.si.edu/collections/interviews/oral-history-interview-rosanne-somerson-13618#transcript

Pellegrin, B. (2012, January 15). Collectors give '80s postmodernist design 2nd look. *San Francisco Chronicle*. Retrieved May 2021, from https://www.sfgate.com/homeandgarden/article/Collectors-give-80s-postmodernist-design-2nd-look-2517937.php

Slesin, S. (1988, April 14). *Furniture by Women on Exhibit.* Retrieved August 2020, from *The New York Times*, Home and Garden: https://www.nytimes.com/1988/04/14/garden/furniture-by-women-on-exhibit.html

Chapter Five

Contemporary profiles

In the forward trajectory of this research, the present preceded the past; that is, most of the interviews conducted for the contemporary profiles took place before the full scope of the social and cultural history came into focus. There was no clearer reassurance that the narrative aligned as when the major themes that had been identified through conversations with makers began to play out over the course of woodworking's history: Education, economics of production, community, and sustainability. Once the history was written it was also clear that the interviews comprised a history of the present, so to speak, and were best understood in the profile format since, in each case, the narrative is ongoing, alive, and well. Thus the decision to present them as a separate yet continuous part of the narrative, allowing more of the makers' voices to speak about their realities, experiences, triumphs, and dreams.

Education and equity

In conversations with makers from Rhode Island to San Diego, and spanning multiple generations, it was more often than not teachers who were cited as mentors. History has shown us that it is not enough to simply have a woman or gender non-conforming teacher. Alison Croney Moses (Profile pp. 172–184), for example, is building racial equity deep into professional development at the Eliot School in Boston, recognizing the gaps in experience and perception between a mostly white faculty and a student community that's largely Black and brown. And we know from countless studies that students' sense

DOI: 10.4324/9780429345418-6

of possibility is shaped by seeing people who look like them at the head of the classroom or, for our purposes, the lead bench in the woodshop.

Critically assessing the curriculum also matters. Beliefs about—and standards of—quality are not neutral; nor are ideas about whether joinery is made visible or hidden. They are bound up in cultural narratives and histories that have too often served to exclude. Teaching the history of woodworking in Western Europe as *a* history and not *the* history of wood and furniture also matters; Rosanne Somerson's (Profile pp. 322–332) desire to expand her knowledge base when Folayemi Wilson (Profile pp. 333–345) was admitted to the MFA program at RISD opened up a rich learning relationship that benefited professor and student.

In the early 1970s, only about one quarter of middle-class workers had any education beyond high school, and most American workers trained for a career path in which they would spend their lives. But as the decade went on, globalization and emergent technologies intersected, and good union jobs that required only a high school education were increasingly scarce. These shifts in the economy and job market in the 1970s exerted new pressures on vocational education programs, challenging them to meet student needs in a changed landscape. By the mid-eighties many teachers, activists, parents, and educational reformers were calling for educational equity; despite the legal advances of Title IX, vocational education was seen as a form of racial and class-based tracking and gender segregation that undermined equity-based reform. Whether through overt or unconscious bias, students were tracked into programs that trained them for the jobs that school policymakers and teachers associated with their identities, thereby both mirroring and replicating inequities and undermining economic mobility.

Today, school districts from Massachusetts to Tennessee are working at reinventing vocational education so that all students leave high school college *and* career ready. However, work remains in many districts across the country: In the course of this research we heard stories about districts in which the shop tools aren't suited to the curriculum requirements, and school administrators—many of whom have no shop experience themselves—are resistant to the investments required to align them. We also heard stories about advocates and educators like Girly Shop Teacher who are traveling around the country bringing new ideas to educational conferences, community groups, and social clubs about shop culture, curriculum, and learning models. Char Miller-King's (Profile pp. 288–299) presence and passion for teaching both online and in her community—and her willingness to talk tools for days with a broad audience—helps students of all ages discover their own agency through her teaching practice.

The economics of production in the twenty-first century

The economic conundrum intrinsic to the Arts and Crafts movement—reconciling handcrafted labor with affordability in a capitalist system—is as much a challenge today as it was in 1850 or 1950. In late capitalism it is perhaps more of a challenge in some respects, even as small-scale production tools continue to advance and become more affordable, and the internet gives makers access to multiple markets.

Every maker interviewed for this project is grappling with the same challenge: Addressing the economics of contemporary production in complex, strategic, and multifaceted ways. SIOSI (Profile pp. 311–321) uses social media to cultivate a community that seeks a relationship with the producers of their household goods and has the resources to do so. Sean Desiree (Profile pp. 185–196) also began their career as a maker by using Etsy as a marketplace; today they consider practices that bridge that accessible market with higher-end consumers, as well as grants and opportunities for public art works. Yvonne Mouser's (Profile pp. 300–310) *Bucket Stools* are designed by the artist in California and fabricated by Amish makers in Pennsylvania, a small-scale manufacture model rooted in cultural history.

KG MacKinnon (Profile pp. 243–252) and Nancy Hiller (Profile pp. 197–206) both operate in the marketplace of custom built-ins, helping their clients imagine and create spaces both beautiful and maximally functional. And where furniture and woodworking education is rooted in academic settings, many maker-professors appreciate that the salaried position frees them to do speculative, risky, or innovative work without the same imperative to sell it. There isn't one answer, and most of the profiles speak to this as an evolving conversation, with makers changing and bridging strategies at different points in their careers.

Collaboration and community: Building community-centered spaces

More than ever, women and gender non-conforming makers are creating and joining woodworking communities of all kinds across the United States and beyond. Building and sustaining such spaces isn't easy: The right balance of inclusion, expansiveness, dialogue, accountability, and horizontal leadership is both demanding and time consuming to create and sustain. Whether, like Workshop of Our Own in Baltimore and Girls Garage in Berkeley, they are constructed as a space for women, girls, and gender non-conforming makers; or co-educational like The London School of Furniture, Philadelphia's Tiny WPA, or blkhaus-studios in Chicago; or simply a shared shop space without a name, communities are created to share resources, provide networks of mutual support and learning, or serve as spaces to design and create community-driven solutions to the challenges of our cities.

In community-based educational settings, balancing the political vision and the rigor of making—an emphasis on craft—can be a challenge; programs often privilege one or the other. Emphasis on the politics might look like a rapid-fire program where the intention is to expose as many girls and women to power tools as is possible. For Emily Bunker—founder and Executive Director of Girls Garage—they are deeply connected: Creating a thing that is beautiful and well-crafted changes your perception of what you're capable of.

Resources and sustainability

Nothing is inherently trash.

(Strasser, 1999)

According to Executive Director Susan Inglis, when the Sustainable Furnishings Council was founded in 2006, "we were the only voice for life cycle assessment, and even for life cycle thinking, in the furniture industry" (Fire, 2020). Fifteen years later there's much more awareness of the life cycle of materials, driven by consumer demand for healthier materials and greater transparency in supply chains. There remains, Inglis observes, a knowledge gap among manufacturers, while focus on sustainability is growing within the design community.

Figure 5.1: Girls Garage, 2019, *We Are Builders*

Until the consumer revolution of the second half of the twentieth century, Americans on the whole produced relatively little trash. Most goods were sold in bulk, things broken were repaired, and clothing that no longer fit was passed down to a younger sibling or other community member. In the first decade of the twentieth century, the average American worker made four to eight dollars a week; a new piece of furniture could cost a week's wages. In San Francisco, as in other cities across the country, in the years before and during WWII, the ragman made his way through neighborhood streets with a six- by ten-foot open cart drawn by a single horse, calling out, "rags, bottles, sacks," drawing neighbors out to the street to sell these recyclable and reusable goods for pennies. One might sell old newspapers in the salvage yard for a penny per pound, $20 for a ton. These reclaimed goods were understood to be resources for domestic production.

Sixty years later, in 2002, William McDonough and Michael Braungart issued a thoughtful, popular call for a new industrial revolution, termed cradle-to-cradle design, with the subtitle and call to action, "Remaking the Way We Make Things." They called for a radical reimagining of product design and manufacture in which, at the end of their life cycle, products could provide nourishment for the next generation of products. Using nature as a model, their book reconceptualized our current "cradle-to-grave" life cycle. The World Counts, a Copenhagen-based organization that gathers environmental data from large and small sources across the world, estimates that, globally, the amount of furniture we buy corresponds to the total economic output of Sweden: $18,000 every second (The World Counts, 2021). This level of manufacture and consumption is hard to comprehend, and harder to gauge in relation to the makers in this book; however, it points to the scale and complexity of resource consumption when we think about furniture. In the United States the majority of deforestation occurred prior to 1910; the pace has since slowed, but issues of habitat fragmentation and the transformation of forests in a changing climate remain paramount.

Louise Brigham's early twentieth-century box furniture integrated a social, environmental, and economic philosophy, reskilling urban workers by repurposing locally available and adaptable materials, thereby reducing waste and resource consumption. Today the use of recycled materials focuses on two intertwined but distinct threads: Not wasting materials (which relates to future need) and the impact of industrial waste (pollution and other harms) (LaFarge, 2019). Inglis suggests that concern about sustainability in mainstream furniture manufacture today seems to be driven most by a personal concern about healthy products in the home, but a 2017 study by Capstrat Public Policy indicates that more than fifty percent of American consumers would be willing to pay more for more sustainable products (Chrinian, 2017).

To consider sustainability in woodworking and furniture is a social, economic, and material effort: Most of the makers in this book are choosing domestic hardwoods, conscious of the impact of deforestation on tropical forests. Desiree (Profile pp. 185–196) rarely buys wood, working largely from found materials; Christine Lee (Profile pp. 231–242) is reconsidering materials and resource consumption at virtually every level of her practice and pedagogy; and Wilson's (Profile pp. 333–345) work on community-driven design has other implications for rethinking consumption and the design of our neighborhoods.

Shop settings can teach us about our bodies and help us see ourselves as agents in the design and creation of our environments, whether we end up working in wood or not. And in art school settings woodworking and furniture most often sits in a context of creative problem solving, what the RISD program terms "critical making," using wood and furniture as a medium for creative engagement with our histories and the challenges we encounter both as individuals and a culture. The makers profiled here are doing just this in manifold and inspiring ways.

Maker profiles

JENNIFER ANDERSON
Joy in Mudville

Figure 5.2: Jennifer Anderson at her workbench, 2018

There's something there and I can't figure it out ... I am working with these materials that are so closely related to the environment that I grew up in ... I'm shaping these highly ornate objects literally out of dirt. I come from an extremely agricultural landscape. I went to school with a bunch of ag kids and farmers and so I'm wondering if that had something to do with where I am ... or I just stumbled on an interesting material.

From Stockton to San Diego, California

Jennifer Anderson was the child who liked to make things, stringing chains of flowers and ropes of rubber bands, and weaving string around her room to form giant cobwebs. She was born and raised in Stockton, a mid-size, hard-scrabble city in California's Central Valley, and her hometown continues to inform her perspective on life and the ordering of high and low culture. The city's European-American roots are in the Gold Rush, and before it was called Stockton it was known as Mudville, rich in peat soil and located on a navigable channel east of San Francisco (City of Stockton, 2016). When she goes home today, the Stockton Anderson describes is a particularly American vision of rural and small-town life, of pickup trucks and dusty roads which "shaped … and explains a little bit of me," Anderson says.

Although she self-describes as a woodworker, Anderson frequently makes furnishings from mud. Construction is technically challenging, requiring the right soil composition, control of cracking and drying, and a strong metal armature. For Anderson, there is power in the use of dirt, an unexpected but ubiquitous material, to make objects of definite cultural value. Growing up Anderson admired her maternal grandmother, a resourceful child of Portuguese immigrants and an "amazing artist" who painted on paper and insisted on using both sides of the page. Drawing at her house, "You'd use your whole sheet and the backside as well. You didn't get another piece because paper cost money!" One can almost hear her grandmother's voice in the celebration of the humble material, her lessons on cost and value paired with the investment of craft imbuing Anderson's works with special meaning.

But Stockton and mud are just one aspect of Anderson's persona; she is also a consummate fine woodworker, a craftsperson exploring materiality, an artist whose work is collected by museums, and a professor at a long-running and well-regarded cabinet making program at Palomar College in San Marcos, California, just north of San Diego.

~

Anderson's form and style resist easy categorization: Just as there isn't a singular material or technique, there isn't a particular look to her work. She constructs a wide range of styles, from iconic mid-century modern-style chairs to elaborate, Rococo chandeliers—traditionally glittering objects bejeweled with faceted glass droplets that mimic precious stones; rendered in mud they are matte, elemental. The tension in this duality—the juxta-position of high and low, valuable and mundane—both physically and metaphorically—is woven throughout Anderson's work.

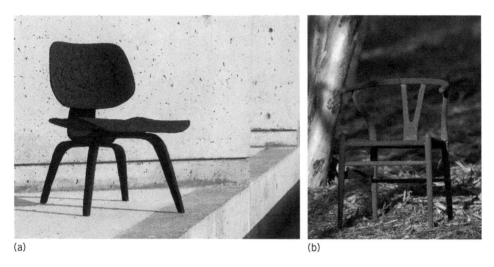

(a)   (b)

Figure 5.3a and b Jennifer Anderson, (L–R) Mud chairs, *Eames Study #1*, 2009. (Jason Anderson); and *Wegner Study #2*, 2008. (Larry Stanley)

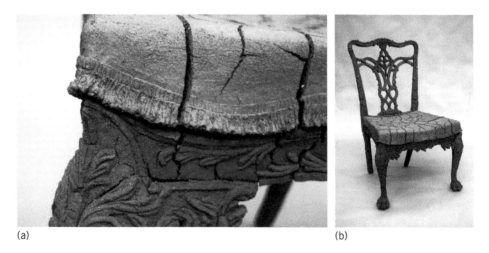

(a)   (b)

Figure 5.4a and b: Jennifer Anderson, *Cadwalader Chair*, with detail, 2014. (Heather McCalla)

Experiment and fail

Anderson borrows from historical or recognizable forms as a platform for exploring the meanings embedded in materials and objects. Her desire to explore the breadth of material possibilities is paralleled by another: To broaden the audience for finely crafted objects. To that end Anderson fluidly integrates various modes of production, from singular pieces to small batch manufacturing using **Computer Numerical Control (CNC)** technology, moving comfortably between wood, fabric, soil, and felt. Her graduate experience at San Diego State fueled her desire to keep learning from materials. "I think most people learn a material and learn everything about it. They master it and that's where their career takes off, or they become known, or maybe things get easier." By contrast, she feels drawn to experiment, finding the edges of how she can manipulate them or work in non-traditional ways. "It's a constant learning process. It's experimentation—experiment and fail, experiment and fail—and then perhaps you stumble on something that doesn't fail, that actually works."

Sitting at the far edge of Anderson's material explorations, the mud chairs have a solidity that takes you by surprise, and the sculptural detail in her *Cadwalader Chair*—mimicking the foliate carving of its eighteenth-century namesake—is as evocative as the landscape-like expanse of the seat, whose cracks mimic historic photographs of drought-ridden agricultural regions. Anderson uses soil mixed clay and an adhesive, sculpting the mixture to create the structural forms. "The process is fascinating because I'm forcing the material to do something that it naturally doesn't want to do. I'm forcing it to be something—a shape, a form, a structure—that it would just obviously never be without my hands manipulating it into that specific form." **Tolerances** are very tight—measured in millimeters—giving her a sense of control. "I've got it perfect and I walk away, and no matter what, it completely changes, and the funny thing about it is that it usually changes for the better."

Some of Anderson's works, like *Stitched*, a pair of plectrum-shaped side tables in mahogany with bent laminated rails, one with the rails below the top, the other with the top captured by the rails, are well-proportioned, with an informed wood selection, excellent craftsmanship, and a clearly articulated combination of curved and straight elements. The three elements that make up one of the tabletops are stitched together with copper wire, an unexpected transposition of a joining technique from one craft to another. Within what is otherwise a fairly traditional approach, Anderson blurs the boundaries between materials and subtly draws attention to the very act of joining disparate elements together. In *Pattern Study #2*, Anderson's

(a)   (b)

Figure 5.5a and b: Jennifer Anderson, *Stitched*, 2003. (Larry Stanley)

three-legged beech stools (Figure 5.6a and b), she combines a minimalist and familiar form with curvilinear shapes carved on a CNC machine. The deep, landscape-like crevasses reference topographical maps or sand dunes and are accentuated with exuberant color applied with milk paint. In each instance something is revealed about underlying forces or material structure.

In recent years, Anderson has embarked on two projects with her partner, woodworker Brian Newell. Keeping with the exploration of small-scale manufacture, they are developing a line of wooden shoes inspired by a pair of Swedish clogs that Anderson tried to throw away several times but kept retrieving from the trash: They were too comfortable to give up. Anderson and Newell's shoes will be batch-produced using a combination of hand and machine techniques: They start from hand-carved soles, models which are then cut by a CNC machine. They will then shape and attach the leather uppers in their workshop. It is a project of some complexity, and just as she always seeks to learn and explore, Anderson relishes diving into a new technology and combination of materials. It requires her attention to detail and her understanding of three-dimensional **shaping** for both aesthetics and comfort, as well as her ability to collaborate with others. The shoe project also demands the collaborators develop a big picture vision for marketing, packaging, and pricing, and, for Anderson, where this fits into her life and work.

(a)   (b)

Figure 5.6a and b: Jennifer Anderson, *Pattern Study #2*, 2011. (Yuki Batterson)

Figure 5.7: Jennifer Anderson and Brian Newell, shoe maquette with felt, 2018

Doing it all

Juggling the complex demands of her creative life and her teaching, Anderson is seeking to create a workable system to find an oftentimes elusive balance. While community colleges don't share university expectations that faculty do research and publication—or creation and exhibition—they *do* require that faculty take on abundant administrative work. At Palomar, in a department that used to have five staff people, they now have two—including Anderson—who are expected to do the administrative work of the department while teaching full time.

The program at Palomar has a strong reputation, and as is also true of many two-year colleges, an extensive community that has taken courses over many years and fostered a unique culture. Faced with programmatic changes or new college administrators, those community members often resist change, whether to new key and access policies or changing curriculum. Anderson experiences some of this through the lens of gender. The program faculty used to be all men, teaching in an environment that was in no small part defined by older male students pursuing woodworking and craft as continuing education. Coming out of the arts, Anderson's approach is often more defined by a tactile relationship to the material. When many students are used to measuring something in the 1/128 of an inch, the linguistic and cultural shift can be a site of resistance, with some of those students according less respect to a female faculty member who takes a different approach to the material.

It takes a village

> In my most productive and happiest times in my own work, I've been in an environment that's supportive, and now I want to create that environment, not only for myself, but for other people as well.

Anderson's workshop is in a nondescript low-rise area, between a massage parlor and a pawn shop, around the back of the building, next to a parking lot of cracked pavement and weeds. Providing directions, Anderson said, "When you think you're in the wrong place, you're there." The ground floor workshop—a warren of ten spaces for different woodworkers—sits adjacent to the machine room, which is equipped with heavy duty industrial machinery. Anderson's workspace is bright and clean, well-lit, organized, and intimate. She had numerous projects underway at the time of our visit: Oak stools with CNC carving in various stages of completion for a demonstration at World Wood Day; prep work for classes at Palomar; and Danish cord for a mid-century modern chair repair. A mud chandelier and a pair of Queen Anne chairs, also in mud and with cast bronze feet, had recently left for the permanent collection of the Chipstone Foundation at the Milwaukee Art Museum.

Anderson "both hates and loves the shop" because, as one of three primary lease holders, she can't come in and immediately start working on her own pieces. She has to deal with shop operations: Dull cutters, tool maintenance, and tidying up. On the other hand, it is a readymade community of woodworkers, with the potential for friendship, mentoring, critique, and collaboration. Community matters: Anderson's education was a series of tightly knit, intensely focused groups, and she seeks to replicate that experience here.

As an undergraduate Environmental Design major at UC Davis, Anderson found "her people" in furniture design; not only was it the right scale for her, but the group hung together in a way that mingled work and life and an obsessive search for form. She graduated in 1995, and by 1999 had found a place at the College of the Redwoods Fine Woodworking Program in Fort Bragg (now The Krenov School). Despite some initial reservations about the "woodiness" of the place, she fell for it within a week and says she has "been looking for [*the community at*] CR ever since." To some extent Anderson found it again with Wendy Maruyama (Profile pp. 273–287) and her fellow students in the graduate Furniture Design and Woodworking program at San Diego State University, a cohort of artists and makers with whom she is still in touch fourteen years later.

With her demanding job, Anderson is not at the studio as much as she used to be; it's easier to get there if working to a deadline. A big part of her work today is nurturing communities that are rooted in woodworking and making. In teaching she's sharing the skills of furniture design and fabrication; in San Diego she's a leading figure in a community woodshop; and up in Fort Bragg, where Newell lives, the couple has created a woodshop from a renovated milking barn. When they started out, the complex now known

Figure 5.8: In both 2019 and 2020 Cypress Street Barn hosted the Midwinter Show of student work from The Krenov School. (Laura Mays)

as Cypress Street Barn was little more than a redwood shell on a concrete slab. Today the shop is well-equipped and filled with natural light, accommodating a handful of local woodworkers who rent bench space and access to the machines. City permitting requires that a portion of the building has a public function, so Anderson and Newell have turned a quarter of the 3,300 square-foot interior into a retail space and gallery. "The idea is that it becomes part of the community up here, with a gathering space for openings, social events, and so on." It is a project that involves shaping intangible materials: Space and community.

ALISON CRONEY MOSES
Identity in making

Figure 5.9: Alison Croney Moses in the studio, 2021. (Todd Dionne, courtesy of The Eliot School)

Boston, Massachusetts

Born in Fayetteville, North Carolina, in 1983 and raised in Winston-Salem, Alison Croney Moses was shaped by crafty, resourceful parents who had immigrated to the US from Guyana. Her father was from the capital city and her mom was a farm girl with fifteen siblings. Although he was a city boy, Moses' dad "knew his culture and experiences," and together they raised their three children to value making things. Her mother sewed the kids' clothes—not everything, but everything important. "For the Christmas holiday we were in plaid, Christmas-y outfits. And my mom made my prom dresses, everything. Making," says Croney Moses, "was part of life." For his part, her dad taught her foundational drawing skills, and—in a workspace tucked away in a corner under a carport—used hand tools to turn pine boards into furniture. Croney Moses worked with him and together they constructed step stools, a desk for Croney Moses' sister, and various other items for the house. Though partly born of financial constraints, the greater value was learning to use your hands to construct your material world.

Growing out of the creative making she did at home with her parents, Croney Moses became an art kid, though she was equally good at science and math. She attributes her ease with the sciences to "those experiences of making furniture with my dad or doing things with my hands at home, like holding a hammer. You really embody these things that you learn about in science, like kinetic energy or friction," she explains. "Because I was able to make stuff, it came easy. I understood it in the abstract because I understood the physicality of it."

Early on, realizing her daughter was spending more time in school socializing than studying, Croney Moses' determined mom secured the scholarships needed and sent her three children to private school in a wealthy and mostly white neighborhood of Winston-Salem. One of only a couple Black kids in the school, Croney Moses learned to navigate it successfully, and by high school she was elected student body president. She inherited the ferocity of her mother's conviction: "Don't tell her no,'cause she will do it." In high school Croney Moses took as many art classes as she could and only applied to art schools; her mom still had designs on her becoming a doctor. Though today she's supportive of her daughter's creative work, "Pursuing a career in the arts was not necessarily on top of her list. 'Are you sure? Are you *sure*?' So I've had to say yes, I'm sure. Yes. I need to prove this. Yes."

Croney Moses recalls her first moment of "pride, pride, pride in the work": The drawing in kindergarten of a clown for which she received a blue ribbon. Later, her middle school art teacher provided Croney Moses a creative space when her young student had just lost her father. "I hung out in her classroom. She knew the first boy I kissed … all the things," Moses recalls. "She was the space for the emotional support and the art skills, and the space to be whoever I wanted to be, no matter what was going on outside." And then there was Uncle James Melvin, a family friend and a successful artist on the outer banks of North Carolina who allowed the young, aspiring artist into his world. "There are these moments, and sometimes they're surprising and sometimes you don't realize who's actually supporting you and mentoring you."

Rhode Island School of Design

I showed up. I didn't know really what I was getting into. I didn't even know what college really was. I just knew it was away from home studying art and being part of a whole new community.

Influenced by her experience with Melvin, Croney Moses signed up for graphic design as a freshman at RISD. It seemed like a practical career choice; graphic designers can earn a living. But she wasn't good at it, and worse, hated it. She talked to her friends in the furniture department, who appeared to be having fun and learning, so she switched. Recalling her work with her dad, it made perfect sense. "It was the best decision I could have made. I learned a craft from knowing very little to having a foundation that can get me probably anywhere within the field. I know enough and I know where to look to learn more." Along with a respect for—and knowledge of—tool use and care, Croney Moses says that after starting off making crazy sculptural, ugly, painted things, she found her own visual sensibility. "I know what feels right, like identity in making."

Through teacher and maker Don Miller, Croney Moses discovered bent lamination, a way to create curves that wasn't a gouge. She also discovered that you don't have to paint everything, but that it can be used sparely to articulate the curves. She started to trust that you can let the process speak for itself. Miller continued to mentor her in the technique, developing an especially valuable and poignant relationship in context. "Being a Black woman in a wood shop, I think about how people treat you based on your identity. It comes up in very subtle ways, and for the most part, my first year in the furniture department, the professors did not engage with me and my work in meaningful ways."

Moses observed that with male students, most faculty—principally male and white—evidenced a casual ease in stopping at her male peers' worktables to chat about their project, even those who didn't sign up for a

Figure 5.10: Alison Croney Moses, *Redwood Shell*, 2018. (Michelle Davidson Shapiro)

desk critique. By contrast, she knew that if she didn't sign up for a desk crit, she might not talk with most professors for a week or longer. "Looking back, I recognize that those subtle moments—when a professor pays attention to someone and their work, when it wasn't scripted by who signed up—that tells you that what you're doing is valid and who you are is valid. And in fact, what you do and who you are, it's *more* valid than other folks in this space. And that's the subtle difference." By contrast, Miller responded to Croney Moses' obsession with curved forms; he connected to her work, and when she pursued an independent study with him, he labored with her over the projects, feeding her confidence and fueling her curiosity.

Engaging in community

Art is something that saves lives. There are all these things that we experience as a young person that no one knows about. And if I did not have art, I cannot say that I would be here.

The complexity and challenges of Croney Moses' own story are many: Losing her dad quite young, some mental health issues in the family, and limited financial resources among them. In describing her work today, she will say that she is "a product of the programs I try to create and ensure that kids have access to. We as an industry, we as the department, we as whatever we want to call ourselves, why would we not be constantly thinking about how to engage younger folks in this work and encourage hands-on making, because it is a way to ensure survival?" This passion, intimate personal knowledge, and desire for connection fueled her pursuit of community practice at RISD.

Over the concerns and even objections of her senior thesis advisor, Croney Moses channeled her mother's refusal to let anything stand in her way. "I listened and nodded and kept doing the work I had to do. (You) talk to me about the community engaged piece and you don't have a framework to actually critique it well, so I'm just going to do it and learn what I can and learn from who I can." RISD alum and Director of the Office of Public Engagement, Seth Goldenberg set up a structured program at RISD as his thesis project that invites students to integrate community collaboration into their education. Goldenberg mentored Croney Moses in pushing outside the boundaries of what most faculty understood to be the makings of a furniture design degree, supporting her desire to bridge her art practice with community engagement. He also mentored her through both how to think about and give language to her community work, and to navigate the college systems to attain her degree with this as her thesis.

Goldenberg connected Croney Moses with Blackstone Academy, a local charter high school serving mostly Black and brown students. She moved intentionally into the slow, sometimes uncertain, unfolding relational work of community collaboration, letting the project take form through the dialogue with students. Croney Moses' work with Blackstone students integrated skill-building workshops with design and problem solving. Together the high school students did their own research with students at a local elementary school, ultimately imagining and prototyping furniture they thought would enhance a playful learning environment for the younger students, who were then able to provide feedback on the models. Of the three large works built from that process, one was Moses' emergent vision, a form with moveable skins that could change shape, turning from animal into fort or other imaginative form.

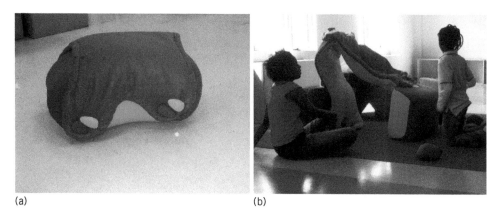

(a)   (b)

Figure 5.11a and b: Alison Croney Moses with youth and furniture from the collaboration with Blackstone Academy, 2006. (Alison Croney Moses)

As an undergraduate working with community, Croney Moses kept her own making separate, working slowly and painstakingly on a chair that integrated the bent lamination work that she'd been refining. White faculty often make the mistake of assuming that their students of color are making work about their identities, and that the white students are just making work. In the tensions of this context, Croney Moses wanted her faculty and peers to simply talk about her work. "That work I didn't want to connect to my identity. I wanted it to be looked at as its own and critiqued as its own," she explains. "One of my necessary processes was separating—in my communication and my presentation—my identity from my work in order to be treated more equally, in order to be respected in the furniture department.

"You don't always have the words to explain what you're going through, but I remember now that I was like, 'No, don't talk about who I am. Talk about the work for the work, because otherwise you are not looking at it in the same playing field,'" she continues. "It's not on the same pedestal; it is looked at as less than because you have attached the brownness of who I am to it, or the femaleness of who I am. And I didn't want that to be a part of it because I was into the craft of it."

I am inspired by the process of making

At RISD Croney Moses learned the tools and techniques of furniture: Mortise and tenon joints, dovetails ... all the things that allowed her to cultivate

Figure 5.12: Alison Croney Moses, *Walnut Chair*, 2005. (Mark Johnston)

what she thinks of as the gearhead in her. "There's these things that I find really gratifying in that process. I like the structure of bent lamination and I like **coopering** as a process. I also like shaping, although I've shaped a lot of walnut in my life, which is probably not a wise decision! I like the look of it and the smell of it, but it is hard to shape." Croney Moses can obsess about technique and work to get a **glue joint** just right, "but I am not restricted by rectangles and sharp corners. In a way I feel freer to do it, you know?" She figured out that a circle didn't have to be divided into perfectly equal pieces with the same angles, that she could cut the angle and adjust it until it feels right.

It is easy to assume that Croney Moses' inspirations are natural forms: Seed pods, ferns, or shells. Though she loves nature, she finds her inspiration elsewhere. "People imagine my studio full of objects like that, but it's more full of lines, of obsessive curved lines, because the feel of the line that you make is what is interesting to me." Reflecting on the *Walnut Vessel* that is now in the collection at the Boston Museum of Fine Arts (Figure 5.13), Moses remembers the drawings, made on big brown paper early in her education at RISD—obsessive vessel forms that were not symmetrical. Mad at being told it had to be symmetrical, she chopped off the top of it. "I remember being like, 'Why? Why? We *can* make it!' And then Miller said, '*You* might be able to. I don't know how to, but for your first bent laminated project, you probably should just make it symmetrical.'" The challenge of it, working at making wood do something that it doesn't want to do, through a process she's confident in, is exciting. "How do you mess up making a barrel to make something beautiful that you want to touch and you want to scoot inside of?"

After graduating from RISD in 2006, Croney Moses entered a second summer of work in the wood program at Anderson Ranch, where she came to a juncture that will be familiar to countless art students: On one path an exciting winter residency at the Ranch; and on the other a job in community engagement at the Museum of Contemporary Art in Denver (MCA), which promised a salary and a measure of security. She chose the MCA.

"That was a transition from saying, okay, I'm going to do art. That decision determined that I'm going to be primarily in art administration rather than a maker full-time or even majority, or even half time." In a 2014 study, entitled *Artists Report Back: A National Study on the Lives of Arts Graduates and Working Artists*, the authors, who all identify as artists and art school graduates, tackle the realities, tensions, and myths art school graduates face in continuing their creative work while earning a living in this economy. They found that only ten percent of arts graduates make their primary living as working artists (Jahoda et al., 2014). "From that moment, I haven't made a lot. I try now to make a couple of pieces a year. But now there's actually motivation (an exhibition opportunity) and I'm going to rent a shop space, so hopefully I'll be making more."

It wasn't simply the economic stability that the Denver job offered. Making beautiful things felt, in Croney Moses' words, masturbatory; this is a tension that many makers we spoke with feel. "I'm just making things for

Figure 5.13: Alison Croney Moses, *Walnut Vessel*, 2004. Collection of MFA, Boston. (Mark Johnston)

Figure 5.14: Alison Croney Moses, sketch on notepaper, 2021. (Alison Croney Moses)

the sake of making and they're beautiful. And it feels good to make it. And it looks good and people are going to buy it, which makes me feel good. But many people don't have money to buy it!" Croney Moses connects this feeling to the fact that she'd already separated that work from her identity as the maker, "like that work would stand on its own. And of course, that's actually not possible. Your identity always influences your work." Unable at the time to hold the integral relationship between her identity, community, and creative practice, it was, "like, what the hell am I doing it for?"

Though planning to head back into the woodshop in the near future, Croney Moses doesn't regret the decision to pursue arts administration and education, and feels like she's making an impact. As educator and advocate, she's the Program Director at the Eliot School of Fine and Applied Arts, a Boston-based institution with roots in the late nineteenth-century manual training movement, now offering craft and art classes to all ages.

The Eliot School maintains a strong relationship with the Boston Public Schools to support student access to art and craft education. "We serve more youth within Boston communities than we do in our schoolhouse. We do work to ensure that kids who have hardly any access to art—or no access at all—get it." Though the work Croney Moses describes that she did with the Blackstone kids reads like a liberatory pedagogical model, engaging the end user in the design process, she's also aware of the value of coming into a collaborative partnership or community art setting as an artist not already ensconced in educational theory. The pedagogy emerged through the process of working with the young students, with Croney Moses bringing in a distinct skill set and thinking like an artist. It's easy to draw a line from her undergraduate project to the work she does today at the Eliot School, especially as she maps programming in response to a changing consciousness of student and community needs today.

Moving from avoiding conversation about identity as an undergrad to engaging conversations about racial equity in craft education today is,

Figure 5.15: Alison Croney Moses, *Cedar Pods*, 2016. (Nora Bilal)

Croney Moses argues, a question of power. "I recognize that at every moment, people are able to bring their identity to the forefront (to the degree they can at that time). ... being an art administrator, it gives me a certain amount of power," she explains. "A position to be able to determine things .... There's a platform for me to be who I am and be a lot more intentional about it. And there's an appetite for it. I'm on zoom calls with arts education folks saying, 'Let's not forget who we actually are serving.'" Rooted in the belief that teachers should be prepared to meet the social/emotional needs of students—helping them both to gain skills and develop pride in who they are—Croney Moses made professional development in racial equity, decolonizing curricula, neuro diversity, and accessibility a priority for the Eliot School teaching staff. The trainings recognize the identity and experience gap between teachers and students in a system in which the majority of kids in the Boston public schools are Black or brown and the majority of teachers are white. "If we are not actually talking about our identities and giving teachers and students skills to work with upfront, we're doing a disservice to those students. And to the teachers. I'm privileged to be able to do it; I know all folks of color are not able to right now." Holding fast to the value of arts education for kids, Croney Moses is equally invested in making the tools of the arts accessible to adults. Uncertain where it will all lead, she is ready to sit in the process, connecting her skills as a maker and educator to her personal history.

Motherhood

Until recently Croney Moses identified more as a woodworker and craftsperson than artist, though she has used all of them to describe herself. Trained as a furniture maker but not making furniture, perhaps she is more of a woodworker, but in creating a commissioned work for the aforementioned exhibition, which is about designing motherhood, she feels more like an artist. Croney Moses plans to pair her sculptural work with embodiment, collaborating with a movement artist to engage moms of color, specifically Black moms. "We talk about the fact that our physical bodies are actually torn apart first," she describes, planning to bring these elements together to create a healing process that integrates her identity and her sculptural work. "I'm interested to see where that goes. Of the work that I make, how does that connect to myself in my community? How am I being really intentional about identity?"

In practical terms, Moses envisions creating an ongoing artistic practice that's sustainable for a mom with a full-time job and two children, one not yet in school. As soon as her children could sit in a toddler chair for more than ten seconds without falling over, she put crayons in their hands. Today they have small easels not far from her in their home studio space. The stability of her job and that of her husband, good health insurance, the satisfaction and ambitions of her work at Eliot, and affordable daycare are helping to create the space for her to return to the shop. And she can envision a time—perhaps even a decade away—when she'll leave arts administration and return fully to the shop to make work.

SEAN DESIREE
Rooted in the now

Figure 5.16: Sean Desiree with two works from *LIFTED: Public Housing, An Aerial Perspective*, 2021. (Sam Tannenbaum)

Hudson, New York

Sean Desiree was a child when they were first introduced to the power of making. Their father, laid off from a job, decided to start sewing clothing and building furniture. As much as observing manual skills or learning woodworking, what Desiree saw for the first time was someone making things as a means to support themselves, of claiming economic autonomy, "right in front of me." Both of Desiree's grandmothers were also makers, quilting and crocheting in their spare time or to keep hands busy, but they weren't trying to make a business out of it; these were instead gifts, demonstrations of care for loved ones and community members. Taking their cue from their father, by elementary and middle school Desiree was weaving necklaces and bracelets on a small loom to sell to raise money for team uniforms.

> Throughout my life within the Black community that I grew up with, there's so many models of people trying to raise money for something through selling, through cooking, through churches and community centers. So that's always been a way to create for yourself. When you don't have, or there's no other, you can't apply for a grant.

Though Desiree showed an early passion for music, art wasn't something they considered for themselves; it seemed to be the province of folks whose upbringing didn't look like Desiree's childhood in public housing in the Bronx. Even when they started building furniture eight years ago in their late twenties, it was the craft rather than art that drew them. The relationships between craft, art, and community began to form when they were living in Hudson, New York, and the result was a project that focused on public housing. Thus, when in the past couple years Desiree did start to think about their work as art, it was rooted in community and the desire to make a meaningful contribution.

A couple hours outside Manhattan, the small city nestled along the Hudson River has—since the late twentieth century—attracted escapees and retirees from Chelsea and other New York City arts enclaves. The handsome and affordable late eighteenth-century architecture of Warren Street, the main commercial strip in Hudson, draws artists, designers, antique dealers, and gallerists who see attractive fixer-uppers within proximity of their New York

City base. Over the past two decades these relatively affluent newcomers to a city that had struggled with poverty, drugs, and declining investment in public schools have increasingly displaced local families by converting multiple-unit buildings to single-family homes, lowering the population and increasing the economic divide. US Census figures in 2019 suggest that 21.3 percent of Hudson's population lives in poverty (that number is nearly identical to the percentage of Hudson's population that is African American) (US Census Bureau, 2019).

In a city with an abundance of artists, Desiree saw little funding for the arts going to public housing residents. Already doing pattern-based work on tabletops, they saw an avenue to translate this process to a mapping of Hudson's public housing. "I was making pattern work, and I thought I could contribute to this community in this way. I could draw attention to these units," they explained. "I grew up in public housing, so it's something that I care about. That's how I came to think of it more as art, because I wanted to put the things I made into the public housing units. It would make me proud to have [what] I made in the public housing unit that I grew up in." Once they started researching public art, Desiree's interest in its potential grew, and their identity as an artist started to take shape, "based on need and want ... and connected to community, not just me wanting to be a visual artist."

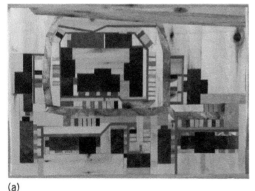
(a)

(b)

Figure 5.17a and b: Sean Desiree, (L–R) Pine, mahogany, spalted maple, ebony, zebra wood, oak; *Crosswinds at Hudson*, from *LIFTED: Public Housing, An Aerial Perspective*, 2019. (Sean Desiree)

Desiree's initial path into woodworking also pivoted on need and want: They wanted a farm table and couldn't spend a thousand dollars to get it in the commercial marketplace. "I was just like, 'Is this something I can do?' Fortunately, I was living with someone who had some tools; he taught me some basics." Desiree's friend had a chop saw, a hammer, a drill, and a crowbar, and a quick search online for table makers turned up free pallets, often constructed from domestic hardwoods. "Being grounded in knowing that it's important to be self-reliant and it's important to try to impact the environment in a positive way ... brought me to just doing it myself. Why not try?" That initial table turned out just fine; it was a learning experience and, most importantly, Desiree enjoyed the process enough that they just kept doing it. Watching YouTube tutorials and following other makers, they developed their skills and took a class at the Arts Center of the Capital Region in Troy, New York. That experience helped fill in the basics and gave Desiree more access to a broader array of tools. From there they joined a local makerspace to have consistent access to a woodshop.

Throughout their early twenties Desiree held a variety of jobs, doing everything from corporate layouts for a company that customizes sugar packets, to working in the tax department of a kids' bedding company. It's difficult, Desiree says, to work for someone else's vision; they felt in each of those roles that they had to "dim" part of themselves to fit in. Woodworking,

 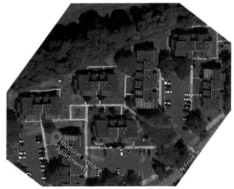

Figure 5.18: Sean Desiree, *Hudson Terrace*, from *LIFTED: Public Housing, An Aerial Perspective*. Pine, spalted maple, oak, African padauk, mahogany, ebony, beech, cedar, 2019. (Sean Desiree)

by contrast, held the promise of self-reliance, of the autonomy modeled by the entrepreneurs they grew up around. Desiree positions their work within a tradition of self-reliance born of racial discrimination and disenfranchisement. Black people in America have always had to "make a way out of no way" in a country where they couldn't rely on government, fair employment, or access to the means to succeed. "A lot of it is, well, I still need to survive. My work is very much connected to that." The desire to be self-reliant, to have control over their own life, is a profound inspiration. Moreover, "woodworking allows you to be in the now and meditate on something," they reflected. "Through the use of your body you could work through a lot of trauma or give yourself positive affirmations. I like to feel that every day, to feel like, 'Oh, I accomplished this.' It is very monumental for me. I very much am someone who needs that."

Desiree attributes the classes and tool access at the Arts Center and makerspace in Troy with their ability to shape their life as a woodworker. Resource availability has a deterministic effect; lack of access to tools in one's community is too high a barrier to overcome.

> The trajectory of your life could really change depending on the resources that you have and what is made available to your community. That was the only way I could have done it. I got a scholarship to do those classes at the Arts Center … also having a makerspace available in Troy … those are the ways that I was able to really see that vision through. So many people have so much potential to do so many things, but it's really about the people in your life; your community can really dim that, or really allow you to see it through.

Desiree's pattern work is inspired by the women's quilting tradition of Gee's Bend, Alabama, bold and vivid, abstract and improvisational patchwork quilts that both relate to the rich tradition of patchwork quilting in African American history and have a shared language born of geographic isolation and intergenerational dialogue. Like so much quilting, it was also a way of reusing resources, and the denim quilts particularly—with scraps sourced from the local Sears factory where many of the women worked—reference or invoke the labor history of a community descended from persons enslaved on the local Pettway plantation. "Okay, they turn these scraps into *that*? It's

Figure 5.19: Sean Desiree, *Young Coffee Table*, inspired by Annie Mae Young, Quilter from Gee's Bend, AL, 2019. (Sean Desiree)

inspiring what they were able to do with [what] they had. I'm using scraps also, whatever I can find; I don't really buy wood for the most part."

In the Gee's Bend quilts Desiree found an encyclopedia of patterning that has helped them grow as an artist. The arts are traditionally an industry of opinion, according to Desiree, one that consistently chooses the same voices as worthy and valuable. We are drawn to what we've already been told is beautiful, as we're drawn to value neighborhoods we're told are safe. Absent a conversation about race in America, we—consciously or not—perpetuate a standard of white supremacy. Maybe that's changing gradually, as more Black artists' work grows in visibility, but it remains a challenge because white artists are still able to view their racial identity as transparent, taken for granted. "My practice as an artist is to use our reference, the history, the different histories within my community, and do something different with that," they elaborate. "It gives me the courage to do it. And it gives me a way to do it that isn't referencing just a European aesthetic—what (has already been) presented as beautiful, as art."

~

In a field of practice dominated by cisgender white males, Desiree is African American and nonbinary; in a shop setting they describe being met first with uncertainty. "I feel like if you're not a cis man, it's difficult to be seen as a whole person. Your opinions and your abilities aren't really fully recognized or seen and respected. They don't automatically give you the credit that you know what you're doing." As is also true for many women in a shop, men frequently offer Desiree unsolicited tips and opinions. Being nonbinary adds an additional layer: Initiatives aimed at supporting women in the woodshop also don't quite fit; without erasing part of their own identity, these opportunities are out of reach.

> It's a hard dialogue to have because obviously women are more marginalized, but they also don't see you, so it's kind of like, 'Hey, you're not the only one marginalized here. There are people that are further marginalized than you, so as far as solidarity, let's try to be as inclusive as we can.' I am also someone who recognizes that there are some spaces that are important for women to have, and also nonbinary people to have. But I think in trying to uplift people, it's important to be inclusive.

Like most makers outside the conventional mold of the woodworker, Desiree has developed strategies to address the social dynamics of the woodshop, though they come at a cost. "Sometimes you just have to be cold, which is hard. But it's hard to open yourself up every time for someone that most likely is not going to meet your expectations. So sometimes I don't want to be bothered; I don't feel like engaging. I just don't have it in me to make small talk or whatever." It's difficult to open oneself up time and time again when too often you'll be disappointed, hurt, or enmeshed in exhausting emotional labor. "I don't want to be closed off, but at some point I just have to protect myself. If someone is worthy of your engagement, that

Figure 5.20: Sean Desiree, *Franklin Housing*, inspired by a painting by Jamaal Peterman, 2019. (Sean Desiree)

will show over time, but if you let someone in and they say or do something that is hurtful, then I have to make another decision," Desiree explains. "Am I going to say something to them? That's going to bring up all their feelings that I have to deal with. Or do I just eat it?"

For the most part, Desiree's impulse is to put their headphones on, put their head down, and focus on work. Last year, though, they did two workshops at Soul Fire Farm in Grafton, New York, fifteen miles east of Troy, an "Afro-Indigenous centered community farm committed to uprooting racism and seeding sovereignty in the food system" (Soul Fire Farm, 2020). Soul Fire Farm is connected to a land reclamation movement that "claims the rural as a safe place and as a place of land ownership and autonomy." There to both learn and cofacilitate workshops on stick and timber framing, Desiree felt able to connect with ease with Black and indigenous makers in an environment where sharing knowledge and "skilling people up" was at the center.

This profound experience wasn't Desiree's first as a teacher. They also teach at Emma Willard School, an all-girls boarding school in the Troy area. During the summers Emma Willard offers classes to girls aged six to fourteen with GirlSummer. Desiree teaches project-based classes using both hand and power tools. "All of them are capable, you know, and it's so much fun!" The girls are eager and ready to build from the first moment they step into the shop space; even while Desiree is still offering tutorials, they're asking when they can start to build. "Can we just start; can we just start making things?" Some of the projects are directive, like making your own stepstool, and others are more open-ended, like "making your own crazy world." Desiree likes teaching and appreciates that it forces them to slow down, not take skills or safety for granted, and reminds them about precision and detail.

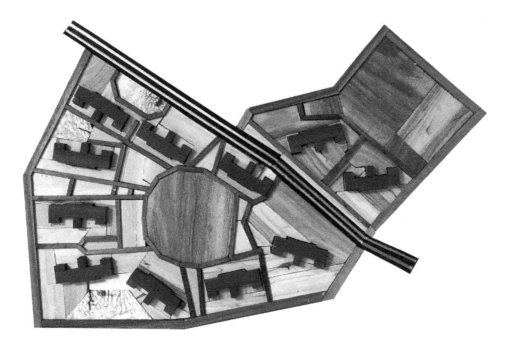

Figure 5.21: Sean Desiree, *Marble Hill*, from *LIFTED: Public Housing, An Aerial Perspective*, 2020. (Sean Desiree)

Artist or furniture maker or both?

I definitely call myself an artist and a furniture maker now.

Today Desiree claims both "artist" and "furniture maker," with permission to be flexible. The research they did about art—and specifically public art—in creating their series about public housing in Hudson expanded their sense of what is possible with their skills. "Art for me and many people is a way to deal with reality. You can create a magical space that is hard to make in reality." Integrating their growing knowledge of furniture with that of structural building, Desiree aims to design life-size structures and sculptures that act as sanctuaries, protectors, and symbols of empowerment for BIPOC queer, trans, and nonbinary people, much as the Maroons created small communities throughout the Americas when they escaped chattel slavery. What does safety look like in the present? "What will that look like as far as being a nonbinary person? What can I do to create my own safety? If it was an art project, what would that look like? What would I need to fill it with?" While making change in the world can feel out of one's control or overwhelming, as an artist Desiree can fill that gap, creating spaces much as people create altars in their homes.

I have control over my own fantasy. If I can make it available to the public, I can give some solace to other people. Ideally it would be wonderful to have my work in a playground, to do the pattern work on the ground. It could be the neighborhood that the kids actually live in, mapped out on the ground as another element of play.

Understanding the marketplace

The momentum of doing, doing, doing is demanding, and Desiree wants to make work of which they're even more proud. They recently put their successful Etsy shop on pause; seeing ways to improve their work, they took an intentional hiatus to work on skill development while focusing with similar intent on understanding the marketplace for their work. As a furniture maker in this economy, you have a few options, and Desiree wants to be strategic about where to place their pieces. Are they a craft furniture maker that sells on Etsy or other online distribution platforms for a commercial clientele? Or would they rather create objects more closely connected to the art community that could potentially sell for a lot more? Having more flexibility about which world to move in means for Desiree a focus on the rigor of their work, from seamless joints to impeccable finishes. Then they'll send out their work to a few more venues and see where it fits, rather than automatically placing it for sale in their Etsy shop. "I want to be making at the cross section of art and furniture for sure. I want it to feel like an object of art and also be something that people could use."

Figure 5.22: Sean Desiree, *Sculptural Table*, 2021. (Sean Desiree)

These are tensions faced by virtually every maker with whom we spoke, even those who aren't relying on their woodworking for the majority of their income. Desiree is considering having different work for different platforms or scaling up the pieces so that the relationship between time committed and income makes economic sense. "How does that all work? You know, what makes it different? What makes this furniture just furniture? I want my work to be affordable to people and I also want it to be a means for me to sustain myself," they contemplate. "Taking a pause and playing around with the shapes of things and being a little more experimental will help it to live also in the object world. I'm trying to figure out if that's even possible." The commitment to the ongoing development of their work is paired with the inspiration to reclaim space for Black and indigenous communities, teaching the structural and building skills that seed self-reliance.

It's very powerful to have that skill. I didn't know. I wanted to learn how to build, but now that I have that knowledge, I very much feel like it's necessary. It feels very powerful. It's important to have more options of who you could learn from, like another person of color or someone that isn't a cis man. People want to learn from someone else that has a different approach. That's something that I could add to the world, add to a knowledge set and maybe encourage other people who wouldn't normally do it.

NANCY HILLER
A cabinetmaker's life

Figure 5.23: Nancy Hiller at her table saw, 2018. (Nancy Hiller)

Bloomington, Indiana

Nancy Hiller's home and woodshop are situated in rolling countryside a few miles outside of Bloomington, Indiana. Sitting in her cozy house, surrounded by pieces of her furniture, the kitchen lined with cabinets she built, and upon a floor she laid, the work of Hiller's life is all around her. She is unique amongst women woodworkers in the longevity and shape of her career: A cabinetmaker since dropping out of university at age nineteen, almost all her income comes from the output of her one-woman shop. Hiller trained formally as a cabinetmaker in the City and Guilds, an English training system and—except for a few times when she tried to quit—has been making her living as a cabinetmaker since. Woodworking is the thing she can turn her hand to quickly and easily, and she has succeeded in shaping her career and her life around her skills and interest in architectural and furniture history.

Specializing in cabinetry and built-ins, Hiller is attentive to context: The room, the house—its specificities, peculiarities, and history. She describes this as "putting her ego on hold," focusing instead on interpretation and reflection as a manifestation of the respect she pays to each project. Hiller isn't making speculative work in the hope of a future buyer; instead, she does custom work for clients with whom she has a contract. She is working to their specifications, wishes, requirements; she's solving their problems. And the resulting works are extraordinary in their range and attention to site and historical and material references.

Hiller is outspoken, informal, and unpretentious; words pour forth from her; she has given much thought to a huge variety of subjects, turning ideas around, exploring them from different angles, and is eager to share her

Figure 5.24: Nancy Hiller, cabinetry designed to re-use architectural salvage from clients' family home, 2005. (Spectrum Creative Group)

stories. There are a multitude of projects on her bench: There's a kitchen for a couple moving into a new house in Bloomington; this requires keeping costs down. Drawers will be **rabbeted** and nailed but, she says, "They're just the kind of clients I want, which is to say they have modest means, they're very thoughtful, they're critical thinkers, and they don't want to be consumers. But they have this place built to retire."

On the drawing board are a kitchen design for a woman in Michigan's Upper Peninsula; a walnut dining table, clean-lined, straightforward, and made to the client's size specifications; a "really cool sideboard" in ambrosia maple; and—finally—an "out-there tabletop," the ultimate problem-solving venture. The clients have a small house and a grand piano. There's no room for a table, which means no friends over for dinner, so Hiller is creating a top for the piano that will turn it into a table when necessary.

Family expectations

Hiller was born in 1959 and grew up in Miami, Florida. Her grandparents and great-grandparents were Eastern European Jews, and her parents were brought up, as many second-generation immigrants are, to aspire to the American Dream. For her father that meant Harvard Law School and then a job in advertising on Madison Avenue; for her mother it meant forgoing art school and focusing instead on marriage to a man with a well-paid, white-collar job while she maintained social relations for the family. The bubble burst when her father could no longer stand the rampant materialism and superficiality of advertising and quit his job. Her parents' marriage broke down soon after, and in 1971 Hiller's mother moved her two daughters to England. She also wanted the girls to experience something other than middle-class American culture.

Hiller's descriptions of 1970s England in her 2017 memoir, *Making Things Work: Tales from A Cabinetmaker's Life*, are both hilarious and depressing; however, she did well academically and earned a place at Cambridge University. But it was not for her; it wasn't long before she dropped out and took a job in a metal-castings factory. She and her then-husband had no money to buy anything, so she began to make furniture from scavenged and scrap wood. Hiller had little previous experience of woodworking, but goaded by a challenge from her stepfather over her efforts

Figure 5.25: Nancy Hiller, *Edwardian Hallstand*, 2002. (Spectrum Creative Group)

to furnish her house, she signed on to a year-long furniture making course at a vocational college. She was a twenty-year-old American woman and a college-dropout in a class of sixteen- and seventeen-year-old boys, most of whom had taken woodworking classes in high school or were even employed by local companies. "It was only my determination to make my stepfather eat his words that got me through the year-long training. During the first week I spent two whole days trying over and over to cut a simple lap joint with a saw, chisel, and mallet." Frustrated and near tears, Hiller "hid behind my workbench, pretending to look for a tool on the lower shelf." Only the prospect of admitting defeat helped her prevail. "By the end of that day I had made my first well-fitted lap joint" (Hiller, 2017).

With her City and Guilds certification, in 1980 Hiller started working in a series of small country shops in the south of England. She learned joinery, scheduling, and fixing the inevitable mistakes, gradually building skills and confidence, and perhaps more importantly, gleaning some insight into how business operated and what it was like to be a woman in such a male-dominated field. It was, in her words, a liability, and certainly when compared with her observations of being a woman in the woodshop today.

Hiller is definitive in calling herself a cabinetmaker. "In England, there was always a divide between the art woodworkers, and the 'just fucking get on with it, you're a cabinet maker' woodworkers, many of whom had City and Guilds or other training," she explains. In cabinetry you could make a living. With a trades background rather than an art school education, Hiller declares, "I'm not in the art woodworker world. I have spent a lot of time in the construction industry, working with remodeling contractors, working with houses. I like houses. I don't just like furniture; I like houses."

During this period Hiller also made her first attempt to leave woodworking, though she still kept her portable Black and Decker Workmate in the dining room and continued to make furniture for herself and her husband. By 1986 her marriage had ended and Hiller decided to return to the States. To earn money for the move, she landed a job as a carpenter's assistant at an aviation museum. There, newbie Hiller was subjected to the peak of misogyny that she would encounter. Today she reflects that her education in an all-girls high school allowed her to weather the experience. "It never occurred to me until recently that it gave me the freedom to just be who I am." Sitting in the tea-room with the guys at the museum, she told herself,

" 'Yes, you are making fun of me … You are a bunch of sexist pigs, but also … you are actually letting me look at your cool shit and use your tools'."

Returning to the States, Hiller worked in Vermont and Montana before moving in 1990 to Bloomington to run a custom furniture business with her second husband. She soon made her next and final serious attempt at quitting woodwork: She completed a degree in Religious Studies at Indiana

Figure 5.26: Nancy Hiller, reproduction of a Lebus sideboard, 2007. (Spectrum Creative Group)

University. By 1995 Hiller was again single and looking for work. She didn't want to teach at the college level, and high school teaching required yet more training, so she again turned to what she knew best. She started NR Hiller Design Inc., the business she runs today.

From the workbench to the desktop: Research and writing

In recent years, Hiller has increasingly concentrated her effort on period work—late nineteenth- through early twentieth-century interiors—and kitchens. This led her to the field of historical research, which in turn has led to writing. She writes in her spare time, principally on weekends, for the love of sharing knowledge. After decades of identifying as a maker, Hiller is writing up this research, and her output is prodigious: She writes or has written for *Popular Woodworking*, *Fine Woodworking*, *Old-House Journal*, *Furniture and Cabinetmaking*, *Huffington Post*, *American Bungalow*, and *Bloom*, as well as nine blogrolls on her website and a lively Instagram account. Hiller's writing revolves around her work, exploring the prosaic, historical, and technical. She describes writing as a way of gaining a "meta-artifact;" not only does she make an object, but she then has an opportunity to reflect on it, examine, and draw lessons from it. She covers a multitude of subjects: Historical research, the trials and tribulations of a life in woodworking, more abstract ideas of value and morality, her own personal history, being a woman in a male-dominated field, and more. Just the titles of some of her recent blogposts reveal the breadth of her curiosity: "Replace a Base Cabinet Door with a Trash Pullout," "Put Your Tool Where It's Not Meant to Go," "5 Tips for Dealing with Difficult Clients," "Nancy Hiller's Reality Check(list)," and "Ruskin's Moral Elements of Gothic: A Foundation of the Arts and Crafts Movement."

Hiller has a forthcoming publication on kitchens with Lost Art Press, as well as having completed books on the Hoosier Cabinet (a particular type of free-standing kitchen cabinet manufactured and marketed in Indiana from the end of the nineteenth century through the 1930s) and *English Arts & Crafts Furniture: Projects and Techniques for the Modern Maker* (2020). The latter is classic Hiller: A blend of erudite history and biography, sociology, firsthand research and interpretation, and three how-to projects for the contemporary maker, complete with working drawings and photographs of pieces under construction on Hiller's bench. These contributions are a reminder that woodworking is not the only field in which it is difficult to consistently earn a living: "The books, in effect, pay nothing. The magazines at least pay something, but it's not enough to cover my overhead and operating expenses, let alone live on" (Hiller, 2017).

Work for our bread; work for our delight

Hiller's philosophy aligns closely with that of the English Arts and Crafts movement, particularly Ruskin. The idea that a person and their work are deeply enmeshed was at the movement's heart, and is deeply culturally embedded, particularly for the so-called "creative class." She raises a complication in the entanglement of making and morality: People have a misconception, she observes, that "if you're an excellent craftsman you must be an excellent human being, but that is clearly not true." Hiller further writes:

Figure 5.27: Nancy Hiller, kitchen for 1915 flat in Chicago, 2014. (Spectrum Creative Group)

[*The Arts and Crafts movement*] brought urgently needed attention to the human realities behind the objects that furnish our lives ... the idea that the things we make express our values and influence our actions; that we have an ethical obligation to consider the quality of life experienced by those who produce the things we use in our daily lives; and that work, ideally, should not be a mere means to income, but should engage our capacities and afford us opportunities to improve ourselves.

(Hiller, 2018)

Hiller is deeply rooted in the materiality and labor of wood. "I'd like to think that my work is literally grounding. My hands are in material every day, I am doing manual work a lot of the time." Her work is also grounded in an ethic of doing the best job she can for her clients, evolved from Wisconsin-born Craftsman furniture manufacturer Gustav Stickley's motto and mark: *Als Ik Kan*, a Flemish phrase which means "the best that I can do." Hiller is consciously at odds with what she fears has become a cultural norm: "It's fear of the style over substance thing. Not that you can always, or necessarily ever, really distinguish, in an absolute way, between them; you can't. But there certainly is a spectrum where the style/image/veneer vastly exceeds the substance, and vice versa."

Hiller talks about the value of her work, both monetary and intangible, something with which a lot of makers struggle. "A lot of people say, gosh, it's so hard to put a value on your work. Well, not if you charge this way: $60 an hour plus materials!" It's a simple and honest formula that Hiller appreciates. "This is my hourly rate. This is what I think it will cost. I will write you up a proposal and I would love to do the job." Pricing her labor in this straightforward and transparent manner is appealing. Hiller gets to choose her clients—a critical part of creating one's world—and prefers to work for middle-class clients who exhibit gratitude for what they have. "At the end of the day they stand there, and as one of them said, 'Honestly, Nancy, it's an embarrassment of riches.' The fact that he can have that perception of how lucky he is to be living the life he is, is beautiful to me. I want to be with those kinds of people."

Hiller has spent her working life dealing and negotiating, not only with materials, tools, clients, contractors, sub-contractors, publishers, editors, husbands, employees, fans, and correspondents, but with herself. Her work

Figure 5.28: Nancy Hiller, oak coffee table built from a downed tree on the client's property, 2015. (Spectrum Creative Group)

ethic and commitment to excellence has taken its toll on relationships: She has often privileged work over friends and family. Yet she has harnessed her inner vulnerability, quashing it where necessary, sometimes masking it, and at other times making it the subject of her work. Only in recent years has Hiller been willing to examine the fact that she's a woman in a still male-dominated field. "I've spent most of my life being like, 'So what, let's not talk about gender, let's not give it power by talking about it.'" There were no role models for her, no images of other women. It wasn't cool to be a woman; it was a liability. "For a long time it was like 'I'm just Nancy Hiller and I do what I do.' Now I will post more pictures of myself working on Instagram just because I realize we need more."

KATIE HUDNALL
Practice makes imperfect

Figure 5.29: Katie Hudnall, summer 2018

I've realized that my way of making connections and figuring things out
and moving through the world has its own kind of successful outcomes,
but they don't look a thing like other peoples'.

Indianapolis, Indiana

Katie Hudnall lives on a quiet, leafy street in Indianapolis in a scene so
quintessentially middle American that it stands in stark relief to her work,
which is anything but. The house is set back on a green lawn sloping slightly
away from the house. Everything is symmetrical. A straight path leads to a
quaint early 1910s Craftsman house. There's something reminiscent of Tim
Burton or Pee Wee Herman about the whole scenario.

Inside Hudnall's house there are collections of things—acorns, shells, pens, cookbooks—arranged on shelves and on the windowsills. Against one wall is *Spirits Cabinet* (2011), functioning like conventional furniture, filled with stacks of plates and bowls. Despite its unconventional nature—one door opens upwards and, viewed end-on, it is essentially a see-through cabinet—it fits well in the tidy, warm room. Like many artists, Hudnall is inspired by and uses reclaimed materials in her work. *Spirits Cabinet* includes a piece of reclaimed wood from every place she had lived until its making and so, though she sells most of her work, this one is personal and not for sale. There are no tricky woodworking joints; instead, she most often uses cold connections—screws, cotter pins, rivets, nuts, and bolts—which become a visual and material element in work that is witty, often obsessive, and sometimes outright hilarious. Hudnall's pieces are true contraptions, created where Rube Goldberg met the falling down barn in a wheat field.

As much as *being* furniture, Hudnall's work *alludes* to furniture, which she calls "furniturish." These might be floor cabinets designed to contain, but whose capacity for holding is so particular to a singular object as to

Figure 5.30: Katie Hudnall, *Spirits Cabinet*, 2011. (Michelle Given)

verge on the absurd. Like your grandmother's drawer labeled "strings too short to use," Hudnall built a storage cabinet for screws that failed to have the slots milled during manufacturing, and a beautiful magnifying display box for a wingnut, playfully illuminating the humanmade objects created to provide for very particular human needs. In another instance it's a lamp poised like a spider ready to pounce, or a wall cabinet that invites the user to peer through a porthole at the contents, which seem to peer right back. These are furniture works that invite us into a set of unexpected relationships; the ways we think of opening and closing a cabinet door or putting stuff away are taken to logical yet unexpected conclusions. Hudnall's work resides in a world where we live *with* our furniture, where the side table might not stand complacently at the end of the couch.

Born in 1979, Hudnall grew up in the eighties in suburban Washington, DC; slow to read, she was placed in classes for students with learning differences. With testing it emerged that the issue was how she sees, both literally—she is nearly legally blind—and perceptually. When asked in vision exams which way the letter was pointing, she would respond, "What do you mean, *pointing*?" Glasses helped enormously, as did her supportive parents.

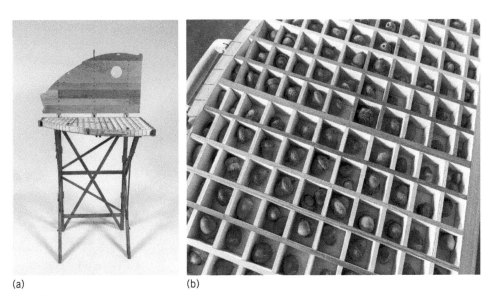

(a)   (b)

Figure 5.31a and b: Katie Hudnall, *Nutcase*, 2019. (Mary McClung)

Like many kids, Hudnall enjoyed playing soccer, biking, and walking around the neighborhood and up and down the Potomac River near their home. The rest of the time she drew anything "that would sit still long enough." She paid particular attention to small things, perhaps because she couldn't see the big ones: "I had no idea there were leaves on trees that you could really see until I was ten."

As a teenager Hudnall attended Catholic school, but there was no soccer, she found the uniforms restrictive, and her grades plummeted. She found sanctuary in the theater club and the art room, which felt to Hudnall the only subversive space in the school. She became part of the stage crew and learned to make things, "building sets badly." When it came time to thinking about college, her dad suggested art schools. She chose Corcoran College of Art and Design in Washington, DC—not far from home, but far enough. Hudnall quickly realized that there were people there who were better at drawing, in a technical, representational sense, so she gravitated toward sculpture. "I certainly wasn't the student that anybody thought was still going to be making work twenty years later, because most of my cohorts aren't now," she reflects. "There's a couple of us, but very few. I learned that making good work has a lot less to do with natural talent than with practice."

Growing up Hudnall had loved going to the Museum of Natural History, fascinated by the drawers of rocks and shells, and in the mundane realm of a trip to the post office, she found an affinity with the walls of tiny doors, each representing a person. For her final project at Corcoran, Hudnall built a head-shaped cabinet with compartments inside which she envisioned as a material manifestation of the inside of her brain, doors opening and closing, hiding and revealing, and perhaps presaging the future direction of her work.

Upon graduation, Hudnall accompanied her girlfriend to Spain; they landed on September 11, 2001. Unable to speak Spanish, for those next few months Hudnall wandered Valencia in the company of Sheepy, a sheep who lived on the pages of her sketchbook, and Fred, another character who reminded her to stay out of trouble. She even made a pilgrimage to Scotland to see the work of Charles Rennie Mackintosh, with whom she was obsessed: "Tall, skinny, uncomfortable chairs? I thought they were the bees' knees." Hudnall moved back to Oberlin, Ohio, where she became increasingly interested in resuming the nascent woodworking she had begun as an undergraduate. She found work with Palli Davis, a sculptor, and her husband, Michael Holubar, a specialist in Frank Lloyd Wright furniture. They taught her some basic woodworking skills and urged her to think about graduate school. Using recycled pallet wood stitched together with copper wire, Hudnall created a portfolio and applied to Virginia Commonwealth University (VCU). She got in.

At VCU Hudnall was one of two woodworking students. While she was trying to make **dovetailed carcasses** and more traditional, formal furniture, her notebooks were filled with "weird furniture that's walking around." All of her professors encouraged her to create the work that animated the pages of her sketchbook, but it was Susan Iverson, a textiles professor, who phrased it most succinctly: "Where's the humor in this work and where's the line quality? Why do you keep trying to make stuff the way other woodworkers make stuff? You draw stuff this way, why don't you make it the way you draw it, not the way you see other people doing it?" It is difficult to imagine Hudnall's work not always being what it is now—a world of its own with a self-contained, absurdist logic. With permission and encouragement, she realized she could be her own kind of woodworker. Once she was introduced to cold connections Hudnall realized with relief that she could transfer this technology of fasteners to wood.

The first piece Hudnall made following this revelation was the four-legged *The Pirate Stool* (2004) (Figure 5.32), which has a peg-leg that can be swapped out, dressed up or down. For her MFA thesis project Hudnall invented a character and then constructed their environment (Figures 5.33 and 5.34): The mad tinkerer—essentially Hudnall herself, or the scientist/maker she hoped to be—and her tools. A chess board and table rotated on four wheels so the tinkerer could play against herself. When the viewer approaches, the game would be half-played. "And then I made stairs going up to the window, and covered the window with a door, so it looked like a way out. And I put in a fake floor that made all these crazy sounds when you walked into it. There was a little woodworking bench, and drawings all over the walls, and these weird rafter things that I just sketched in space." The installation was, Hudnall describes, "like walking into an illustration. That was the idea." And there was more: The door at the top of the stairs had a door cut in it, and that door had a little door cut into it, and again and again, until the last door had a window. Hudnall had created a microworld for her work.

Figure 5.32: Katie Hudnall, *The Pirate Stool*, 2004. (Taylor Dabney)

Figure 5.33: Katie Hudnall, *A Tinkerer's Studio* (thesis installation), VCU, 2005. (Katie Hudnall)

Hudnall has not continued to make installations—partly because of space constraints, but largely because she realized a piece creates its own context, the terms on which it is to be encountered. "I figured out that when you make an object, it has to be good no matter how far you zoom in. And that was something that the installation taught me: That the detail should be as good, if not better, than the piece from far away." This is one of the remarkable aspects of her work: The confidence of its internal logic.

On leaving VCU in 2005, Hudnall moved to Bumpass, Virginia, forty-odd miles northwest of Richmond, where she lived with her then-partner on their family farm. All around them was rural infrastructure built and repaired by the previous seven generations: Utilitarian buildings informed by function and expediency, and an aesthetic integrity fueled by rationality and utility. Though by the time Hudnall moved to the farm the buildings were mostly falling in, the experience proved quite formative. "Being able to see all the

Figure 5.34: Katie Hudnall, *A Tinkerer's Studio* (thesis installation), VCU, 2005. (Katie Hudnall)

solutions, all of the ways that the doors closed with just a pivoting latch—it was really beautiful. You can follow the logic of how everything's made."

It was a busy and productive period: Hudnall was making a lot of work, exhibiting as much as possible, teaching adjunct at VCU for one semester per year, and working in commercial cabinet shops. She was learning speed and efficiency at the commercial shops, developing a pedagogical style, and consolidating her aesthetic. In 2008 she was awarded an $8,000 scholarship from the Virginia Museum of Fine Arts, which was not only a boost to her confidence but allowed her to build a website and pay for professional images of her work, both of which increased her visibility.

After a residency at the University of Wisconsin, Madison, and another at Anderson Ranch in Colorado, Hudnall applied to a full-time teaching position at Murray State in Kentucky, where the department was looking for someone able to talk with equal ease to the students drawn to sculpture and those attracted to woodworking. She was the right candidate at the right time. Both the academic politics and Kentucky itself came as something of a culture shock. Hudnall was the only openly gay faculty member in a conservative Christian town, to which she responded by growing a mohawk. But she describes the department as a good introduction to teaching: Other faculty were gentle with her, easing her in slowly, and she enjoyed her students. After three years she decided it was time to move on and landed a position as Associate Professor of Furniture Design in Herron School of Art and Design at Indiana University in 2013, and was there until the beginning of academic year 2020–2021 when she moved to the University of Wisconsin at Madison to lead their woodworking program.

~

An early riser who is drawn to the quiet, the solitude, and the lack of social media, Hudnall often spends those early morning hours sketching. In fact, she sketches a lot, and not furniture per se, using the medium instead as a way to store, process, and discover her thoughts and impressions, whether she's at a faculty meeting or taking a line for a walk. The drawings resemble her furniture in line quality and humor, but not as representations for a particular piece or a plan of action. Hudnall is introspective and self-reflective, and there's a playful and sophisticated blend of the ordinary and the extraordinary in her way of being in the world, and in her work, which is unusual, hetero-geneous, and recognizably hers, with referents to contemporary art history.

Hudnall's work privileges line quality over form or mass. In some cases, the work appears relatively delicate, almost fragile, and because of its accretional nature, she simply adds more linear elements until the structure is strong enough. In other works, the apparent lightness of line weight has more in common with the logic of a suspension bridge, a complex array of components carrying weight that defies expectation. Her favorite illus-trators—Edward Gorey, Quentin Blake, and Shel Silverstein—are all darkly funny. She is particularly drawn to Gorey for the intensity of the detail: "Edward Gorey's people will be in a room that's got wallpaper and he's drawn the fucking wallpaper. It's amazing," she marvels.

Hudnall is particular about the specifics of line: She doesn't just use the pen or pencil that happens to be in her hand, instead choosing the rather fussy and sometimes messy technology of refillable drafting pens. Hudnall attends to her workspace with the same deliberate consideration, constantly resetting, or "**knolling**," it. Her use of cold fasteners means that

(a)   (b)

Figure 5.35a and b: "Sketchbook niblets from a couple of weeks where I haven't been able to make it to the non-paper studio much. Even when I'm too busy or tired to do woodworking I sneak a few minutes in my sketchbook (during meetings, yes) each day and it helps keep me connected to making and allows me to keep a little artistic momentum." (Hudnall, 2019)

she has literally hundreds of connectors to organize in her shop, a fact that seems to fill her with joy. She refers to organizational structure as the exoskeleton which keeps her brain on track, a concept and approach she tries to communicate to her students. "They leave their benches a total mess, and I constantly reorganize mine, and clean. I call it resetting. I'll constantly reset my space because I'm really scattered as a thinker, and if I don't have a structure around me, I'll just be looking for my pencil for like 400 hours and never actually make anything!" Her workshop is indeed tidy and organized, and unusually animated, which in Hudnall's case means that inanimate objects have faces and sometimes names, and there are notes on the wall, both to and from Hudnall.

Some of Hudnall's students are drawn to her classes because they've seen things on Instagram that they want to be able to make, but while they may start by wanting to replicate that resin table they saw, they're open to trying new things, Hudnall says, and they're getting more sculptural.

Figure 5.36: Katie Hudnall, workshop, summer 2018

Sculpture is about human skill, about things the size of furniture, things the size of something you can hold. It's about being human, whether it's new technology or traditions or something blended. Fine art sculpture feels like it's about fine art sculpture; you would have to understand the history of sculpture to understand it. I don't think you have to understand the history of craft to understand some of these sculptural craft pieces. You just have to have a body.

Hudnall goes on to argue for the importance of the knowledge furniture makers bring—of material, scale, and utility—to creating sculptural work. "Some of the most interesting sculpture is being made by furniture makers. Some of my colleagues in the sculpture department would be mad at me for saying that, but they are not here!" She's also excited about fibers and ceramics, likewise materials best worked at a human scale.

The excitement Hudnall brings to both her work and her classroom is infused, too, with deliberation and a patience for the learning process. Indeed, when asked for any advice she would give a young woodworker, there are clearly lessons Hudnall has taken to heart:

Your head will get a lot further than your hands and you have to be patient with yourself. You'll have ideas for things that you want to make that you're just not capable of making at first. Be patient and tenacious and remember that so much of the world is made up of wood. Look at it, pay attention to it, because there's so many different ways to do things, and if it works you've done it right. There's not one way to do stuff.

YURI KOBAYASHI
Believing

Figure 5.37: Yuri Kobayashi at Anderson Ranch Arts Center, 2019

It feels like I found my water to swim in.

Tokyo, Japan

Born in 1971 and raised in Tokyo, Japan, Yuri Kobayashi is most at home these days in the United States. It suits her way of being in the world; it lets her *be*. Growing up as the elder of two daughters, Kobayashi was not content to slide into the normative and gendered role that society offered her. Her father—who spent his career with the Tokyo Police force—held traditional views of gender and didn't see this self-identified tomboy with equanimity. Kobayashi was raised with ideas—spoken and not—about how girls should walk, talk, eat, or even laugh. There was no discussion: In his household, he was right.

Kobayashi's kindergarten school uniform included a skirt, but as soon as she got home, she changed into shorts and headed to the sandbox. She grew early and by elementary school was among the tallest of her peers. With fewer boys than girls in her class, teachers often treated her as they would a boy. She reciprocally acted more like one, and by middle school also found boys' social politics easier to manage than those of her female classmates. The child who loved soccer, make-believe swords, and bows and arrows became the high school student excited about sports, making things, and solving puzzles.

Both of Kobayashi's parents came from fruit farming families in the mountains, where cousins and grandparents still live. Intrigued by the traditional wooden houses in which they lived—so different from the buildings in Tokyo and its suburbs—Kobayashi was curious about how they were put together, and when it came time to think about what to do after high school, architecture was her natural choice. Though she was choosing in some part to satisfy her parents' professional ambitions for her, her father was disappointed. He had been the only one of his siblings to go to university and move to Tokyo; he wanted her to pursue medicine or law, each with clearer markers of professional success and familial advancement than architecture offered.

In Japan, entering university is competitive and stressful, and Kobayashi gained a place at Musashino Art University in Tokyo, a small and prestigious art school with an architecture department that emphasized design rather than technical engineering. Though she says she developed a habit of finishing projects at the last minute, she would work until the last train left—or beyond—and then catch the first train home in the morning. The school curriculum paired beginners with more senior students, a tradition in Japanese school systems: "Freshman or sophomores got to work with seniors on their projects, helping with model building and drafting, and sharing struggles and sleepless nights. I enjoyed that mingling, learning not only from the professor, but also from upper class students." They also interned in professional architects' offices. In school at just the moment when the field was shifting from hand to digital modes of working—when older architects didn't want to learn the new methods—Kobayashi, like many of her peers, was paid to learn to make AutoCAD (**computer-aided design**) drawings. Just out of college, she put her model-making and AutoCAD skills to use, working at several firms, big and small, around Tokyo. In a country enjoying intense economic growth, Kobayashi made good money.

After a little more than a year, Kobayashi realized that, despite the money, this wasn't how she wanted to spend her life. The models were fun, but they were still scale models, representations of rather than the thing itself. Kobayashi came up against the frustration that haunts many architects: The building contractor actually *knows how* to build things and the architect can be as much an impediment as an ally. So she took a summer to travel around Japan, visiting craft studios with a focus on wood, fiber dying, and clay. She found a private woodworking school a remote 200 miles from Tokyo and, without her parents' knowledge, applied.

~

The school was Shinrin Takumi Juku in Takayama City, founded in the early 1990s by Osamu Shoji, a master craftsman, and Masatoshi Tsukuda. The school had an allied manufacturing facility, Oak Village, where in return for free tuition, students in the Production Training Course worked on real products in a manufacturing environment. The aesthetic and attitude of Takumi Juku and Oak Village was, and continues to be, one of respect for wood. It takes every tree decades—perhaps centuries—to grow, and the object built from it should last equally long. Though not particularly interested in the Shaker-informed design they employed, Kobayashi respected the program's ethics and integrity.

On top of learning woodworking techniques and hand tool care, the student-apprentices at Takumi Juku learn the fundamentals of business: Quality, delivery date, cost, and profit. As the school's vision states, "There is no point learning these things if you end up with desk theory. It is always learning through the body in real movement" (*Takumi Juku*, 2021). In practice that means students work in teams on large production runs, 500 to 1,000 pencil cases or mirror frames, and smaller batches of perhaps ten chairs, benches, or tables. Kobayashi loved it. The repetition instilled muscle memory and increased speed and fluidity while maintaining quality. Planning to a production deadline meant scheduling, and if the scheduling was wrong, apprentices worked after hours to catch up. Kobayashi knew from the very beginning that she'd found her place:

> As soon as I walked into the woodshop—with its unfamiliar machinery, workbenches placed in order, piles of lumber, jigs, templates, and hand tools hanging on the wall, I felt it: This is it! In orientation on day one, twelve of us—the new students—were each assigned a different task. The staff told you what to do, and what to pay attention to. Without knowing exactly what we were doing, we filled in an assembly line to fabricate a product. The piles of wooden parts on a dolly, the smell of the wood, the sound of cut, and the repetitive activity … doing the same thing over and over again, for hundreds and hundreds of pieces … I just loved it. I still remember that day. I fell in love with woodworking day one, and felt okay, "I did the right thing and made the right choice."

After two years as a student, Kobayashi didn't yet have the confidence to step right into a company or start her own business. Instead, she worked as a staff member at the school, supervising students, managing the assembly line, maintaining machinery, ordering supplies, and handling communications. The school hosted lectures and classes from visiting woodworkers, including James Krenov, whom Shoji *sensei* admired and whose principles were quite influential on the ethics and aesthetics of the school. Another visitor was Wendy Maruyama (Profile pp. 273–287), longtime friend of Shoji and program chair of Furniture Design at San Diego State (SDSU), who visited several times, first when Kobayashi was a student, and again when she was on staff. The third time Maruyama came, she arrived with a grant for an exchange program at SDSU. Kobayashi applied. She was taken by Maruyama and her iconoclasm. Kobayashi remembers her demonstrating the application of milk paint to wood: "I was like, 'Wow, she's putting color on the wood?' Everybody's looking at each other, unable to hide our surprise, going 'Wow, is that what American furniture makers do?' It was totally shocking." Kobayashi describes meeting Maruyama as the single biggest influence and impact on her life. Shortly thereafter Kobayashi immigrated to the US to study with Maruyama at San Diego State.

San Diego, California

With Maruyama's logistical support, Kobayashi was able to navigate the language and immigration requirements for SDSU and moved to San Diego to pursue an MFA in Furniture Design and Woodworking. She arrived to find herself in a student community that members have described as a dream team: Jennifer Anderson (Profile pp. 163–171), Christine Lee (Profile pp. 231–242), Kimberly Winkle, Mia Hall, Matt Hutton, and Cory Robinson, who welcomed and nurtured her. They became a tight group of friends and colleagues, spending countless hours together in the shop over the three years.

Applying paint to wood turned out to be just the tip of the iceberg: The diversity of woodworking practices in the program and in the United States at large transformed Kobayashi's sense of what was possible with the medium. Woodworking could be an individual and expressive activity, and furniture and wood could be carriers of meaning and objects of communication. If in Japan Kobayashi had worked as part of a team—making objects both conceived and designed by others—in San Diego she was being asked to make pieces that were expressive of her inner self, manifestations of thoughts and feelings.

Despite the long and heralded tradition of woodworking in Japan, there was no development of anything comparable to studio furniture through the twentieth century, in no small part because furniture itself plays a different structural and social role in a traditional Japanese home. Instead, during the period when studio furniture in the US emphasized the development and expression of personal aesthetics, small-scale furniture factories were

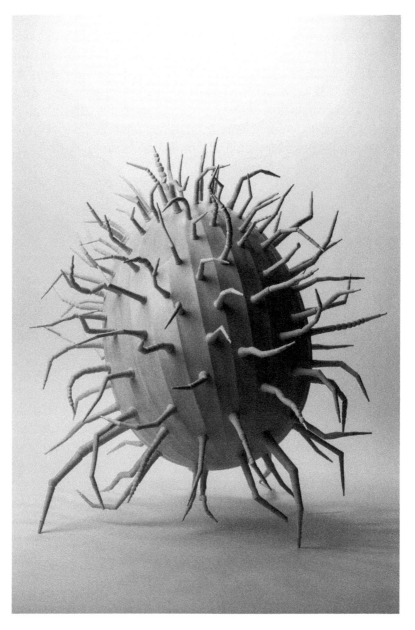

Figure 5.38: Yuri Kobayashi, *Curio*, 29"w × 30"d × 29"h, 2015. (Dalton Paley)

developed, often with high manufacturing standards and a clean modernist aesthetic derived from mid-century Scandinavian furniture.

Kobayashi's experience at San Diego State was revelatory and challenging. Not only was she being asked to express herself through the objects she made, but also, as an MFA candidate, through spoken and written language—*and in English.* If form, or the shape of objects, is ambiguous and open to many interpretations, context and shared cultural references aid in the process. The verbal statements—being able to give language to what one has made or intends to make—can establish the framework of inquiry. For Kobayashi, inserted into an English-speaking world, this created something of a barrier. She chose to focus on what can arguably be considered universals of human experience: Emotions that transcend language and culture. As examples, she mentions the grief we experience in the break-up of a relationship, or a belief in a power larger than ourselves.

> When we experience a break-up of a relationship, we get sad, mad, disappointed, regretful, etc. It doesn't matter how old, or a boy or a girl, or Japanese or American; it doesn't matter. I wanted to capture the kind of emotional experience that everybody can share.

Rockport, Maine

Kobayashi left SDSU in 2006 with as much interest in sculpture as in functional furniture, and she continues to oscillate between the two. If the formal and structural characteristics in her work sometimes blur the edges, she thinks of them as two distinct modes of practice: Furniture has strict parameters of function—ergonomics, comfort (especially if it's a chair or sitting object), and a focus on the end user—while sculpture, on the other hand, emanates from her emotional life and experience. When making sculptural work she is not thinking of a viewer, focusing instead on the best means of expression. In furniture mode she often goes to other makers for input and advice; when making sculpture she does not seek external feedback but relies on herself for judgment as to whether the piece is successful.

Having been trained in traditional woodworking in Japan, Kobayashi now moves fluidly between sculpture and functional furniture, employing a shared visual and material vocabulary in both realms. Contemporary and

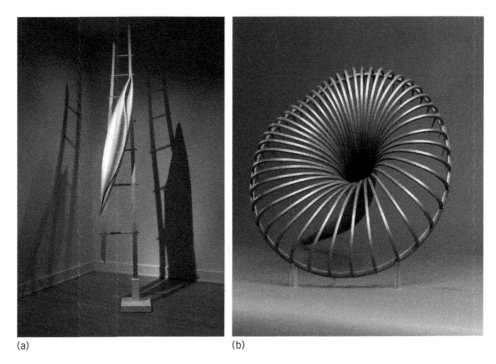

(a)   (b)

Figure 5.39a and b: Yuri Kobayashi, (L–R) *Will*, 20"w × 20"d × 132"h, 2009. (Joshua Laieski); *Whisper*, 36"w × 16"d × 18"h, 2012. (Mark Juliana)

monochromatic, the furniture can look abstract and sculptural, and the sculptural pieces suggest a function one can't quite identify. The radiating elements of *Believing* (Figure 5.40), for example, are reminiscent of the spokes of wooden wheels or the engraved lines of mill stones, but the luminous and evocative structure—spare, lightweight, and ascendant—defies utility.

When choosing materials, Kobayashi exploits the possibilities of ash—a wood both flexible and strong—bending, weaving, and joining it. The focus is on what the material can do, rather than a modernist reverence for the beauty of the grain or figure. The works, often built from multiple, steam-bent linear elements, have volume without weight or mass, reaching out to define both negative and positive space. Elegantly executed with a precision and refinement that is as impressive as it is reassuring, Kobayashi's work often achieves the primal beauty of a sinuous curve through space, perfectly executed, like the trajectory of a skilled gymnast.

Figure 5.40: Yuri Kobayashi, *Believing*, 74"w × 20"d × 74"h, 2009. (Craig Smith)

Kobayashi has been teaching one semester a year at Rhode Island School of Design. The rest of the year she does residencies, often at the Center for Furniture Craftsmanship (CFC) in Maine.

Being involved at the Center for Furniture Craftsmanship, it's great! [*There are*] always excellent woodworkers, furniture makers around me that I get feedback from and I listen to them. But with sculpture, no matter what they tell me or suggest to me, I totally ignore them. "Thank you but I'm doing this." And then if that doesn't work, I'll figure it out. [*With*] a chair, it's, "Yuri, I think that's not going to work." ... But with sculpture, I don't listen to them at all.

For all makers, the determination of what kind of work to make and when, is strongly influenced by the demands of the marketplace and the nuanced relationship between the markets for *art* versus *craft*. Kobayashi spoke of a strong preference for working in "sculpture mode," making furniture only when commissioned or for a group show. For example, for a two-person show with Thomas Hucker at Gallery Naga in Boston in summer 2016, Director Meg White specifically asked Kobayashi to make furniture, feeling more confident the gallery could sell furniture pieces. In a recent meeting with the curator at the Center for Maine Contemporary Art in Rockland, Kobayashi was told that her sculptural work is "too heavily craft oriented" and that "it wasn't going to open a door into the contemporary art field." This uneasy relationship between art and craft leaves many artists and makers trying to make judgments about how to promote and market their work, balancing questions of creative freedom, utility, rigor, and valuation. Despite Kobayashi's conception of the division between her sculptural and functional work, the encounter with the curator seems to have left her uncertain about where to position and promote her work as she hopes to move more singularly to making sculpture. As much as theorists, educators, and artists work to break down these barriers, the perception of difference between the worlds of art and craft remains a powerful narrative in the field and driver in the marketplace. Where the lines sit can be uncomfortably subjective, their location difficult to discern.

Teaching undergraduate skills and technique classes in Furniture Design at RISD, Kobayashi wrestles with a related struggle, questioning the value and relevance of rigorous craft training for a contemporary student community, many of whom are taking hands-on courses but hope to pursue design. As the sculpture department's curriculum integrates more film, performance art, and other time-based media, Kobayashi's classes attract sculpture students seeking kinesthetic and material skills, taught through the lens of furniture and craft. Operating again in the spaces between sculpture and furniture, rigorous craft and personal expression, Kobayashi remembers how much she learned from the upperclassmen when she was in college, and wonders if it is generational and they would benefit from more contact with emergent makers.

At CFC, on the other hand, the emphasis is most definitely on the technical: "They're passionate about improving their craft skills; they want to do well." Teaching at art and craft centers such as Anderson Ranch capitalizes on Kobayashi's expertise in the craft of woodworking. Moving between these practices and the identities they offer, she vacillates, sometimes drawing strict distinctions, sometimes blurring or deliberately not seeing boundaries,

Figure 5.41: Yuri Kobayashi, (L–R) *Sui*, 2016; *Lin*, 2015. (Mark Juliana)

navigating the relationship between art and craft, sculpture and furniture, in an ongoing way and in every realm in her life: Negotiating, disrupting, adding to and subtracting from, creating sculptural furniture and rigorously crafted sculpture that references furniture traditions.

Snowmass, Colorado

In summer 2019 Kobayashi was at Anderson Ranch Arts Center in the small town of Snowmass, high in the mountains of Colorado, teaching a week-long course on bending wood. Each of the dozen or so students was doing a different project; Kobayashi was buzzing, moving easily from bench to bench, cajoling, supporting, encouraging, demonstrating, and asking questions. **Steam bending** is time sensitive. Wood has to be moved promptly

Figure 5.42: Yuri Kobayashi, sketchbook page of the beginnings of a chair, posted to Instagram, July 30, 2015. (Yuri Kobayashi)

from the steam-filled chamber to a form and bent quickly and smoothly. Too abrupt of a movement can cause the wood to crack; too slow and the wood will lose its temporary pliability. Kobayashi, an expert at the technique, moves fast and with surety. Her students were clearly enjoying the class, and it seems she gains as much energy from teaching as she puts into it. Kobayashi was in her element.

CHRISTINE LEE
Material things

Figure 5.43: Portrait of Christine Lee, 2015. (Blake Lockard, courtesy of Anderson Ranch Arts Center)

As soon as someone says, "Are you doing sculptural work?" I'll say yes, but then I'll make a functional piece. And then someone might say, "You're doing mostly speculative functional pieces." Then I'll have just finished some type of large-scale installation. So I stopped identifying with the disciplines specifically and I started focusing more on just material exploration as a way to describe what I'm doing.

Tempe, Arizona

The child of scientists, Georgia-born Christine Lee approaches a new material scrutinously: She spends time with it, getting to know it and then playing with it, breaking it apart, reconfiguring and manipulating it without preconceived expectations as to how it might or should behave. The relationship between Lee's investigative approach and her upbringing is evident; before focusing on the arts, she studied chemistry at the University of Wisconsin at Madison. Both parents were from large, frugal, and hard-working South Korean families, instilling their strong values in their eldest child. "There was a real emphasis on appreciating what you had and not wasting anything, from aluminum foil to wrappers." Lee reflects. "They just didn't throw stuff away arbitrarily. I think that really informs a lot of what I do; I don't like throwing things away without thinking a little bit more about what can be done with it."

The family moved from Athens, Georgia, to Philadelphia and then to Chicago, where Lee (b. 1973) spent most of her childhood and early adulthood. In college, halfway to the chemistry degree, it was clear that she was deeply unhappy: Though she had pursued science in part out of respect for her parents' hope for a secure and well-paid career, they encouraged her move to art. Then, in a printmaking class, a friend noticed her cutting deeper and deeper into the wood block—unnecessarily so—and suggested she look into woodworking. She signed up for the furniture design program, and graduated in 1997 with a Bachelor of Science in Art degree.

Over the next couple years Lee consolidated her woodworking skills, developed her portfolio, and applied to the furniture program at San Diego State. There, she decided, "I'm just going to go for it. I'm going to make the work that is spontaneous, challenging ... whatever I feel ... I'm not going to make stuff that is just pretty to look at." The piece she made next was a bench from padauk—a prized hardwood from central and West Africa recognized for its rich color and durability—and recycled newspaper used on edge, so that it becomes soft and almost fluffy as the paper fibers wear. Lee was interested in the cultural context, perceived value, and lateral materiality in the dramatic contrast in materials: Their texture, rigidity, and resistance. She thought, "I'm going to do it because I see potential here. And so that was very freeing for me to do that because ... I felt like I had nothing to lose."

As if a switch had been flipped, Lee started to think differently about materials, to explore their intrinsic qualities freed of perception about utility and value. The questions and potential meanings of unusual and undervalued materials had some shared resonance among her peers in the

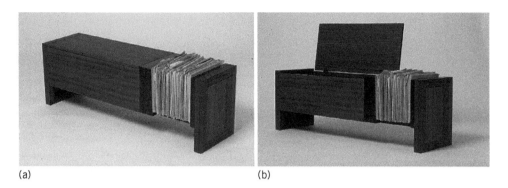

(a)   (b)

Figure 5.44a and b: Christine Lee, *Newspaper Bench*, 2002. (Michael James Slattery)

program, including Jennifer Anderson (Profile pp. 163–171) who had begun using mud to make chairs. Risk-taking has become Lee's deeply held creative value, to the point where she's uncomfortable being comfortable. An insatiable curiosity has overtaken the inevitable doubt: "Push it. Do things that I'm not sure how it's going to turn out but go for it."

Graduate school offered community and the chance to be challenged critically about her work. In Program Chair Wendy Maruyama (Profile pp. 273–287) she found a mentor and role model—as so many others have—and a team of colleagues that included many who've continued in the field as makers and educators, including Anderson and Kobayashi (Profile pp. 219–230). Supportive and nurturing, Maruyama continued sending Lee emails years after she finished the program, encouraging her to pursue opportunities.

Deeply knowledgeable in the tools and techniques of furniture, Lee uses familiar materials—**caning**, wood, veneer, or concrete—in unconventional ways. She will reconceive the whole framework of a given material: Fire hoses might become a screen, or construction-grade shims might become the tessellations of a crystalline landscape. In this open-ended and exploratory process, Lee's work moves between art practice and industry with a graceful seamlessness of thought and intention. A single material, undecorated and uncolored, used repetitively—its intrinsic qualities explored and manifest in a manner that simultaneously challenges our assumptions about the material—is characteristic of Lee's work.

In March 2019 Lee was installing a site-specific caning piece at the Museum of Craft and Design in San Francisco a few days before the

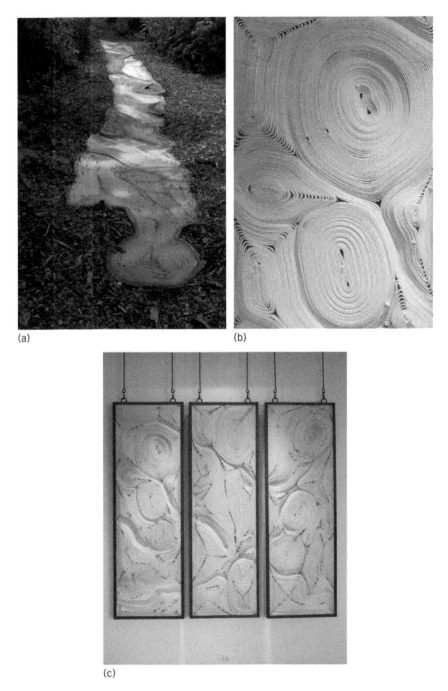

(a)

(b)

(c)

Figure 5.45a, b, and c: Christine Lee, (L–R) *Between Twelve and Three*, 2004. (Shawn Goodell); *Terrain*, detail, 2003. (Christine Lee); *Terrain*, 2003. (Christine Lee)

exhibition opened, weaving a large vertical grid of **rattan** that entwined the wall and adjacent column, becoming part of the architecture while transforming it. Strands of rattan, the material used in caning chair backs and seats, are flexible when wet, tighten as they dry, and remain straight and taut over 16 feet. The translation to an architectural form reveals a playful understanding of the material and the technicalities of its use, and—like so many crafts—an investigation of building up multiple parts into a complete whole. As Lee worked, she gave a crash course in the practicalities of caning.

You want to make sure it's not twisted as you're weaving. I'll tend to go in and out and maybe like about ten inches, or eight inches. And I'll just pull it as close to the plane as possible; it seems to be easier. Then go another ten and end up there. What you're actually looking at right

Figure 5.46: Christine Lee, *Intersection*, 2019. (Christine Lee)

here is four layers. You have the first verticals back here; the second one is on top of it; the third one is to the right of every first vertical, and then the fourth one is where you actually start weaving. The fifth and sixth layers run on the diagonal, with the fifth traversing the grid from upper left to lower right.

On the wall, the grid of caning (and its attendant shadow) within a wooden frame is reminiscent of the cross-hatching of a drawing or the comforting grid of graph paper, but then the grid pulls away from the wall and wraps around a column, revealing itself as flexible and three-dimensional.

Lee is also intrigued by rattan's historical roots and connection to the natural world. Native to parts of Asia and Africa, rattan is found most commonly today in Indonesia, growing in narrow vining stalks in tropical forests; the shiny, non-porous cane is the skin or bark of the stalk. Used in beds and caskets for centuries, caning first appeared in colonial era European furniture in seventeenth-century Holland, England, and France. Lee loves diving deeply into a tradition that is centuries old; once she understood caning in furniture, she began to think about how else the material

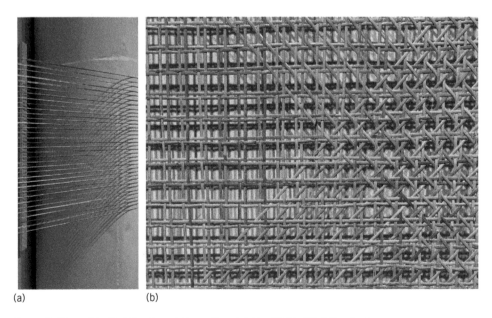

(a)   (b)

Figure 5.47a and b: Christine Lee, *Intersection*, details, 2019. (Christine Lee) could be used. "Before we had books, before anything, we were starting somewhere. It's very instinctual, it's very embedded in us, and there's a lot of direct interaction. To me, the fact that it's been explored all this time and it hasn't gone away, that's what I love about this process."

Sustainability

For nearly a decade after leaving San Diego in 2007, Lee moved around the US as an artist-in-residence at, among others, Anderson Ranch Arts Center; Recology, Workshop Residence, and Djerassi Resident Artists Program in the Bay Area; Purchase College in New York; and Indiana University (IUP) in Pennsylvania. Participating in an array of exhibits, Lee's work was also purchased by collectors and institutions. It was a migratory and somewhat unsettled lifestyle, offering no opportunity to put down roots or form long-term relationships. On the other hand, she got to know the field broadly, and made deep friendships with others on similar trajectories.

A 2010 residency at University of Wisconsin, Madison, offered an unusual combination of research and artistic practice. Lee collaborated full-time with Forest Park Laboratories' mechanical engineer John Hunt to develop a "non-toxic, biodegradable and recyclable, engineered wood composite panel made from sawdust and post-consumer recycled fibers without added formaldehyde." By contrast, most man-made timber board products—**plywood**, **MDF**, **particle board**—contain formaldehyde-based glues which off-gas carcinogens. Able to fully allocate her time to research, Lee recalls a rich learning environment without the demands of teaching. Back in the woodshop, Lee was building things with lumber that was generating sawdust that went back to the lab and was integrated into the composite boards. "I was creating this really interesting cycle of material use from the by-product that I was generating from **milling** wood," she says. That residency culminated in a show at the Madison Children's Museum of objects made from the boards they had developed, *and* a provisional patent for "Binderless Panel made from wood particles and cellulosic fibers," filed with Hunt in 2012 (USDA, 2012).

~

Since 2016 Lee has been the Senior Sustainability Scholar of the Julie Ann Wrigley Global Institute of Sustainability and Assistant Professor in Wood/Sustainability in the School of Art, Herberger Institute for Design and the Arts, at Arizona State University in Tempe. She teaches a sustainable practice class, a special topics class like Art and Sensory Acuity, and all levels of woodworking to undergrad and graduate students, and to art majors and students from a variety of disciplines across the university. Juggling teaching and making, bureaucracy and committee requirements, Lee never actually completes the workload. She is also tenure-track, and required to have a one-person show, even though her work is commonly collaborative and cross-disciplinary, and not necessarily well-suited to a gallery space.

Lee approaches students and syllabi, course descriptions, and learning outcomes as she does sculptural materials: With the same open-minded curiosity and without a predetermined outcome. A success is a student who has expanded their definition of who they are and what they are capable of. She described a business student who came in wanting to make traditional furniture, kept coming back, and left making a sculptural chess set. "For me, that's a triumph. Here we had someone who came in with his mind set, and in the end … ended up making really sculptural pieces … that's an outcome. How do you come into a class and challenge yourself, and really think critically and differently about your work?"

To achieve this transformation, Lee encourages her students to hold a responsive attention to wood as a material, with the following introduction: "I say in Beginning Wood, it's like you met somebody at orientation and you realize you have some things in common. Intermediate Wood is where you actually feel like you want to become friends with that person, and then you get to learn more about what that friend likes and dislikes, their nuances and tendencies." Working with wood in the same way, you learn to handle the tools and material with care and respect. "They kind of laugh when I explain to them. It really doesn't make sense to shove the medium through in a different way without respecting what it should do or how it should be presented. You don't force yourself on people, so why would you force yourself on the material?"

One of the benefits and challenges of working with a material in such an engaged and attentive manner is that it demands slowing down. "Especially

Figure 5.48: Christine Lee, *Stacking Order*, site-specific installation for *Making a Seat at the Table*, 2019

today, where everything is moving so quickly, none of the students have time to reflect on anything they've done because you just keep moving forward, we lose the ability to work at a normal human pace." They rarely have any idea of how much time it takes to make something, that there's a series of steps and processes aligned with the pace of the human body and its movements. "They can't rush using a tool on a piece of wood, because A, it can be dangerous, but also, B, they just don't get the quality results. And they are forced to deal with that because they have no choice."

Just as Lee doesn't force her preconceived ideas onto materials, similarly she lets the students discover for themselves through experience, until they get to the point where "they just love being in the shop." Being in a space that's filled with wood is deeply inviting, so much so that Lee wonders why other faculty don't offer classes in the shop even if it's not a woodworking course. "Going from a classroom that's so minimal and sterile, to something that has evidence of character and use of things," she reflects. "You're there to do stuff, and it's going to make a dent in something. It's not about keeping it super clean; it's not about *not* leaving any crumbs anywhere; it's a place to work. So I like that the space, the environment itself, is conducive to creative thinking, creative brainstorming. Once again, we are asking them only to do what a human can do, at a pace that's reasonable." The shop invites us to be attuned to how we move rather than how technology moves. "They can still use machines. It's not all about hand tools, but it's just that there's a sequence, there are steps, and there are processes. Processes that require focus and concentration, but also just a different pace."

~

Though Lee's work engages many different materials, wood is the one she started with and to which she most often returns. She compares wood to clay and to steel: Wood is the Goldilocks material, neither too hard nor too soft, with just the right degree of resistance. Clay is too "mushy," betraying every indentation of manipulation; working metal, on the other hand, requires too much force. "Seeing the different degrees of refinement that you could achieve with wood was really eye opening for me. I realized that I need to have some type of major physical element; it has to be something that's really getting the blood moving. I realized that the whole package is what makes working with that medium more alluring."

In summer 2019 Lee was the artist-at-sea with the Schmidt Ocean Institute on the Pacific Ocean west of Hawaii. She found herself fascinated by the coral, plants, and creatures living in the *bathyal zone*—800–3500 meters down—subject to pressure differences and osmosis, and with "fluidity, no hard edges … It's interesting because we work with materials that tend—not always—to be solids at room temperature. But here, everything is liquid or gas or permeable." From the constant dynamic motion of the ship to the demand to think about materials in fundamentally different ways, the experience pushed Lee into new terrain. She worked in a dramatically smaller space than she's used to with only the tools and equipment on board, all of which were designed for scientific purposes. Lee developed three projects simultaneously (a common practice for her): She used the onboard 3D printer to recreate the underwater flora, which she then embossed using the bearings press; used the measurements and patterns of underwater eddies to inform embroidery stitches; and explored pseudo-skins and underwater polyps using origami-like structures.

Like other cross-disciplinary residencies, the aim of the Artist-at-Sea program is for the artist to bring new questions and new ways of thinking to scientific research. It's a project made for Lee, bringing together art and science within strict parameters. She loved the whole experience, saying, "I need to start thinking differently about materials, because that's where I feel like I'm moving forward, I'm expanding. It was very transformative for me. I want to continue pursuing what I started. I need to get back to it!" Moving between worlds, from the Arizona desert to the depths of the Pacific, and disciplines including art, craft, and science, Lee is at home blurring boundaries and seeking a sense of discovery: "It feels unbounded and that's the way I love thinking about ideas. It's like making those boundaries really soft so that you're exploring the universe in your brain."

~

 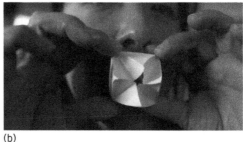

(a)   (b)

Figure 5.49a and b: Christine Lee, (L–R) Blind embossing test using modified bearing press onboard the Falkor, 2019; Folding prototypes of "skins" inspired by the polyps on deep sea coral specimens that were acquired during the dives at the Emperor Seamount Chain in the Pacific Ocean, 2019. (Monika Naranjo-Shepard)

At the Museum of Craft and Design in San Francisco, Lee circles back to the vital, galvanizing roles of both curiosity and risk in her practice as a maker. When that opportunity emerged in the spring of 2019, it had been a while since she felt so alive. "It was because this installation was so risky. I'm onsite weaving this thing, and I hadn't really been able to test it out in a large enough space ... Physically, I felt like, 'Oh, yeah ... This is why I love doing this. I love making!' I might as well have caned myself into it; that's how excited I was about it." In the throes of that installation, knowing that once it was completed she'd head back to school, Lee felt certain that she was—in that moment—exactly where she was supposed to be. "I wish I could just stay here, and everything could be paused, and I could just continue caning." In fact, if Lee could have, she would have kept caning across the whole gallery.

Figure 5.50: Christine Lee, *Intersection*, 2019. (Christine Lee)

KG MACKINNON
The space between

Figure 5.51: KG MacKinnon in their Brooklyn shop, January 2020

Brooklyn, New York

I'm a problem solver. That's the best part of my job, when I create solutions for people. I help people exist in their spaces and not feel like they're too much or that it's too much. We solve problems so that the space becomes the sanctuary that you deserve it to be, that you need it to be, and that you want it to be.

KG MacKinnon walks a line between the knowledge that identity is always present and the desire to not make it primary. Their work is clean-lined, well-made and precise, solid, contemporary, and functional, belying any obvious attempt to associate the maker's identity with the product. Among

243

their freestanding furniture pieces there are a lot of quarter and half-rounds, a kind of geometric friendliness. Much of MacKinnon's work is custom and built-in and, like the freestanding pieces, their site-specific work is clean and precise, with tight, even reveals, and exceptional attention to detail. This work must be highly functional without sacrificing aesthetics.

Being aware of one's body as a tool, engaging weight and strength to move things or operate machinery, is crucial in working with wood. To varying degrees all of our subjects are aware of their bodies in the traditionally male shop space, but there is an acute difference between consciousness of the body's functionality and being made aware of one's appearance by the reaction or comments of others. MacKinnon is very attuned to their body, both in its utility and its presentation, and in the perception and response of others. They're aware of its size and height, weight and muscle distribution, haircut and style; they're also conscious of their demeanor, how much authority they assume or confidence they communicate, how talkative they are, and what clothing they choose. Their body and awareness of it is fundamental to both their work and their sense of self.

I am aware that I'm catalogued as female because in general people default to she pronouns for me. But I am also aware of the hair on my face, the crackling of my voice, and the definition of my shoulders, back, and biceps that testosterone has given me. I am aware of the curvature of my chest that a surgeon has carved for me. I witness people also become aware of these things, which reminds me of them. Luckily in general we all just want to get back to what we came for, which was to do a job.

Field and studio

MacKinnon was born on Long Island in 1982 in a supportive and loving family. They played outside a lot—baseball, soccer, and football—and loved being dirty and running around. MacKinnon also hung out with their father, tinkering in his small home workshop in the garage, where he'd fit out toolboxes with radios for his friends and coworkers. They loved art—particularly drawing—and did well in school. Today they can see the

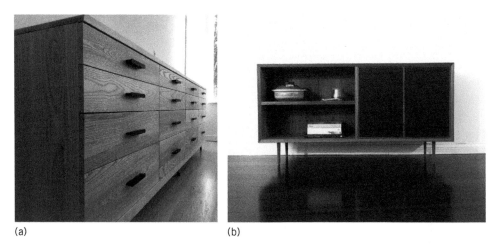

(a)   (b)

Figure 5.52a and b: KG MacKinnon, (L–R) Mid-century modern dresser in ash, 2019; Credenza in teak with dyed leather, 2016. (KG MacKinnon)

overlaps between these seemingly disparate worlds: "I didn't just *like* sports and drawing; I understood myself and the world around me through them, and I still do." Engaged in sports today, MacKinnon can see the many ways in which the physicality of athletics and the spatial awareness gained in youth sports participation have manifested not only in their art but in their woodwork and spatial problem-solving for cabinetry customers. Structure and external constraints, independence and self-reliance, careful observation and internal investigation are threads they link back to early learning on the field and in their drawing notebooks.

Athletics and art continued to shape MacKinnon through their high school years when they played competitive soccer seriously enough to draw the attention of scouts. As in their elementary and middle school years, art remained a parallel and equally important practice. When time came for college, MacKinnon went to SUNY New Paltz, where they "fell hard" for ceramics, connecting to the direct relationship between hands and material, and the meaning and life force embedded in clay itself. A good student, eager to learn and be present for their classmates, MacKinnon also understood themselves as an outsider, willing to resist normative ideas and ideals, finding energy and value in difference. Given their inspirations,

Figure 5.53: KG MacKinnon, *Bricklayer*, stoneware installation at SJSU, 2011. (KG MacKinnon)

it's no surprise that MacKinnon's work was quite conceptual and process-oriented: Their undergraduate thesis project, for example, involved carving one hundred "chairs" from bricks. The discards were arranged by size in vessels and displayed alongside the chairs.

I was interested in process as subject, not as means but as meaning. In an early project I hand pressed 100 molded bricks of clay, deconstructing each into hand carved "chairs" whose remnants were then collected and organized into clay boxes by size and texture. The additive and subtractive production of form, the chair as both an object constructed and revealed through excavation; as a symbol it imbues a sense of the body, yet empty it is also a symbol of absence.

Before MacKinnon arrived on campus at New Paltz they'd been unaware it had a healthy reputation as a "lesbian haven." They "came out" in the second week of being on campus, though it had long been evident to friends and community members who noticed their rainbow paraphernalia and short haircut. "I was taken under some older women's wings very quickly and I liked it and did not turn back," MacKinnon recalls. It was "very obvious to most people; it just wasn't something I felt safe expressing until I left Long Island."

Liminality

After graduation MacKinnon did a year-long residency at the College for Creative Studies, a small private school in Detroit, moving first to Chicago and then to San Francisco, making art and tending bar before deciding to pursue an MFA. MacKinnon returned to their roots, to a time they had felt "centered and grounded, connected to people and myself." They went back to clay and applied for the MFA program at San Jose State University (SJSU), which, in addition to studio work, offers graduate level opportunities to develop and practice teaching skills and style. MacKinnon continued to explore process as subject matter, experimenting with their own body by, for example, smearing themselves with slip and using it to leave traces. They developed simple systems to explore dichotomies, constructing limits, tools, jigs, or repetitive gestures to find the space between chance and control. And they also began to research liminality, this threshold, the place through which one passes on the way to the next, but instead of passing through, making that liminal space the destination.

And MacKinnon made things: "If there was a shop in the school, whether metal smithing or photography, I got pretty thorough experience in it."

They also started to incorporate wood, developing their skills while pushing the traditional pedestal beyond the white box. Knowing how few artists sustain themselves on their studio practice, MacKinnon intended to teach after completing the degree, buoyed by their experience at SJSU. Instead, "I ultimately found myself in a thriving manufacturing community in New York City." Small- and medium-scale manufacturing in New York is bustling, competitive and exciting, and the opportunities are many. In each situation MacKinnon was the only woodworker in the shop, thrown in the deep end, but bringing a breadth of experience gleaned from the sculpture studio. "I've just had to learn on my feet a lot and been lucky to do that."

The work was most often built-ins for residential settings and after the first job, MacKinnon thought about quitting woodworking. "I kept having these encounters that felt a little toxic, so I thought this wasn't my chosen path." They thought about going back to teaching, but an ad on Craigslist for a Brooklyn-based design and fabrication studio seemed to offer work more aligned with their interests. MacKinnon spent three years building with them, until—ready for a change and conscious of the risks of self-employment—they went out on their own.

Today MacKinnon lives and works in Brooklyn, where we met them in a large, shared shop in the gentrifying neighborhood of Sunset Park, historically a warehouse and manufacturing district but now home to "creative work." It's an old-school shop, with twelve or thirteen "old guys" who have been in the business for decades, a great reservoir of talent and experience. The space is divided into large bays, where each woodworker has their own machines and tools, and a shared space with larger, less-often-used machinery. MacKinnon shares their bay with Jack, a buddy, and the only other young guy. Designing, hustling, making, and problem-solving as part of the complex web of production in New York City, MacKinnon launched Līmen, their research, design, and fabrication studio, referring to that threshold, a space both physical and psychological. They speak about their clients and the potent beauty and importance—metaphoric and actual—of spaces in which we feel safe and comfortable to live fully. "Being a part of the process of creating those spaces they've imagined feels like such a privilege. I love that."

~

Figure 5.54: KG MacKinnon, sideboard in sapele, 2018. (KG MacKinnon)

Making an independent and creative living in New York isn't easy; it's demanding and requires constant hustle. And working as a sole proprietor can challenge one's confidence and sense of self, yet today MacKinnon describes themselves as "incredibly lucky and grateful" for their success and ongoing growth as a designer, businessperson, and fabricator. As many makers running their own businesses will attest, pricing can be a

Figure 5.55: KG MacKinnon, residential built-in, Fort Greene, New York, 2020. (KG MacKinnon)

surprisingly emotional and difficult part of the process; MacKinnon wants to value themselves and their work—to run a profitable business—while remaining accessible to their own community. They ask for input on pricing from other makers, and take diligent notes throughout their making process, keeping track of the time expended on any element of a project, taking note of all that goes into each piece. Only five years into self-employment when we spoke, this all still feels new.

In custom built-ins, getting things to look inevitable and almost unnoticeable is sometimes the hardest work, whether getting a run of doors to all sit in the same plane, or keeping grain pattern consistent or even continuous across drawer fronts. It is about working with someone else, the urban client, designing and building contemporary cabinetry that will improve their lives, in the context of a marketplace whose inhabitants are mobile, changing address and lifestyle more often than suburban or rural customers.

Figure 5.56: KG MacKinnon, residential built-in, Carol Gardens, New York, 2020. (KG MacKinnon)

What's next?

MacKinnon has ambitions to grow their business as a designer and builder. They'd like to employ an assistant and—attracted to the possibilities of overlapping trades and skills—pursue opportunities to collaborate, which might take the place of the business partner they'd once assumed they needed. "For a while I thought that I needed a partner for my business to really grow, but I think that collaborating might be a more interesting way to think about growing. And more exciting," MacKinnon reflects. "Maybe helping somebody else who's helping me create something that couldn't exist by either of us alone ..." MacKinnon loves learning and loves using their body, "so if I can keep doing those things and creating and feeling, solving problems, I feel really excited to do that."

There are other possibilities, too, among them a small cafe, "heavily curated," filled with handmade objects in use. For someone who worked a long time in restaurants, being the one to create that space is a compelling possibility, creating "a collective space, a gathering space, a community space." MacKinnon goes on: "At the end of the day a lot of carpenters are like, 'I don't want to talk about work.' You don't make enough money, your body hurts," and, MacKinnon acknowledges, "the clients, architect, and the contractors can be difficult, and so most completely check out at the end of the day. I don't feel that way and I make it a point to try to have good relationships with everybody I work with. I'm not afraid to talk about creating after creating all day."

KRISTINA MADSEN
Just a hunch

Figure 5.57: Kristina Madsen, January 2020

I carve because I love it. I'm quite consumed by it; I love pattern making.

Western Massachusetts

Twenty-eight years ago, Kristina Madsen (b. 1955) moved back to the New England house in which she grew up to care for her parents, both of whom had been raised in the Southampton area in families involved in agriculture. Madsen's parents tended the land around their home and sustained a large garden, putting up food each fall for the family to get through the winter, a tradition Madsen maintains today. Neither parent was a woodworker, but the women on Madsen's mother's side were dexterous, skilled craftswomen in various kinds of needlework and textiles. "My mother was a needleworker of the highest order," Madsen recalled. "She did exquisite work, and she set me to stitching when I was a little girl. I was using all the needles, sewing

Figure 5.58: Kristina Madsen, sample carving done in Fiji, 1991

needles, knitting needles and the like, so I've always been inclined toward handwork and precision."

In high school Madsen became very involved in the art and theater programs. When the time came to do her senior independent study, though she'd never taken carpentry or woodshop, she sought a woodworker with whom to study, but couldn't find one. When asked what her impulse toward woodworking had been, she replied, "I have no idea! It was just a hunch … I was seventeen. There's no accounting for it … I had no familiarity whatsoever with fine furniture building.

"Then the year after high school I met (master woodworker) David Powell in a bar," Madsen continued. "A mutual friend actually talked him into taking me on … When he asked me what I wanted to build, I told him a wheelbarrow and a ladder. Go figure." With one semester of university education under her belt, Madsen was hooked. Powell, who had trained with Edward Barnsley, had a small shop in an old potato barn in Hatfield, Massachusetts, outfitted with hand tools, a work bench, and a table saw. "For the first two years, I just used hand tools because that's what he was trained on," Madsen recalls. "Barnsley's shop just had a treadle circular saw, and everything else was hand tools. You can see in his tool chest all of that lineage."

In her first apprentice year Madsen was making pieces Powell had designed, from a hand-sawn octagonal cutting board to a bookcase to a coffee table to, finally, a chest. "He was very demanding," she recalls. "I think one reason he gave so much to me was because he could see that I had the inclination for precision and that I was focused and persistent." In the second year Madsen completed a type case of her own design for a bookbinder. After the second year of taking on apprentices, Powell (now Powell and [John] Tierney Woodworkers) formalized the training program as Leeds Design Workshops. Madsen eventually started teaching there. With twenty students at a time, she remembers that there were never more than two or three women in a class, and Madsen isn't aware of any that are still working in wood. She suspects that the women in the program likely had the same experience of Powell, their reserved and unapproachable yet "stunningly skilled" instructor, that their male peers had.

In 1979, Madsen emerged as a maker into a world that was rich with opportunities. The studio furniture movement was blossoming: Galleries along the eastern seaboard were mounting exhibitions, and the marketplace offered opportunities for commission, representation, and collection. Except for one summer in her early twenties when she worked as a seamstress, Madsen has made her living since as a furniture maker, an extraordinary and rare accomplishment.

> I had opportunities—I think we all had opportunities—that people getting into the field today don't have. There was a great sense of camaraderie throughout the growing field, especially amongst the small group of women makers. For instance, one year,'83, Wendy [*Maruyama*] and Rosanne [*Somerson*] and I all were residents at Art Park in New York. We were there as friends and coworkers during that time. It was really lovely to be part of that.

Figure 5.59: Makiti Koto, *Kini* (paddle club), 1988

Learning from Fiji

In 1977, living in Northampton, Madsen was lent a catalog that would shape the rest of her life as a woodworker: A large, coffee table-sized book of the Oceanic Collection at Chicago's Field Museum. This was her first exposure to the exquisite carving of the Pacific Island region northeast of Australia. "I would pore through that borrowed book," she recalls. "I eventually found a copy for myself ... and then, when I was invited to the University of Tasmania, I [went] to New Zealand on my way over and Fiji on my way back: ten days in New Zealand, a week in Fiji. That was an extraordinary opportunity," she says. "I was saturated with that work and really pursued it."

In Fiji Madsen was introduced to a carver named Makiti Koto and arranged to spend a day with him in his village. When Madsen returned to the States shortly thereafter, a friend encouraged her to apply for a Fulbright Grant. Without a college degree, she applied in the "at-large" category, which recognized makers or scholars with ten or more years of experience in their field of practice. She received the award and went back to Fiji in 1991 to work with Koto for nine months. In his forties and with a young family, Koto spoke English fluently, had traveled to New Zealand and the West Coast of the US, and was willing to take on a young and enthusiastic American. Madsen spent five months with him on the main island of Viti Levu, and another three in his home village on Fulaga, one of only two Fijian islands where carving is done.

In the complex intersection of personal relationships in a global and colonial political and economic landscape, an American's presence afforded some economic and social capital to Koto's family.

We worked in the shade under his house [built on pilings]. Often, there were one or two other carvers working with us. Makiti was a great storyteller and as we carved, he schooled me in *nai vakarau vakaviti* (the Fijian way). On Fulaga, where traditional mores were still intact, I couldn't carve with the men, so I sat and carved next to Makiti's mother. I was quite a curiosity to all of the villagers, who were patient with me as I made plenty of blunders navigating village life.

In addition to studying the language, Madsen was doing as much reading in the library as she could take in, and absorbing Koto's conscious efforts to help her understand Fijian culture and history. She returned from her Fulbright experience in February 1992, building a new body of all carved work. The relationship formed that year changed both of their lives creatively and personally. It's clear that she's as enlivened today by the possibilities of carving as she was when she first fell in love with that catalog of Oceanic carving.

Patterning and process

Throughout time and across cultures humans have decorated surfaces. We have a natural, innate desire for decoration. My work is one link in this ever-lengthening chain of tradition.

With her history of stitching and needlework, it's no surprise that when Madsen started to make furniture with carved surfaces, textiles served as her primary pattern reference. "Fabric is as much of an interest to me as wood is," Madsen explains. "The wood has come to dominate, but they're very interrelated. And the carving is now quite similar to some of the more rhythmic stitches, like the knitting or crocheting. It's very repetitive and quite meditative. You just get into the flow of it." Nowadays, botany is also a major design source. "Pattern work is ancient; it's everywhere in nature, complicated, beautiful patterns. We're surrounded by them," she says. While in Fiji Madsen met a professor at the University of the South Pacific who introduced her to the book *Symmetries of Culture*, which became "one of my primary sources of pattern research. It's a mathematical analysis of plane pattern; all symmetries have a formula that can be applied to them," she explains. "I couldn't read the book because it was pure mathematical analysis of pattern, but it's rich in imagery. Many of the early patterns on my post-Fiji work were influenced by Oceanic patterns, tapa cloth in particular." Madsen's furniture design and fabrication—completely intertwined in physical demand and quality of time, and designed simultaneously—are distinct from the energy and focus required for the carving. While she uses the furniture form on which to carry out the carving, she also loves the building and problem-solving aspect of furniture. Sometimes the idea of

Figure 5.60: Kristina Madsen, *Dining Chair*, 1993. (David Stansbury)

the pattern comes first, and sometimes it's the furniture piece that first takes shape in Madsen's imagination. Never easy, Madsen describes it as *brain strain.* "I have to work really hard to get a project going. The building is active, upright. I'm moving around all the time. And then, when I get to the carving stage, I'm sitting for weeks or months at a time, and it's very focused and more tiring," she explains. Little of the carved pattern is drawn onto the completed furniture form; in fact, often she draws only the layout in broad strokes, later doing the thought-intensive work of refining it. "The final effect of light reflecting off of the carved facets is never completely apparent until the last coat of finish is on it. There's always some surprise. Always." *Poppy Cabinet* (2019) (Figures 5.61 and 5.62) beautifully demonstrates the way she works to combine the furniture form with the carved pattern.

In 1997, after her father had died and her mother needed more care, Madsen settled in and built a shop for herself about thirty paces from the

Figure 5.61: Kristina Madsen, door detail, *Poppy Cabinet*, 2019

home where she and her mom lived (her mother passed in 2007). Madsen is now the steward of her family's acreage, and she and her sister are in the midst of creating a conservation easement for land that feels sacred to her. Forty years into her career, Madsen is making work that is more ambitious than ever. They're large pieces, complex in structure and extraordinarily intricate in detail. And, while remaining passionately engaged in the shop, in the last couple years other opportunities have been enticing.

When Pritam & Eames—the gallery that had represented Madsen for twenty-five years—closed its physical space in 2017 and moved entirely online, an anchor for studio furniture was lost. The closing propelled Madsen to consider new paths. She contemplated returning to school to pursue the degree she'd left behind years ago. Yet after exploring various options, she realized there is still too much she wants to do in the woodshop. She set her sights on an exhibition that will combine completed pieces held by private collectors and a series of new works. "I have a limited amount of time to pull this off; it's now or never. I'm excited. We'll see where I can take it."

Figure 5.62: Kristina Madsen, drawer front for the cabinet base, *Poppy Cabinet*, 2019

SARAH MARRIAGE
A bench of her own

Figure 5.63: Sarah Marriage in the shop at Workshop of Our Own, Baltimore, MD, 2019. (Princeton University)

For masterpieces are not single and solitary births; they are the outcome of many years of thinking in common, of thinking by the body of the people, so that the experience of the mass is behind the single voice.

(Woolf, 1929)

Baltimore, Maryland

Sarah Marriage was born in Tulsa, Oklahoma, the middle of three children. Her dad edited an engineering journal at night, and her mother taught high school religion but stopped to be a full-time stay-at-home mom. Marriage was early to read and do math; she and her brothers had been identified as "gifted," with talents their parents proudly encouraged and displayed. She spent part of her childhood carving out a space between her brothers—one an athlete, the other a scholar—and her mother, a strong and sometimes contradictory and domineering personality, whom Marriage describes as equal parts controlling and supportive. "My way of dealing with that was always like, just live in your own world that also follows the rules of hers." Marriage created a place for herself within a strict framework infused by serious and personal expectations: Her grandmother had died young from cancer, and her mother had her first bout with the disease when Marriage was three or four. She charged her daughter with finding the cure.

When Marriage was ten years old the family moved to Anchorage, Alaska; she remembers it as cold and dark, but *cool*: A place where you feel the vastness of the natural world, the interiority of the individual, and the precariousness of human beings in a stark environment. Even now Marriage self-identifies as an Alaskan, proud of the outsider status the state confers.

An activist is born

As she grew older, Marriage showed interest instead in the sciences. In high school she did a mentorship with an environmental engineer and another with a geneticist. She was particularly drawn to the genetics research, which offered not only problem solving and math but moral and ethical questions with real-life implications. School clubs and societies offered Marriage organized interactions that were easier to negotiate than the subtle dynamics of the teenage social scene. Soon she was the president of the Science Club, and with her brother set up the only Alaskan branch of the

Pugwash Conferences on Science and World Affairs. This organizational affiliation sent her to Washington, DC, in the fall of 1996, where she saw a presidential debate between a socialist and Green Party candidate and witnessed parts of the United States that were new to her. "I was probably 17, and it was really eye opening to see the blatant institutionalized segregation that exists in the United States." Acknowledging that it is everywhere, even Alaska, was a new and vivid realization. She was also in Washington, DC, to see the AIDS Memorial Quilt the last time it was ever displayed in its entirety on the National Mall.

When it came time to apply to college, Princeton University was Marriage's first choice. She moved between physics, math, computer science, and architecture classes. Drawn to building but troubled by the labor of enslaved people that built most of the "great" buildings of the last few centuries, Marriage struggled to find an ethical way to construct. She referred to Robin Evans' observation that, "'Architects don't make buildings; they make drawings of buildings.' I just wanted to build stuff." At Princeton, there's a graduate class where students actually build a portion of a house or a complete tiny house; that's what Marriage wanted to do. In the undergraduate courses she was struggling, unable to connect with the material and doing poorly. "I hit this roadblock of, 'Oh, the thing I really like, I don't really like right now.'" In her junior year—disenchanted and depressed—she dropped out and returned to Alaska to live with her parents.

Starting to make furniture

Back in Alaska Marriage started volunteering for a youth group, where she met Jodi Corley, who became her best friend and collaborator. They began making "really bad furniture" from thrift store and yard sale finds, dismantling and reconfiguring the wood and sheet material components that were available and easy to work with. Marriage's parents let her set up a makeshift shop in their garage. Yard sales only happen in Alaska summers, so the two spent Saturdays together cruising around in Marriage's Subaru, newspaper in hand, making the rounds of all the sales. "We'd just load the entire back, the whole fricking car full of junk, and then cut that apart to make new furniture. I had no idea how to put two pieces of wood together!" Marriage and Corley used metal brackets and screws where connectors were needed. "I wanted to make stuff and I wanted to learn. I didn't find a lot at the library, so I would go to the used bookstore and sit in that *How to Make Things* aisle and look at all the books."

Marriage's mother's cancer returned in 2002. In the midst of her mother's decline, her father was also diagnosed with cancer. Marriage nursed both of them through their illnesses; she doesn't dwell on this period, but it was clearly harrowing. Her father recovered, but her mother passed away in early summer 2003. Marriage tried Princeton again for Studio Art and then Religion but once again dropped out. She got a job in a physics lab, where she learned CAD (computer-aided design). In 2010 her brother invited her to Baltimore to see the house he and his wife had just purchased. "Though abandoned for ten years and in need of a ton of work, it was this gorgeous, gorgeous house in Bolton Hill. I was just supposed to come out and do the as-built drawings and help them find a contractor. I ended up falling in love with the house, stayed for a year, and worked on it myself."

In summer 2011, Marriage enrolled at the College of the Redwoods (CR) in Fort Bragg, California. CR (now the Krenov School) Director and lead instructor Laura Mays remembers Marriage as hardworking, ambitious, and smart, with a ready technical and spatial understanding and facility. "From the beginning she made quite challenging and spectacular pieces."

It was CR that pushed me into craft more. I'm naturally inclined to be someone who wants to learn everything about a thing, then do what I will with it. I don't realize that when you try to learn everything about a thing, the process changes you. I came out the other side a little different.

Marriage was thinking, reading, and writing away from the workbench, too: She co-founded and co-edited an online quarterly and instigated a reading club with other students. She left her two years at the school on a high, having sold both of her second-year pieces, one to an instructor, the other to a private East Coast collector through the prestigious Pritam & Eames gallery on Long Island. But life after CR wasn't easy. Three months later Pritam & Eames closed for good, without showing the piece for long nor ever getting it onto their website. "I never got the benefit of the PR push of being represented by that gallery. I dropped the piece off, and it was at

(a)   (b)

Figure 5.64a and b: Sarah Marriage, (L–R) *Fiddler Mantis*, 2012; *Leviathan Rolltop Desk*, 2013. (David Welter)

a purchaser's home a week and a half later." Busy doing paid work for her shop mates, Marriage was still making things and trying to develop products. "I never really found a footing and I didn't have a regular income stream from it. I wasn't sure how I was going to make it a more permanent gig." Back on the East Coast, Marriage rented a workbench in Thomas Hucker's shop in Hoboken, where four or five other woodworkers also rented space, and faced a constant barrage of micro-aggressions, which never feel small:

> I did a craft fair (at the museum) in Princeton, and so many of the people who came up were like, "Who made this? Did your husband make this?" My name is on the top of the ten-foot booth. And they're super liberal folks, and when you tell them it's you, they're terribly embarrassed. But it just would drive home how people just don't expect it.

In 2014 Corley died tragically, and back problems that Marriage had treated with surgery years earlier flared up. She was making rattles and toys, unsure of where her work should go in a larger sense: Design-led, batch production, or studio. She joined the Board of The Furniture Society, assisted Jennifer Anderson (Profile pp. 163–171) to teach a course at Haystack, and did a three-month residency at the Center for Furniture Craftsmanship in Maine. It was during this period that she had a conversation with Christie Byrd and Jess Osserman, also a CR graduate; "That's when Christie says, 'You guys should just form a bad ass all-women's shop up in the Hudson Valley, or something.' ... A place where you just happen to be all women running a shop together."

Marriage will tell you that she got a "little bit activist about it." The idea felt like a good and necessary strategy, and she assumed that using social media she and other women woodworkers out there—likely more than she knew—could support each other. She sought advice from Laura Zahn whose Allied Woodshop in Los Angeles was offering both full- and part-time bench spaces and classes of varying lengths. Marriage also looked at shared cooperative shops where tools are variously individual and collectively owned. She put aside the gym membership model that characterized maker-spaces like the TechShop franchise—requiring a core staff without building a core community—and, just a handful of years into working as a full-time professional woodworker, designed A Workshop of Our Own.

In 2017, A Workshop of Our Own (WOO) opened in Baltimore, Maryland. Launched with a $25,000 John D. Mineck Fellowship award, WOO is a woodshop, a community, and an educational facility for women and gender non-conforming makers. Women's spaces and institutions have a long history, from women's colleges founded in the nineteenth century to the radical feminist art spaces of the early 1970s. WOO gives more than a nod to second-wave feminist art spaces, including its eyebolt logo, which was designed by artist Sheila Levrant de Brettville for the Feminist Studio Workshop in Los Angeles in 1972 (Chicago et al., 1972).

To get to WOO the visitor dips under an interstate and drives along a thin strip of land between train tracks and a canalized river. The area is cool, still rough around the edges but ripe for the inevitable influx of coffee shops and microbreweries. The shop is a gritty, industrial cinder block construction with murals down the length of its exterior that blend easily into graffiti.

Figure 5.65: A Workshop of Our Own, logo. (Phoebe Kuo)

Marriage chose Baltimore for its affordability and the availability of industrial spaces. The shop is two long rooms—6,400 square feet total—oriented
end to end, taller than they are wide, and each with a huge roll-up door. The
first, which is flooded with abundant natural light, is the bench room and
includes a kitchen area and Marriage's office; the second and windowless
room is the machine room, crowded with equipment carefully annotated with
safety instructions and filled with donated tools. Romeo the shop cat—who

Figure 5.66: A Workshop of Our Own, a table project in process, 2018. (Phoebe Kuo)

has a few hundred Instagram followers of his own—lounges strategically for maximum visibility.

In the machine room the names of every donor are painted on the wall, both a reminder of how much support Marriage has garnered for this project and an example—one of many—of how well she has created and managed a graphic and consistent visual identity. The wall of names calls out to be photographed, which also means it's most likely to get posted to plenty of social media accounts. The hot pink of the logo is carried through all their promotional material and up and down the exterior walls of the building. Though the name derives from the 1929 essay by Virginia Woolf, "A Room of One's Own," and the underlying philosophy from 1970s-era radical feminism, Marriage makes excellent and strategic use of contemporary social media, bridging past and present with an eye to building a community of interest.

Marriage initially imagined that full-time woodworkers would form the backbone of WOO. That hasn't been the case. Instead, to generate income

Maker profiles

Figure 5.67: Sarah Marriage with WOO community members, 2018. (Charlotte O'Donnell)

(a)   (b)

Figure 5.68a and b: A Workshop of Our Own, 2018. (Charlotte O'Donnell)

beyond membership fees, Marriage and WOO take on various paying woodworking jobs at a variety of scales. During our visit in 2018 she was working on a batch of small folding screens for a local Dungeons and Dragons club. They've also made conference tables for other Baltimore non-profits, and the church pews in the corner were slated for repair and restoration. On a subsequent visit in fall 2019 we joined Marriage on a trip to a recycled building materials yard. WOO had earlier built a sample tinier-than-tiny house in the parking lot out front, vividly illustrating the potential reuse of materials in the yard. This time Marriage was among a group of artists asked to create something for display using recycled materials. She'd created an automaton: A discarded bathroom cabinet was transformed into a vignette of a workshop, a workbench with a maker on each side. As you turned two handles the people sawed and hammered at the bench. It was a sweet window into Marriage's playful side, and an indication that she and WOO are increasingly embedded in the local art and making scenes.

WOO takes many forms, including a series of one- or two-day-long workshops focused on a single activity; sometimes outside teachers come in, and at other times Marriage is the lead instructor. For example, in summer 2019 WOO offered "Tree Milling 101" led by Larissa Huff and Elisabeth Arzt. In early spring 2020 Marriage led a two-day cabinet class called "The **Doorway Effect**," referring to the phenomenon of forgetting things after walking through a doorway into a different room, which psychologists tie to the ways we compartmentalize memory (Brenner and Zacks, 2011). Marriage explored this "event boundary" both conceptually and practically as a framework to teach the basics of cabinet making.

WOO is still taking shape. Though Marriage was initially opposed to it, filing for non-profit status will allow her to seek grants and financial assistance. And she'd like to build out the classes with more offerings, and most importantly to find renters for benches, preferably full-time professionals. Though drawn to Baltimore for the affordability of industrial space, the building that houses WOO has been repeatedly threatened by the vagaries of the city's property market, but despite acquisitive landlords and multiple changes of ownership, they seem today to have found a measure of stability.

Marriage has a sense of both urgency and vulnerability in the wake of her mother and grandmother's early deaths, a complexity of emotion that drives a fierce work ethic and ambition. She doesn't yet draw an income

(a)   (b)

Figure 5.69a and b: A Workshop of Our Own, 2018. (Phoebe Kuo)

from her work and "lives on fumes," investing every last ounce of her energy into WOO. It's an ambitious vision and a daily commitment, an expression of a vision for a present and future where anyone—regardless of gender or expression—can find their way into the woodshop. Her hope is that it ultimately affords her a bench space of her own in the shop, and maybe even—after a while—someone could be hired to run the space so she could return to full-time making.

WENDY MARUYAMA
Culture and craft

Figure 5.70: Wendy Maruyama in her studio, 2018

For four decades Wendy Maruyama has been at the forefront of—and central to—studio furniture. Woodworker, artist, educator, and advocate, Maruyama has consistently challenged boundaries as well as the preoccupations of both craft and concept that have at times defined the field. She helped usher in postmodernism—which became central to the momentum and aesthetics of the studio furniture movement—and through three more decades has continued to investigate its leading edge, always with accessible, connective vocabulary. Maruyama's work seeks to understand woodworking and furniture making in the context of domestic spaces and the social relations furniture suggests, prescribes, and sometimes constrains. It also demonstrates a profound curiosity, and a deep capacity to engage wood as a material for the expression of—or carrier for—meaning.

As an influential educator and mentor, Maruyama's impact has been felt nationally and will have ripples for generations. For decades she headed up Furniture Design and Woodworking at San Diego State University (SDSU)— one of the most prestigious and influential MFA furniture programs in the country—and has enjoyed shorter stints in several other renowned craft and woodworking programs. Her influence is felt across this book, as she has touched the lives and creative practices of many of the voices who are shaping the craft of woodworking today. While continually exhibiting her work, Maruyama has also volunteered for the organizations that are shaping and supporting this field. For many years she was on the boards of The Furniture Society, Haystack Mountain School, and the American Craft Council, and is now working with CERF+ and GreenWood Global. All are active, engaged boards, several of which support scholarships and plan conferences for educators and makers. Maruyama is an advocate for diversity in programming and in the nomination of other board members, arguing that it matters who is in leadership positions; as gatekeepers they shape what questions are being asked and what work is being seen and valued. "Because of the political climate, there's this real need to make sure that we're thinking globally and with diversity. Are we representing a wide enough group of people through publications and shows?"

Though Maruyama does not theorize or intellectualize in conversation, her work has consistently explored complex issues outside of the craft's traditional purview. With characteristically self-effacing humor, Maruyama opened our conversation stating, "I'm not a great woodworker." She is talking about technique: "Making a perfect joint doesn't come naturally to me. It's quite a struggle, actually. So I frustrate myself because you always measure yourself up with other woodworkers and think, '*Oh fuck.*'" In fact, Maruyama is perfectly capable of exemplary technique. While pursuing a two-year program at Boston University (BU) she made a **compound curved** blanket chest in walnut, with sides that bulge out in both directions (Figure 5.71); the piece is remarkable in the complexity of its construction and execution and was later featured in *Fine Woodworking Biennial Design Book*. Once she'd mastered technique, it wasn't long before she saw its limitations, and the fun that could be poked at its pursuit. Technique only goes so far; the pursuit of technical perfection can become a holy grail, a distraction from the other work that furniture can do, the meaning it can hold.

(a)   (b)

Figure 5.71a and b: Wendy Maruyama, blanket chest with compound curves in walnut, 1976. (Wendy Maruyama)

Decoration vs. desecration

In the MFA program at Rochester Institute of Technology (RIT), Maruyama created *Writing Desk*, an angular writing table in maple, an asymmetrical assemblage of multiple slabs that conjure tectonic plates. The tenons from the support structure do not reach all the way through the top, and the remaining eighth-inch void of the mortises is filled with red resin. After assembly but before finishing, she made a large "scribble" of green crayon on the surface, the swooping gesture of a cursive M or W—it is after all, as Maruyama said, a *writing* desk—and subsequently sealed in the crayon mark with lacquer. *Writing Desk* demonstrates Maruyama's almost uncanny knack for presaging the defining ideas of studio furniture in the ensuing decades. With this single piece she introduced both color and the visible addition of materials other than wood. In subsequent works she would look outward to design movements like Memphis Group and explore furniture's relationship to the body and to cultural history as a context through which to explore personal narrative, ethnicity, and gender. Maruyama moved beyond the traditional confines of furniture to explore other materials and create an expansive and conceptual vocabulary for wood.

The pedagogical is personal

Maruyama is the big sister in her family. Born in 1952 in La Junta, Colorado, of first-generation Japanese American parents, Maruyama was the eldest of three daughters. Her father was a small-scale farmer, and when she was young the family moved to the San Diego area to be close to speech and hearing therapists: Maruyama was born with a hearing impairment, 60 or 70 percent loss in one ear and 80 percent loss in the other. Her parents sent her to a public school with good support programs for children with a variety of learning differences rather than to a school for the deaf, for which Maruyama is very grateful: "I would have been isolated. I would have been in some sign language class in some place and never would have done my work, probably." In school Maruyama excelled in her arts and craft classes. "I just couldn't wait until it was time to make clay dinosaurs and stuff" (Pritam Johnson and Eames, 2013, 213).

Maruyama diverges from the stereotypical woodworker in three important ways: Ethnicity, gender, and hearing impairment. Any one of these might have been enough to either prevent Maruyama getting into a woodshop in the first place or from thriving and learning once there, let alone becoming a renowned maker and a woodworking teacher herself. Maruyama posits that the combination of the three created challenges and shaped her experience. She describes the male students she encountered at BU in 1976, the first year that female students were admitted to the woodworking program there: "They were like a bunch of dogs, you know what I mean, marking their territory and lifting their legs everywhere. The guys were terrible to each other at times" (Pritam Johnson and Eames, 2013, 218). In this regard, perhaps Maruyama was spared some of the worst of masculine competition, though at other times she recalls suffering at the hands of an "asshole teacher" nicknamed Coach. The male students loved him, but he made fun of her hearing loss as well as her gender. Maruyama says she got through just by focusing on her work, paying no attention, and building a shell around herself—as she puts it, she "turned down the sensitivity."

Maruyama's earlier entry to the woodshop at Southwestern Junior College was much more propitious. The woodworking instructor in the introductory craft program, Joanne Peterson, had just had a child. She made a cradle for her son and brought it into the shop. "I thought, 'A woman was working in wood!' and that was very important ... I remember the excitement of doing something that I thought was reserved for men." "Having kids," she says, "was never part of my plan. I do not have a single maternal bone in my body. I don't!" That said, her insight into her students, their creative development and professional aspirations, and even their relationship choices, is profound. She talks with sensitivity about managing critiques, the differences she observed between her male and female students, and dealing with students whose sense of self and ego can be hard to tease apart from the work on display.

A couple years later, at SDSU, Maruyama thought she wanted to be a metalworker and jeweler, and so studied with Arline Fisch. "Arline was a very strong figure, very intimidating, very active in the American Craft Council. She was constantly flying to foreign countries ... I remember I wanted to be just like her." Those two early mentors were instrumental in allowing Maruyama to see herself as a craftsperson and a woodworker.

Over the course of her education Maruyama had several important mentors and teachers, each of whom, in their way and drawing on their own passions, helped to support and advance a distinct dimension of Maruyama's work. At SDSU Larry Hunter saw woodworking as an expressive medium and introduced Maruyama to Tommy Simpson's *Fantasy Furniture*, which had a profound effect on her. Alphonse Mattia introduced much more refined joinery techniques at Boston University (BU). Pushing Maruyama beyond the stack lamination and dowels she had used at SDSU, Mattia encouraged a playful and sculptural approach. Jere Osgood, also at BU, was "the guy from who you learned how to transform ideas on paper and to make them out of wood ... He was able to explain things and make a lot of sense."

In a small book put together in 2015 at the time of her retirement from SDSU, Tanya Aguiñiga wrote: "Wendy treated all of her students like family and became personally invested in our education and our careers." Jennifer Anderson (Profile pp. 163–171) echoed Aguiñiga's experience of a professor deeply engaged with teaching as an endeavor both pedagogical and personal: "My time studying with Wendy has had such a huge impact on my career that it's difficult to put into words ... I can't think of a better mentor and friend" (*A Long Engagement: Wendy Maruyama and Her Students*, 2015). Each of the thirty-six students featured in the book speak of how much energy she put into their work and the development of their career possibilities, nurturing them, whether by example, mentorship, or by opening doors.

Defining appropriate craft

Maruyama was among those at the forefront of exploring furniture's capacity for making visible personal and cultural narratives. She understood early and intuitively the cultural zeitgeist of postmodernism and was prescient in introducing it into the world of craft. Playing with pastiche in *Mickey Mackintosh*, Maruyama quickly understood one of the central tenets of postmodernism: Bringing awareness to the distinct identities of both the maker and viewer. In 1981, the year after *Writing Desk* appeared in *Fine Woodworking*, Maruyama was engaging with the postmodern interest in historicism, and she did it with her typical levity. She made a tall-backed side chair, a design that traditionally sits against a wall, so its emphasis is uni-directional and frontal (Figure 5.72). Notably vertical, the back is two straight tall planks, each topped with a three-quarter circle. The chair's form is a deliberate reference to the very tall-backed chairs of Charles Rennie Mackintosh, the late nineteenth-century Scottish designer and architect. The three-quarter circles are clearly Mickey Mouse's ears; the chair is titled *Mickey Mackintosh*. The joke is in the unexpected conjunction of two cultural icons from very different spheres. It is a quick, smart, visual pun, a playful elision of high and low culture. The piece is finished with faux Formica: White paint flecked on a dark grey background. While Formica imitates other materials—marble for example—this finish imitates the imitation, a "poor man's" fake finish. Formica was one of the materials of choice for the Italian Memphis group of designers, so in addition to employing the postmodern practice of pastiche and its concerns with surface, pattern, and authenticity, Maruyama is signaling her awareness of the wider design world.

For five years in the 1980s Maruyama worked at the Appalachian Center for the Crafts in Smithville, Tennessee, where she collaborated with other craftspeople, including the resident artist in glass, Hank Murta Adams. Together they worked on a series of chairs that integrated glass and wood in unconventional ways. As Maruyama described it:

> Glass is usually smooth and sexy and clean, but we used it in a very thick, rough, textured kind of state. We cast it in sand and made little

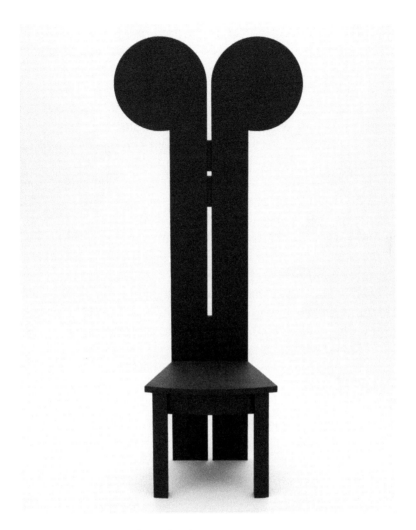

Figure 5.72: Wendy Maruyama, *Mickey Mackintosh*, polychromed poplar, 1981. (Wendy Maruyama)

indentations in the mold so that the glass stuck out. We drilled holes into it and epoxied it together ... I think it's difficult to collaborate with a strong-headed artist if you are pretty strong-headed yourself, but it was a very nice process dealing with another person and listening to other ideas in combination with your own. Some strong work came out of it.

(Pritam Johnson and Eames, 2013, 226)

This was a generative period for Maruyama, ensconced in an intimate and dynamic community of makers. She continued the explorations started in graduate school without the constraints of an academic setting or the commitments that come later in life. Giving herself permission to follow her insatiable curiosity, she established the pattern of her life: Combining teaching and professional work, using travel and residencies in new locations as generative opportunities, and looking up from her workbench to see what else is happening in the world. She also gave herself permission to rupture the oftentimes conservative field of woodworking. Maruyama describes those years as "a great experience, one of the best five years I've ever had."

Throughout the 1980s Maruyama continued to expand her work, integrating new materials and approaches. "Furniture tends to be very static at times and I think color gives it a sense of movement that we were never able to experience before, other than by using highly figured wood." Instead, Maruyama used epoxy resin **inlays** and neon lights, painting and carving texture into furniture surfaces. By the end of the 1980s the forms were becoming more expressive, too; for example, 1989's *Cabinet with Neon* (Figure 5.73) is a rectilinear grey painted box supported by bright green and red frond-like organic shapes held away from the box on small supports. The neon elements are all inside the grey box. Maruyama describes the piece:

> All the neon stuff was hidden between the two walls and the tubes come out momentarily and then go back into the case and come back out. They become sort of a gestural element to the outside of the case, which was very straightforward and static, but it had these organic forms supporting it.

Leaving Tennessee at the end of the decade, Maruyama moved to the San Francisco Bay Area and the California College of Arts and Crafts (CCAC, now CCA), where she joined forces with Gail Fredell and taught in the Furniture Design program. Years earlier she and Fredell had been the first women to graduate from the furniture program at RIT. Together again at CCAC, they introduced a diversity of practices to a relatively traditional department. Maruyama describes their approaches as complementary, with Fredell bringing a more design-led practice, while Maruyama made singular works referencing an array of cultural and art-world influences.

Figure 5.73: Wendy Maruyama, *Cabinet with Neon*, 1989. (Wendy Maruyama)

Figure 5.74: Wendy Maruyama, *Kyoto Series*, 2000. (Wendy Maruyama)

Maruyama's attention to issues of identity linked to post-colonial theory emergent in the 1990s, an exciting time of resistance as the country wrestled with the legacy of Reagan-era conservatism and the Culture Wars. Queer artists and artists of color brought the pluralism and complexity of their experiences to the fore, rather than being subsumed into a presumed universality of experience that had been defined largely by white middle-class men. With all this in mind she explored concepts of femininity embodied in furniture forms such as the dressing table, as well as the ideas and traditions associated with her Japanese heritage. *Turning Japanese*—a series informed by several trips to Japan between 1994 and 2004—"addresses the contradictions of Japanese culture and its references to both Old Japan, conjured by the spare design and rigorous craft for which it's known, and contemporary Japan: Samurai, Godzilla, zen gardens, pachinko parlors, anime, ukiyo-e, geishas" (Maruyama, n.d.). The project takes its name from the chorus of "Turning Japanese," the English band The Vapors' 1980 new wave/post-punk pop song, and takes many forms, from cabinets and boxes

(a) (b)

Figure 5.75a and b: Wendy Maruyama, *Angry Asian Women* (and detail), 2003. (Michael James Slattery)

to kanzashi (hair ornaments worn by geisha), all the way to a full-scale tea house.

In 2008 Maruyama embarked on a large-scale, long-term, and very ambitious project, notable in her oeuvre for being quite serious and absent of irony. The *Tag Project* deals with the forced evacuation of all Japanese Americans on the West Coast during World War II, the result of Franklin D. Roosevelt's Executive Order 9066, signed on February 19, 1942. The project also marks a departure from furniture forms and, for much of it, from wood. *Tag Project* is an installation of 120,000 paper tags worn by every Japanese American sent to an internment camp. The tags—re-creations of the originals—hang in huge clumps of between five- and twenty-thousand tags suspended from the ceiling and hovering just above the floor (Figure 5.76). Their sheer number is overwhelming, visualizing the profound grief and injustice of the internment. Maruyama worked with hundreds of volunteers in churches, schools, and heritage groups to create the tags, to involve community awareness and engagement in the production of a piece.

As our conversation drew to a close, Maruyama brought us into another room of her studio where work was stacked, some packed for moving out, others readied to go to galleries and museums. We spy a *Mickey Mackintosh*

Figure 5.76: Wendy Maruyama, *The Tag Project*, installation view at Arkansas Art Center, 2012. (Arkansas Art Center)

chair bubble-wrapped in a corner, but Maruyama was keen to show us one of the large elephant heads from the *#wildLIFE project* (Figure 5.77). Life-size, they are made of small pieces of wood resawn into thin sheets and sewn together to make faceted three-dimensional objects. The completed head hangs on the wall like a trophy hunter's display. *#wildLIFE project*, which has traveled all over the country to both craft and art galleries, aims to illuminate the devastating impact of poaching on populations of giant mammals like elephants and rhinoceroses.

Talking about the death of a circus elephant in Honolulu brings Maruyama close to tears. The heartfelt passion and willingness to take risks that she brings to her work—whether in the classroom, at board meetings, or in the woodshop—is consistent across her career and the range of subjects and forms that have captured her interest. Returning to her statement, "I'm not a great woodworker," we see again and again how Maruyama has defined a way of working that is effective, developing her craftsmanship not as an end in itself, nor a measure of success. Rather, she has consistently sought—and found—ways of using craft appropriate to her long-term commitment to bringing cultural relevance to the things she makes.

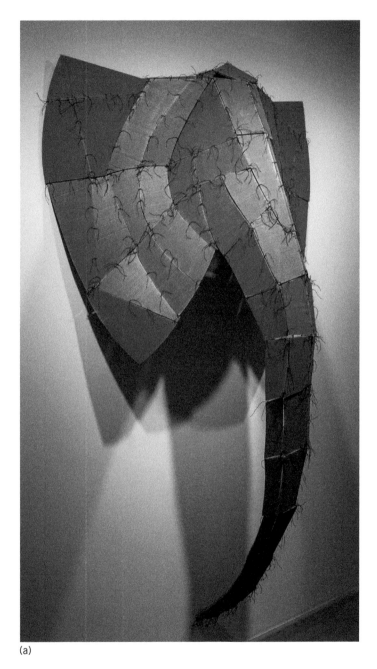

(a)

Figure 5.77a and b: (L–R) *Sonje* and *Lekuta*, polychromed wood, string, 96"h × 40"w × 20"d, 2016. (Scott Cartwright)

(b)

Figure 5.77a and b: (Continued)

CHAR MILLER-KING
Created to create

Figure 5.78: Char Miller-King at the bench, preparing for shop class, 2020. (Char Miller-King)

Atlanta, Georgia

In 2003, recent college graduate Char Miller-King was working at a non-profit internship, not earning much, when she wandered into a store and fell in love with a platform bed. With "champagne tastes and beer money," Miller-King realized the bed—though not fancy—was way too expensive for her. "I kept going back to the store," she told us, hoping "maybe it'll be on sale. Maybe someone will walk up to me and say, 'You look nice. Would you like to take this bed home for free?'"

By about the fifth trip to the store, Miller-King was on the floor looking underneath at the structure of the frame, trying to figure out how it was put together, when a lightbulb went off. "I can make this bed!" She pulled the flip phone out of her pocket, took a picture, and called her Uncle Greg. "I want to make this bed. What do I need?" "Go to Home Depot," he told her, "and tell the guys cut the wood at this length." She loaded the wood into her compact car, borrowed a drill, and picked up a $10 power screwdriver. The process of creating and finishing that platform bed— something she'd really wanted—instilled a sense of possibility, and from there she started building for herself. **Butt joints** at first, simple, functional, but her own. It took her three months to construct it, and she slept on that platform bed for seven years.

Miller-King was born in 1981 and raised in Los Angeles, where her parents, aunts, and uncles were makers, all doing something with their hands: Sewing, designing, cooking. Her father built furniture as well as home accessories with mirror: Doll houses, wall art, trash cans. "He was really crafty and creative," she says proudly; he eventually earned enough from his design and fabrication work to send his daughter to private school. Uncle Greg had taken shop classes in school. At eleven, with a vision for a school project, Miller-King headed to his house and together they designed and built a model school with a little irrigation system. "I've always been a tinkerer, a maker, a creator, but I didn't realize until after college that my actual calling was to create things with my hands. Once I realized it, I was like, 'Okay, now I need to figure out how to do this forever.'"

With a degree in public relations from Clark Atlanta University, Miller-King ascended the corporate ladder, working upwards of sixty hours a week at her job and spending weekends in her apartment building's garage. In what she

Figure 5.79: Char Miller-King, cutting board, 2017. (Char Miller-King)

took to be a sign, that apartment just happened to be across the street from Lowe's; stuck in the midst of a project, she could pull the garage door closed and head across the street for supplies. "I would pretty much spend my money on wood and basic tools, you know, a drill and a circular saw. A work bench was the first major thing that I made. I didn't really know where to go for resources to help me build; there were female carpenters out there, but how do you find them?"

At the time Facebook was in its infancy, and there was no Instagram or Twitter. Miller-King didn't know where to look. She signed up for a few classes—picture frames and basic things like that—and kept spending weekends in the garage. "I don't know what I'm going to make," she would tell herself, "but I'm just going to drill a hole in a piece of wood." One day, talking with a co-worker and friend, she found herself saying, "I was created to create things with my hands." It was one of those moments when the truth of what you're saying surprises you. "Whoa, did I just say that?" she remembers. With two kids, tuition, a mortgage, and a car loan, Miller-King spent the next few years trying to figure out how to make that a reality.

I'm crushing it at work, but I would rather be in the garage just cutting stuff.

The vision wasn't to have a furniture business; Miller-King just wanted to build things from wood. She played out in her head the conversation she'd have with her husband, the one where she tells him she'd like to hang out in the garage and make things. But the conversation turned out differently. Pregnant with twins and approaching maternity leave, she hired her temporary replacement and told her employer that she'd be back. However, like many mothers before her in the workplace, Miller-King returned to work after maternity leave to find the landscape had changed. The promised promotion had gone instead to her temporary replacement, who even asked her to give up the corner office she'd earned. Though she refused, the ground had irrevocably shifted, and she came to understand that she couldn't stay at the job; something had to change. "I left. I came home and I told my husband—and this time I didn't ask, I just said, 'I'm leaving.' He could see the concern in my eyes. And he said, 'How long do I have?' I replied, 'You have two weeks.'"

Though Miller-King is energetic and ambitious and naturally a planner, today she doesn't have a plan; in fact, she says, she's now making it up as she goes along. In 2014 she and her husband created a three-year plan, accounting for the two kids, the house, everything. Within weeks of writing that roadmap seemingly every single element of it started to collapse: Her oldest daughter's school was closing after sixty-five years. The deadline to apply for other private schools had passed, so they wrestled for months trying to figure out her school choice. Miller-King discovered she was pregnant with twins, her husband lost his job, and she gave up planning.

Undaunted, Miller-King hasn't looked back. Every day, she says, is "wake up and figure it out!" She returned to the shop, first putting small things together, and then she built herself a hanging desk. A younger cousin, a millennial, told her, "Oh, you need to get on Instagram." The idea of putting up pictures to get "likes" sounded "pointless," Miller-King responded, but her cousin nonetheless helped her get started by adding hashtags to Miller-King's images. That's how it started, and her audience began to grow. Today she has more than 12,000 followers.

A passion for teaching

In 2018 Miller-King had joined a makerspace not far from home for one reason: Access to a table saw. For her—accustomed to the casual workplace culture of an office, meeting co-workers while getting coffee in

Figure 5.80: Char Miller-King fitting a desk drawer, 2019. (Char Miller-King)

the breakroom—makers can be a little quirky. But she loved it, connected with them, and started teaching, first intro classes for incoming members, and then a basic woodshop class for adults. Her teaching practice grew to include kids, Girl Scout programming, and fundraising events. Teaching—particularly teaching children—is now a passion. "There was something different about teaching children, because many of them see this huge tool (the table saw); it's loud, it's dangerous, and it could cut off your finger or your arm," she reflects. "I knew that my role was to make them confident, to [let them] know that they can use it and use it safely. I would turn it on for them and say, 'okay, this is what it sounds like. This is how it's going to feel when you get ready to use it.'"

Miller-King helps her students, some as young as seven years old, push through that first cut together, and she will tell you that she can feel the exhilarating energy flowing through their bodies. Made on scrap, that first piece gets signed and dated by the maker. When she asks whether they want help the second time through, ninety-nine percent say, "'I can do it by myself.' And that was all the validation I needed. Whatever I said or did or helped them with, they feel like they can do this." Soon Miller-King began to go into schools, including those specifically reaching kids with learning differences, to help them get makerspaces going. Teaching "feeds your soul. Sometimes you don't know how you're helping them, but you are," Miller-King explains. "Sometimes we don't know what it is about teaching; we just know we love to do it. I feed off of the energy in the room, just being around people who want to soak up that information; in exchange, I can give you some of my energy and some of my passion." Miller-King describes herself as a natural nurturer. "I want you to feel loved, but I want everybody to feel loved." Teaching woodshop she brings that side to bolster her students' confidence. "I give fist bumps and high fives in class, and probably a pat on the back.

"I know that I still have a lot to learn, but I'm here and I've been doing it. I probably taught, in a year or so, over a hundred people, a hundred adults, how to use power tools. That makes me feel great." Walking through the makerspace or around town, folks who've taken Miller-King's classes call out to her that they've made a thing, and she hollers back, "'Good! I'm so proud of you!' And that makes me feel great."

When a global pandemic moved teaching online, Miller-King adapted to that, too. "I've worked with a few organizations where we've done online classes; there's one called Tools and Tiaras." Young girls in that class received a birdhouse kit in the mail and they built it together on screen. CNN picked up the story and featured the founder of the organization on a show called Champions for Change. Char also teamed up with another maker who is doing Grand Prix, Derby-style cars for Girl Scouts in Texas. These teaching opportunities both expand her audience but also connect her to community, albeit a national community. "That allows me to teach, that

Figure 5.81: Char Miller-King on her mobile fold-out workbench. "It also doubles as several play surfaces for the kids," 2020. (Char Miller-King)

connects me to the community of girls that I may never have been able to reach out to living in Atlanta, but these girls are from all over the country."

Blossoming flower

Miller-King described what will be a familiar scenario to most women and gender non-conforming woodworkers. She was preparing to teach a birdhouse class for children; the night before she quickly whipped up the pieces for a prototype. When she walked into the makerspace, the male site staff was sitting around. One inquired, "Oh, what do you have there?" When she replied that it was a quick prototype, he took the pieces, said, "This isn't square," got up from the table taking some scrap with him, and rebuilt the birdhouse. "For a few seconds, I was upset, not angry. I was hurt that what I did wasn't good enough. What gave him the authority or the audacity to do that?!"

After just a split second of that feeling, Miller-King gathered herself. "Okay, this is what you signed up for. It's time to start thickening your skin because you're going to be in for this a lot. And that was the last time that I let myself feel inferior or not stand up for myself." In that moment Miller-King committed that she'd no longer be silent when something happened that felt unwelcome or unfair. "I'm pretty sure that he would not have done that to a white male." Faced with the same situation today, she would say, "No, this is fine. It's a prototype. And this is the one that we're going to use. Thank you."

"When I first got serious [in] 2016 or 2017—I did find myself being the *only*," Miller-King remarked. In every class she's taken she's been the only female and the only African American. Initially, she says, she was like the "shrinking flower," only here to do what she wanted to do. And then she came to a transformative realization: "The world that I decided to put myself in was not going to be dominated by people that look like me, and at some point I had to be okay with that."

Today Miller-King writes a monthly column for Atlanta-based *Highland Woodworking*. Every month she highlights a different woman in the field. "People are still amazed that women use power tools. I'm like, 'Guys, get with it.'" Miller-King posts these columns on her own social media, and *Highland* shares widely, garnering plenty of encouragement. "I know that

I won't always be surrounded with people that look like me and today I'm okay with that."

Networking the web

Thanks to Miller-King's growing social media profile, workwear manufacturer Bad North America became her first sponsor. They sent her some of their shirts early on and still maintain a relationship with her today. But what really changed things was an introduction to WORKBENCHcon 2019. The conference was, Miller-King said, "like a high school reunion. Some of these people I [had] connected with online and it was like meeting a celebrity. And a weekend of talking about wood and screws and hardware and sponsors and projects and engagement just blew my mind." Headquartered that year practically down the street from Miller-King's Atlanta home, WORKBENCHcon invites you to "Be a part of the growing network of diyers [sic], makers, influencers & bloggers discovering new techniques, products and skills all while learning how to take their businesses to the next level" (*WORKBENCHcon*, 2020). This is the place where building in wood meets "creating content," where one's audience is primarily web-based, and where part of the learning is not just about building a thing but creating compelling video content to clearly communicate the making process to that audience. It's about sponsors and storytelling; it's about growing one's business using the tools of the internet.

In the wake of a global uprising in 2020 for Black Lives Matter, more companies looked to diversify their brands. "I see myself more now as a brand ambassador, a content creator, a motivator, and an inspiration, and I'll always be a teacher," Miller-King says. "First, I'm different, right? When you look at me, you don't go, 'She's a woodworker. Look at her hands, her clothes.'" She sees this as an asset in the work she's doing as an advocate, educator, and spokesperson. "You'd be hard pressed to find an African American female, mother of four, who is so passionate about tools, right? And who could talk shop with you all day."

At WORKBENCHcon Miller-King had an opportunity to talk with the rep from SawStop, the manufacturer of the saw with the automatic stop on which she teaches at the makerspace. She described it as one of those days when you say something you might not normally say. "Maybe I was feeling really great about myself that day, but I said, 'You guys should consider working with more women, especially women of color. I don't see a lot of that on your site or your feed and I can bring a whole different audience. I think some women would probably much rather watch me use a saw than watch an eighty-year-old white guy use the saw.'" At the time Miller-King had about 3,000 followers on Instagram and the company rep didn't believe she could make a difference to their bottom line. Less than a year later, SawStop called Miller-King back and asked her if she'd be an influencer for them, and whether she knew other women with whom they could connect.

"I'm glad that I planted that seed. We are here, we're not going anywhere, and we will soon make up more than half of your customer base. So I suggest you get ahead of it and get with it." Fueled by the importance of seeing someone who looks like you in a field of practice, Miller-King speaks of feeling deeply "empowered now to speak up and speak out and to be a representative so that more women can get out there. If you don't see anybody like you, then you probably feel like you can't do it."

"Sometimes you have to go through this series of seemingly awful things in order to get to the place where you're supposed to be," she says. "I went through all of that, but here I am on the other side saying I've got a TV show in the works, and I'm teaching, and I've been on CNN, and I've been on PBS and Popular Mechanics works with me." Every day she gets emails with sponsorship and product placement offers, and the once two-car garage—now her woodshop—is filled with tools she couldn't afford five years ago. "I had to go through all of that to get to where I am; looking back, it was worth it."

Who has the time?

The things that excite me are that I get to connect all the dots of all the things that I love. I love teaching, I love making, I love community, and I love helping other people. And I get to do all those things through social media, right? The teaching opportunities that I've gotten were because someone found me on Instagram. And I'm helping them learn a new skill. So I've just connected everything in one project.

Miller-King gave us a rundown of the many projects on her plate at any given moment. There are products that sponsors have sent that are in line

Figure 5.82: Char Miller-King, *Raspberry Pi Radio Station Tower*, 2020. (Char Miller-King)

to assemble. There are also things on the list to build for the kids, and yet other projects that will help upgrade her shop space. Published since 1902, *Popular Mechanics* magazine aspires to cultivate curiosity and teach readers how to "get the most out of life;" they have asked Miller-King to create video content to accompany how-to articles on their site. She recently built a picnic table for them as well as a log rack. They've also invited her to design a desk for them, one which she says will be informed by this moment in time. "I'm looking at my kids and I'm thinking, what do I wish they had on their desk?" There's also a small commission and a photoshoot with Dickies clothing line, and a CNC "that I need to put together like this weekend, hopefully." And the makerspace where she works is building desks for children attending school at home. To date there have been 1,400 requests. "And at some point, I hope to sleep and eat, but probably not."

~

Miller-King is sanguine about the culture of representation on the internet, drawing a distinction between herself and her brand, The Wooden Maven. People find her relatable, genuine, personable. While resisting the part of Instagram that's about looks, she's also realistic. "That's the part about Instagram I don't like; with women, we have to be pretty woodworkers. The men can just be whatever, right? I try not to think of any of it as limiting, just connecting all the dots and connecting people to hopefully enrich someone else's life, which is what I've been able to do every day," Miller-King reflects. "Sometimes I just want to be with my family and just be Char and not put on any makeup or worry about whether the lighting is perfect."

She also wants to talk about things other than woodworking with her family. "I've got to try to make it a point to not take up all of our dinner time talking about the brands and sponsors. You know, they just want mom." But kids are great observers of their parents, and a few days before we spoke Miller-King found the twins making tutorial videos on their iPads. "I can't blame them because they watch me. They're posing in front of the camera and I'm like, so this is what I've created. But it's good. It's all good."

YVONNE MOUSER
Something akin to poetry

Figure 5.83: Yvonne Mouser at work in her Oakland studio, 2019. (Michael Lyon)

I am an artist. I am a designer. I am a woodworker. I am a maker.
What each of those conjures and where you sit in that is a moving target.

San Francisco Bay Area, California

Yvonne Mouser's work sits at the liminal, overlapping, and blurry threshold of art, craft, and design. She is an introvert who seeks to collaborate, a furniture maker who creates jewelry, a woodworker who fabricates with food, a craftsperson who works in sales, and an artist who does production management. Mouser pushes against boundaries, hybridizing seemingly contradictory elements while playfully, questioningly, and unselfconsciously eroding all the edges.

~

Born in San Diego in 1983, Mouser grew up in rural Fort Worth, Texas, on her grandparents' farm, which her parents ran. Far from the long-horned cattle that made the town famous, the family was raising llamas, emus, ostriches, peacocks, and buffalo, among other animals. One of four siblings, Mouser spent a lot of time outside catching crickets and spiders. "I liked making forts in the briars under the trees and yeah, I just liked to get dirty.

(a)

(b)

(c)

(d)

Figure 5.84a, b, c, and d: Yvonne Mouser, (clockwise from top L) *Tetherow Table*, 2019. (Michael J. Lyon); *Barrel Stools*, 2015. (Yvonne Mouser); *Tarik Table*, 2017. (Yvonne Mouser); *Dorothy Bench*, 2019. (Robert Couto)

Climbing trees was my favorite thing," she reminisces. Early on, Mouser knew she was going to be an artist; this childhood connection with raw materials influenced the path her career would take.

Creativity runs in Mouser's family. Her maternal grandfather was a painter who made his way from Indiana to Hollywood, where he eventually ran the titles department at Disney. He bought his granddaughter her first set of paints. Even so, Mouser's early conception of the many possible disciplines in art was traditional; industrial design was not even on her radar so, because she liked to work dimensionally, she took sculpture courses. However, the sculptures she made in college went home and sat in the shed. They were the kinds of assignments common in undergraduate courses, "a self-portrait made in cardboard planes collaged on a blue ocean," Mouser recalls. She decided instead to make things that were functional and focused on furniture.

Mouser initially went to a local university about thirty minutes from home. After two years it was clear it wasn't what she was looking for. She transferred to the California College of the Arts in San Francisco (CCA), where she gravitated to the Furniture Department. Conceptual sculptor Donald Fortescue became her teacher and mentor; Mouser was influenced by his Zen-like approach in the studio. In her final year at CCA, Mouser made a partially burnt and disintegrated table and chair set. More contemporary art than craft, it's emblematic of a personal narrative she explored early on, part of a series of works about making and destroying. "It's hard to do at first. Then it's cathartic," she explains. The table was its "own kind of healing." Despite her enduring interest in impermanence and decay and life's momentary and fleeting nature, Mouser has never felt the need to integrate all of these themes in her work. When it works, it's something akin to poetry. "I'm not a poet," she says. "But I like that I can kind of play with that through objects."

When we met Mouser at her shared studio in San Francisco, it had been more than ten years since she graduated from CCA. Like many emerging artists and makers interested in preserving time and energy for her own work, she has pursued a non-linear career path, balancing "doing her own thing" with part-time jobs and freelancing gigs. It has been, in Mouser's own words, "a hard push." Her first job out of college was with a company that makes small prefab outbuildings. She started in production, stick-framing the walls, before moving to sales, and though she was unfulfilled and unhappy in sales and marketing, she learned the invaluable skills of how to communicate with

Figure 5.85: Yvonne Mouser, untitled table and chair, 2005. (Yvonne Mouser)

people, how to cost jobs, and how to present that information to the buyer. At the same time, Mouser tinkered with paper sculptures in her spare time and continued to show work she had made in school. But she was floundering, stagnant in her creative work and unsure how to have a practice of her own. In 2008—as the economy tanked—she left the sales job and signed up for a two-week class with Wendy Maruyama (Profile pp. 273–287) at Anderson Ranch. It proved to be pivotal. "That was the first time since school that I even thought about myself as an artist again," she remembers. Every day for the first week students were presented with a project on a theme. They made something that day and the next morning there would be a little crit. It was a jump start to Mouser being an artist again, and each object she made in that first week sticks in her imagination.

> One of the things that I made—which was probably one of my least favorite things—was a little scrub brush. It was probably something [*small*] that I carved out of a piece of wood … I sliced up dowels to become bristles. It was sort of odd-shaped, and it wasn't a brush, but it kind of looked like a brush. That was probably the first broom that I made.

Mouser's work that week made an impression on Maruyama, who later recommended her for an Anderson Ranch residency where Mouser continued to work on brooms and stools. In 2015 Maruyama supported Mouser for a second residency opportunity at SDSU. Those two immersive experiences— and the visibility and support that have come with them—have been crucial catalysts for her ongoing development.

A social democracy

In the woodshop Mouser produces archetypal objects for the domestic space: Chairs and tables, brushes, brooms, and trays. Mouser's is a twenty-first-century aesthetic derived from the Bauhaus via a detour to Scandinavian modern with a nod to coziness on one side and minimalism on the other. Shaker design, with its stripped-down aesthetic and merging of morality and making, is another important antecedent to her work, resulting in its social democratic look—affordable and well-thought out in both form and function. Mouser uses techniques deeply situated in our collective cultural history. The *Barrel Stool*, for example (Figure 5.84b), uses coopering, the traditional method of making barrels and milk buckets from tapered staves with angled sides. Yet these references fail to capture the poetic hybridization of forms and techniques which characterizes her work.

Mouser's work is the antithesis of much late twentieth-century studio craft. Spare in form, Mouser's pieces are created from American-grown hardwoods like beech, ash, or oak. There is nothing ostentatious or fussy, and nothing unnecessary. The sheen is low, and the lightly radiused edges are user-friendly. Without obvious toolmarks or evidence of process, there is no clear

Figure 5.86: Yvonne Mouser, *Curb Broom*, 2010–2015. (Yvonne Mouser)

"hand of the maker." In her *Bucket Stool*, at once straightforward and unself-consciously utilitarian, Mouser plays with visual and functional relationships among the object's stool form, bucket reference, and a handle that when upright can double as a low backrest. Both the *Barrel* and *Bucket Stools* play with the relationships between objects and the domestic and agricultural

Figure 5.87: Yvonne Mouser, *Barrel Stools*, 2016–present. (Yvonne Mouser)

tasks which they conjure, in both cases creating playful and poetic hybrids that take on new meanings in a contemporary urban environment.

Mouser's ideology of concept and design is made more apparent in the *Superstition* brush, which has an unusual curved handle. According to an old wives' tale, it's bad luck to rest a brush on its bristles (as well as damaging to them). Most brushes are hung, either with a hole on the handle or a loop of some kind. However, Mouser's design imbues this very simple and seemingly familiar object with a playful and unexpected twist, a gestural, arched form that invites the user to reconsider its possible functions.

Though Mouser's work is more visually and materially aligned with designed objects and moderately scaled production, there are parallels and continuities with the twentieth-century studio furniture movement. She is motivated to retain independence and autonomy over her working life, is engaged with her objects from conception to end user, has control over what and how she produces, and isn't locked into a larger corporate structure of management, marketing, or expensive production facilities. Perhaps most importantly, she sees furniture and other objects of daily use as having the

(a)   (b)

Figure 5.88a and b: Yvonne Mouser, (L–R) *Curved*, *Curb*, and *Shovel Brooms*, 2010–2015; *Superstition Brush*, 2010–2020. (Yvonne Mouser)

ability to hover at the edge of consciousness, to ebb and flow in the user's awareness.

Pinned to the walls of Mouser's studio space and clustered on her desk is evidence of her multi-disciplinary interests: There are sketches and objects—papers in an array of different folds and small maquettes—flyers for food events she hosts, a proliferation of post-its, a color-coded calendar, a dry erase board of lists and notes and reminders, and material studies, including a prototype for an office space divider for a San Francisco-based company. The first batch of *Bucket Stools*, manufactured by Amish craftspeople in Pennsylvania, were stacked high next to her worktable. The production and quality control process revealed the difficulty of communicating with people

Figure 5.89: Yvonne Mouser's studio, 2018. (Michael Lyon)

who don't use modern devices to discuss production details, from how to stop a spinning screw, to the need for color-matching in all the components in one stool. With this project, Mouser was moving into a larger scale of production and sales, figuring out the volume required to get the right cost, and how to reach the consumer.

With a dozen projects in the works—both for herself and for clients—Mouser starts the day with emails, followed by working on the computer or sketching. The food-based events have an ephemeral existence, and she has been working with a woman who does textiles and costuming. In addition to her collaborators, Mouser gets feedback about design and technique from her shop mates, with whom she can consult about construction and practical matters, but the person on whom she relies the most is her housemate, an architect and design researcher.

Mouser is at the end of the beginning of her career or the beginning of the middle, and she has formed a portfolio of diverse activities that give her freedom and flexibility in how she spends her days, and how she puts together an income and, ultimately, a career. As is true for many artists, this flexibility comes at a personal and financial cost; she thinks monthly about getting a "real" job, and has made forays into teaching at her alma mater CCA, where she has taught a couple of workshops and also led an introductory furniture course. The cost of maintaining a space in the Bay Area is high, but the centrality allows her to meet easily with collaborators and to draw on—and contribute—creative energy from collaboration and engaging with others.

~

Coda

In late June 2020, Mouser had moved to a live-work space in West Oakland that's far more spacious than the combination of the apartment and studio she'd maintained in San Francisco. She continues to prototype and refine across multiple materials and collaborative possibilities, seeking small batch manufacturers to put the work into production. A year-long residency at Autodesk—for which she was conceiving of production possibilities for a 100% bio-based resin—was transformed when shops and studios closed to reduce the spread of COVID-19. She hadn't yet had the opportunity to put into practice the software training to use the **5-axis CNC** machine.

The structural limits imposed by the pandemic have, in fact, given Mouser a time to slow down and focus on design, a reprieve from the intense stream of deadlines that marked the preceding months. Her explorations remain broad and today she's focused on understanding the implications of this moment and what it means for makers to respond to a time of upheaval. Whether that's in renewable materials like the bioresin, or in solar lighting for which the cell is a more integrated part of the design, she's working through both possibilities while marketing her woodworking through 1st Dibs, an online commission-based marketplace for design. The move from San Francisco and the possibilities of her spacious studio in Oakland give her room to explore larger works and pursue the single most important goal: To create a sustainable life as a maker.

SIOSI
This is a love story

Figure 5.90: Arrow, Ivy Siosi, and Audi Culver with *Tactile* bar stools, Instagram post, April 3, 2019. (Audi Culver)

Bloomington, Indiana

Girl meets girl.

They fall in love over wood, create a life, launch a business, fashion solid, contemporary furniture, and build a recognized brand.

This is SIOSI's provocative online story.

Audi Culver and Ivy Siosi's engaged and playful, earnest and adventurous social media identity highlights the physical bravado in their work: One or other of them is often captured in mid-leap near or over the latest piece of furniture, or trying new things such as a bigger slab, a new leg design, or diving from a higher rock. Arrow the Dachshund adds a ruddy splash of excitable, short-legged, long hair to several scenes. These are lives their customers want to be part of, perhaps even want to lead, and in that respect their marketing draws on a language well developed by traditional shelter magazines. What makes SIOSI different is that they're targeting an entirely different demographic that has previously never been the market for custom furniture. Many of SIOSI's clients are middle-aged women—suggesting a level of security and financial stability—as well as queer women who want to support other lesbians. These are buyers who, in an age of consumption that is often marked by large, impersonal, and industrial production, want to know the maker, want their piece made by someone. Reciprocally, the buyer gets a grateful mention on SIOSI's Instagram page (as of summer 2021 they have more than 30,000 followers), thus aligning them with an established, like-minded community.

Customers are invited beyond the virtual world and into the creative process with Culver and Siosi, who sometimes end up forming close bonds with their clients, cultivating these relationships with as much care as goes into the pieces they make. With a couple who are wine connoisseurs, for example, the process of developing their table involved a couple of "wine and wood nights," which heightened the pleasure in discussing their design options. Other customers enter into their friendship circle, as evidenced by the customer testimonial on their landing page:

> It's such a great feeling when you get a beautiful piece of furniture for your home. But it's a completely different feeling when you help pick the slab, see it in progress, help with the design and … best of all, make new friends in the process.
>
> J + D Herdrich (SIOSI, n.d.)

It's a seductive offering, an invitation that sets the SIOSI customer experience apart. But in a media landscape where part of what the consumer is interested in is the personal life of the seller, it can be complicated to locate and establish one's boundaries. "It's a balance of showing finished work, and then a portrait. People are hungry for inspiration and personal story," Culver explains.

Ivy's story

Ivy Siosi was born in 1983 in Hendersonville, North Carolina, and was raised by her grandparents until she was three and a half years old. Her grandpa was a mechanical engineer and had a home shop, which Siosi recalls fondly: "I was down in the workshop with him a lot. It was a tiny, semi-damp basement, but he had a lathe and he produced big pieces out of it. It was all knotty pine," she recounted. "He fixed everything from electric to woodworking to working on vehicles. So I think I just have that in my blood." After her grandfather died, Siosi returned to live with her mother. Reflecting on their complicated dynamic she recalls that her mother did not impose traditional limitations on her or her imagination. "No one was there telling me I couldn't do this ... She just was absent," Siosi says. "I think sometimes it's more of a negative to have that traditional mom that's like, 'You're a girl, you can't do that.'"

With few family resources, Siosi learned to make things on her own. "Growing up poor is probably one of the best ways to develop a wide skill set. You don't have a lot, so you've got to work with what you've got, and as long as you've got tools, you can do anything." College did not seem to be an option, but her art teacher entered Siosi's work into the national Scholastic Art and Writing Awards—"probably one of the best things that ever happened to me"—and she won. Having never left her hometown before, Siosi was sent to Washington, DC, to receive the award. There she met Erica Sanger, the curator of the Asheville Art Museum, who would become integral to Siosi's pursuit of the arts. Catalyzed by this experience, Siosi received a full scholarship to Warren Wilson College, only thirty minutes from her hometown, where she majored in printmaking and sculpture. Her thesis project was a small house made of cardboard, positioned in the gallery with windows and electricity. After college, she decided to go to trade school where, channeling her grandfather, she spent a year and a half learning automotive restoration and welding.

313

Audi's story

Audi Culver was born in Indiana in 1983 and grew up between Bloomington and North Webster—about three and a half hours apart— in the northeastern corner of the state. Her father had a water sports business in North Webster, a seasonal living that meant winter migrations to Bloomington, a university town and liberal bubble in a conservative state. The small city of under 90,000 has a vibrant music scene, a wonderful queer community, a supportive entrepreneurial environment, and serves as a thoroughfare for diverse folks who come into and out of town with the rhythms of the academic calendar. Culver was athletic and moved easily through an environment in which every season offered a way to spend time outdoors, but at nineteen, injuries required her to change her focus; she chose art.

In high school in Bloomington, Culver had particularly enjoyed the photography darkroom, developing a practice and sensibility that infuses her work in the woodshop with SIOSI today. It wasn't until she was pursuing an MFA in photography at Indiana University that Culver used her first power tool. She took an eight-week course which focused on a single piece; Culver built a dining table. At the end of that class she had earned ongoing access to the shop and kept building, first a bench for a friend, then more experiments in design and fabrication. Presenting five-foot-long photographic panoramas for her MFA show, Culver reached out to Siosi to help build the sassafras frames.

Crafting a life

The process cemented their relationship, and Culver realized she wanted to make a life with Siosi. For them that meant working together. "Once I finished my MFA, Ivy and I talked about what's next: 'Well, neither of us want bosses and we want to have a career that's creative,'" Culver recalls. "'I have a photography background and you have building and sculpture and printmaking and all this other stuff behind you. How can we combine everything and make a living?'" They went for it: They bought a table saw and a planer and found inexpensive space in a huge warehouse.

Figure 5.91: SIOSI, Audi Culver with black walnut slab table, 2018. (Audi Culver)

The work: Clean, simple, straightforward

The work coming out of SIOSI's shop has characteristically clean lines; it's straightforward, the forms mostly rectilinear, with a few arcs and radii. Culver and Siosi come out of fine arts backgrounds rather than traditional furniture design and fabrication, and it shows in many of their decisions, both about the work and its representation. "We certainly take cues from mid-century modern and Scandinavian of course; they're simple and

Maker profiles

(a)

(b)

(c)

Figure 5.92a, b, and c: SIOSI, (L–R) Ivy Siosi and *180°table*, walnut and white oak, Instagram post, June 3, 2019; Audi Culver and *Lagom* desk, Instagram post, May 5, 2019; Audi + Ivy on *Shortcut* bench, Instagram post, April 9, 2019. (Audi Culver)

functional," Culver explains. "I'm a very practical person, so whenever I'm designing, I'm thinking about how I can make something in its simplest form, but with really delicate details that you kind of have to look for. I've always made art, so woodworking is my current art practice."

SIOSI's objects are practical and made to be used, exemplifying attention to the elemental materiality and integrity of wood. Like Shaker philosophy and much of the mid-century modernism that informs contemporary design, there's an implied morality in the simplicity of form, suggesting a relationship between honesty in construction and a life lived with integrity.

A patchwork of inlays

What distinguishes SIOSI's design and fabrication is the composition of inlay that serves both to repair and stabilize the wood and to amplify unusual grain graphics. Their patchwork technique applied to large slabs

Figure 5.93: SIOSI, *Family Chair* and *Market Dining Table*, 2019. (Audi Culver)

allows them to use planks with imperfections, knots, and cracks, and brings attention to the natural line of the **live edge** as it is juxtaposed with the simple rectilinear lines they impose. Culver and Siosi choose "which flaws to embrace, and which are unsightly or need to be reinforced for longevity." The goal is to strike a balance between the raw, natural beauty of the wood itself and a refined sculptural piece. It is, as the reference here suggests, more than a structural device.

The focus on wood as a material was of paramount importance to the first generation of twentieth-century "master" woodworkers such as George Nakashima, whose *The Soul of a Tree* influenced myriad woodworkers in Anglophone countries to have an almost quasi-spiritual reverence for the dynamics and variability of natural grain. Nakashima and his daughter, Mira, employ "butterflies," a double-ended dovetail key as stabilizer in the order of ¼ to ⅜ inches thick, inlaid in the surface and placed perpendicular to a crack or check in the wood. The double wedge shape prevents the crack from opening further. Most viewers and consumers have come to read them as charming, a demonstrably light touch from the hand of a maker who is preserving the visual and structural coherence of the slab's natural beauty and integrity.

What the Nakashimas achieve through the mostly uniform butterflies, SIOSI achieves through their proliferation of "patches," which vary widely in size, up to about twelve by sixteen inches and down to a half inch square (about the size of a nickel), and the strength of modern glues. The inlays

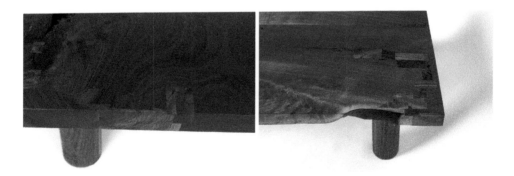

Figure 5.94: SIOSI, *Lowdown Coffee Table* (details), built for *Making a Seat at the Table*, 2019. (Audi Culver)

are put in sequentially, so that they overlap or appear layered on each other; the patches' varying sizes, rectilinear forms, intersecting grain patterns, and variable colors together create a composition that moves easily between two and three dimensions. Positioned in layers of variable thickness, the patches have the slightly destabilizing visual effect of making the wood look like it is pixelated—made of bits and bytes that have started to break up.

SIOSI most often uses the same species for their inlays, though not color-matched to the background. This is both a technical decision—accounting for expansion, contraction, and varying densities of wood—and an aesthetic and conceptual one. "We want you to see the piece as a whole and then wonder, 'Oh wait, what's going on there?' So that's also why we're not adding sapwood or something like that to it; we want you to have to look for it a little bit." Ultimately the surface is flat and smooth, but this intervention creates another layer of engagement, a composition of rectilinear forms contrasting with the more chaotic natural patterns of the wood's own figure. Viewed as a 2-D surface the patches also reference De Stijl painting compositions or contemporary collage.

> It's about the flow of the grain, but it's also making sure that struc-
> turally, it's going to last. It started as, "Oops, I messed up that corner
> a little bit. I guess I have to add another one." There was a practical
> element. But then once you hone that skill, it's more about being
> pleased with the flow of the grain from one inlay to the next and within
> the piece as a whole.

Self-presentation in a maker's marketplace

Eminently practical and resourceful, Siosi and Culver knew their "skill set had to get good, and it had to get good fast." To learn skills they went to YouTube (particularly to Norm Abram and his PBS series, *The Yankee Workshop*); to sell their work, Etsy (before the craft sales platform became saturated); and to market and promote, they set up an account on Instagram, which had just launched: Thus SIOSI was formed in 2012. Along the way they learned about **wood movement**, tolerances, and grain.

A quick glance at a piece of furniture rarely gives the viewer the backstory, but relaying that narrative, in all its complexity, is something that SIOSI works at successfully. Their self-presentation, both their website and social media presence, betrays Culver's background in contemporary photography and a sophisticated sensitivity to design, gender politics, and the maker's marketplace in the early decades of the twenty-first century. The visual language of the photographs—clean and bright, with neutral-light backgrounds, a polished concrete floor, the occasional splash of bright jewel color, and often the makers themselves—references the arts and popular culture. It's quite unlike the standard photographic presentation of fine furniture, where works are generally documented either in the domestic setting where they're intended to be used, or formally against white seamless backdrops. From the outset SIOSI knew that Culver's photography would set them apart and garner more attention for their work. "When you're starting, and there are those really frustrating days when stuff just doesn't go right, it was a nice way to end the day and to document what we had done," Culver explains. "In a way, with a really nice photo, you kind of erase whatever frustration actually happened behind the whole thing."

Buying a piece of furniture from SIOSI is more than a simple financial transaction for a product: It is a way of participating in shared ideas about the nature of labor, community, material resources, and other unquantifiable and intangible values of the personal and small-scale market. Though not for the mass market, neither is SIOSI's work only for the wealthy. A middle-class household could have a table made in America by independent artisans for the price of a family trip to Disneyland. As Culver describes it, "We're made-to-order. We can't afford the materials until you pay your deposit."

Looking into the future

SIOSI's business savvy and their careful curation of their online image has begun to attract the attention of the traditional woodworking world: SIOSI has written an article about their signature inlay technique for *Fine Woodworking*, and in summer 2019 they taught a course at Haystack Mountain School of Crafts in Maine. Their dreams for the future are both practical and philosophical. Conscious of the physical realities of aging, they want to build a practice that's sustainable over time. "At 35 you start thinking about, 'Well, maybe I need to think about retirement,'" Siosi explains. "Our little bodies are not going to be able to do this forever. As we get older, it'd be nice to make less of the big, heavy stuff, and maybe

Figure 5.95: SIOSI, *Lowdown Coffee Table*, built for *Making a Seat at the Table*, 2019. (Audi Culver)

just make two amazing tables a year." The ultimate dream is to have a compound with a house, a workshop, and a guest house for clients to come where they can "create an experience," and the ultimate integration of life and work, where the boundaries are blurred if not obliterated. Located where they are, the dream seems attainable.

Coda

SIOSI, Arrow the Dachshund, and now Win the Irish Setter have purchased a parcel fifteen minutes east of Bloomington abutting Morgan Monroe State Forest. A large pole barn/woodshop and a small house are in the works; they've hired out the exterior construction and will slowly build out the interior themselves. The compound they dreamt of—the house, space for guests, and woodshop—is now closer to becoming a reality. In keeping with their inclusive mission, Culver is thoroughly documenting the process on SIOSI's Instagram.

ROSANNE SOMERSON
Moving doubt out of the way

Figure 5.96: Rosanne Somerson in her home, Rhode Island School of Design. (Cary Wolinsky, Trillium Studio)

Rosanne Somerson first came to Rhode Island School of Design (RISD) as a student in the early 1970s, planning initially to study photography before falling in love with woodworking and furniture. After graduation she developed a rich and varied practice as a furniture maker and designer, one of a handful of women who gained recognition in the field in the mid-1970s and 1980s and were formative in the rise of postmodernism and the studio furniture movement in the US.

Having built a dynamic career as a maker, Somerson returned to RISD in 1985 to teach in the MFA program in Furniture Design within the Industrial Design Department, and a decade later she helped found a Furniture Design Department with both undergraduate and graduate degrees. Somerson taught in and directed that department for many years before rising through upper administrative posts and then becoming President of RISD in 2015. No stranger to wearing many hats, while ascending the administrative ranks of the college, Somerson continued to maintain a studio practice as a woodworker and to raise her two daughters.

Somerson's office at RISD is anchored by an expansive workbench-like ash table and is filled with art by current students and graduates. Both generous and straightforward in articulating the trajectory of her career and its intersections with her personal life, she is poised, calm, articulate, focused, kind, and *very* smart. Born in 1954 on the outskirts of Philadelphia, Somerson was the youngest of three children. Her parents were frugal, hardworking,

Figure 5.97: Rosanne Somerson, *X Marks the Spot.* (Dean Powell Photography)

and intellectual. Her mother, a weaver, dyer, and spinner, did the *New York Times* crossword puzzle in ink every Sunday. Her father, an attorney, had built the family home using the wood from the erstwhile cherry orchard in which the house stood. She ascribes to them her sense of being able to do whatever you set your mind to. If they thought something should happen, they put in the work to get it done. "If you don't think you can do something, it's really hard to try something that is risky or that you haven't done before. I was fortunate to grow up in an environment where there wasn't much doubt about just trying things."

Somerson had two rebellious older brothers: This was the era of hippies and protests against the Vietnam War and Civil Rights injustices. Her middle brother was a photographer and introduced Somerson to the camera; she describes her older brother as something of a bully though, in her typical fashion, she sees the benefits:

> Learning how to stand up to him really served me well in my professional life because I learned to not take it internally or personally, but to really look to remove the personal from the subject, whatever the subject was. Once there was a cause, I could fight for it.

In both middle and high school, Somerson—who was sewing her own clothes and learning photography—tried to sign up for a woodworking class but was refused entry. This was the late 1960s, just a handful of years before Title IX became law, which would have made it illegal to turn her away from the shop. Somerson channeled her energy into academics instead; she was an excellent student and managed to do her courses for both eleventh and twelfth grades in one year and left high school early, effectively giving herself a gap year. By chance she found an ad in the back of a *New Yorker* magazine for a center for creative writing and photography in Jutland in rural Denmark. She did odd jobs and saved up to go.

Somerson loved everything about the experience in what she describes as a "really weird alternative school" in a small, thatched-roof compound in the middle of nowhere. The analog curriculum invited students to use large-format cameras to shoot film that was processed with chemicals purchased at the local pharmacy. "I got really interested in the technical aspects of photography because I was doing everything from scratch. I grew up in a house where my mother never used a bottled salad dressing, so it made sense to do photography that way." On returning to the US, Somerson applied to RISD, drawn by the faculty in the photo area, particularly Harry Callahan and Aaron Siskind. But in the winter session term she was taken by a woodworking course. She wasn't a natural, but as someone to whom academic work came easily, she was intrigued by the challenge of it. As her craft gradually improved, she became increasingly engaged by a sense of possibility as her ideas became real objects. The work itself became an iterative conversation: "I'd make a piece, and I'd be curious, 'Well, what if I did this differently next time? What if I took that idea and then made it in a different context? If I took the thing that I put in a stool, how would it look in a mirror?' I was developing a relationship with my work that became like a partnership."

Somerson's woodworking instructor at RISD was master-craftsman Tage Frid, an émigré to the US from Denmark in 1948 whom she describes

Figure 5.98: Rosanne Somerson, *Berkshires Jewelry Box*. (Jo Sittenfeld Photography)

Figure 5.99: Rosanne Somerson, *Dressing Table with Curl*, 1992. (Rosanne Somerson)

as "an incredible character and really a devoted and gifted teacher." Initially Frid thought she had "ten thumbs," but was quickly impressed by her willingness to work hard: Somerson worked through an entire night dovetailing a large chest for fear of the wood warping if she left it. In a short time, her craft matched her dedication. She was also an excellent listener and observer, and eventually he asked her for help with writing tasks; she even worked with him on his first book, *Tage Frid Teaches Woodworking. Vol. 1* (1979).

On leaving RISD, Somerson worked as a correspondent for Taunton Press, publisher of *Fine Woodworking* magazine and specialist books, and began her own career as a studio woodworker. In an interview with *Smithsonian* she talks about this emergent period: "My first real gallery experience was showing at

... the Richard Kagan Gallery [in Philadelphia]. I showed him a piece that I had made right after getting out of school, and he accepted it, which was a big deal in those days, and then sold it" (Somerson, 2006). Her work was more conceptually driven than most other artists Kagan was showing. Shortly thereafter, Workbench Gallery in New York became interested in exhibiting contemporary furniture, and invited Somerson to be part of a 1983 exhibition of women woodworkers entitled "Women Are Woodworking":

> I was a little reluctant to always be categorized as this "woman woodworker," because I really felt like it just so happened that I was a woman. Early on, I wanted to sort of deny that and just be like anyone else in the field. Later, I reversed that decision and actually realized how much of the content of my work does come from my being female. That was something I grew into.

The Workbench Gallery show was very successful. Somerson sold a number of pieces and received close to two years' worth of commissions; it put her on the contemporary woodworking map. Despite Somerson's initial hesitation to be identified as a woman woodworker, being female in a male-dominated field impacted her most heavily during this time. At RISD she had been primarily focused on learning and acquiring skill. Though Frid was open to having women in the shop, "He was also from a generation that was pretty sexist. He respected us, but he also looked at us a little bit as novelties," she recalls. "He just made that part of the humor of the whole environment in a way that today would be completely inappropriate." In the early seventies his mere support of female students in the shop was considered radical.

As an emerging maker Somerson was creating technically challenging pieces that were exhausting and hard. Staking a claim to the field seemed contingent on technical virtuosity:

> I remember a show that I was in, and Sam Maloof was there. He walked over to this table that I had made—which was super elaborate—and he looked at it. He said, "Who made this?" I heard him. I went over and I said, "I did." He said, "This is unbelievable." For me, that was such a moment to say, okay, now someone is recognizing me not because

they know I'm a woman or they don't, but because they find the work impressive.

As she became more confident in her work and started to win awards and grants, and as she became busier and more pressed for time, Somerson realized that she could make work just as eloquent without quite as much technical complexity. "I started trying to really get at the essence of what I was trying to say in the work and make things that were more edited versions of my ideas rather than putting everything out there." The natural thing at this stage might have been to go to graduate school. Somerson was most interested in the Program in Artisanry in Boston, but because her husband at the time, Alphonse Mattia, taught there, she felt she couldn't study there. Instead, she tried to emulate in her studio the kind of professional growth that she saw people pursuing in grad school. She read all that she could, attended exhibitions, and just worked non-stop.

When Somerson joined the RISD faculty in 1985 she took over the retiring Frid's graduate program within Industrial Design. Three years later she had her first daughter, Isabel, and took a year off from RISD, spending her creative time drawing and sketching, "but I didn't really build much in the studio for a year because I wanted to have that first year with her. Then I started back slowly, teaching part-time." Reflecting on the challenges of balancing motherhood and a demanding career, Somerson notes that the conflicts came up "every day, all day. I mean, it was a constant conflict, and it was a continual juggling act. Daycare doesn't show up; you have a show deadline, you freak out, you set up a play space for your kid in the studio because you need to work." She brought Isabel with her, knowing that she wouldn't get enough work done because, "every minute the kid is going to be saying, 'Look at this, Mommy, and help me hold this, Mommy.' It was really difficult. But I also feel like I've had so much good fortune. I was super lucky."

Somerson and Mattia's work was shown in high-end galleries on the East Coast, notably Pritam & Eames and Peter Joseph in New York. The studio furniture movement was flourishing, and they were both at the heart of it. It was also in this window that Somerson helped to found RISD's Furniture Design Department. It was a period of intense hard work, without even scraps of free time. Then in fall 1997, Somerson and her husband adopted their second daughter, Annie. The timing was a total surprise, but as luck would have it, Somerson was just heading into a sabbatical. She continued her studio practice with assistants, feeding them drawings and sketches, models and mock-ups from which to work, and working part-time herself while caring for Annie and Isabel.

By any measure, Somerson has been remarkably successful in the allied fields of design, building, teaching, pedagogy and curriculum development, and academic administration. Yet even she likely has as much self-doubt and imposter syndrome as anyone else. She has developed techniques to deal with it: Holding her work apart from herself and trusting that the work is a "known good," she is able to work toward its realization. Woodworking—making furniture—is by its nature a matter of externalizing, of making manifest in a physical sense, of placing something of oneself into the physical world for someone else, an audience or a user, to engage with. "It's that sort of dialogue or relationship that you have with your ideas and your ideation. That, I think, was stronger than the worries that I had about not doing things well."

Somerson distinguishes between confidence and drive, considering herself very driven but not particularly confident. She wanted to achieve a result, was driven to achieve it, and so "moved the doubt out of the way." Never satisfied with how things are, she's always trying to improve, whether that's herself—to grow and learn—her work, or an idea: "If you think of it in terms of 'I want to make this thing,' or 'I want to test this idea,' and it's about the curiosity to see the result happen, it's much easier than if you think 'Can *I* do that?'" If one begins with, "'What would it be like to have this new piece or this new curriculum or this new connection between two things that haven't been connected before?' and you're fascinated about that and your curiosity is leading, then you figure out how to do that thing."

Working as a studio furniture maker most often means that one is dealing with people of significant wealth; Somerson wanted to make work that would operate outside of the elite marketplace of galleries and collectors to reach a broader audience. She made a conscious decision to add another mode of practice: Low cost, sustainable furniture based on simplicity and honesty to material. In 2004, when RISD asked Somerson to serve on a committee to select new furniture for recently renovated student dormitories, she found nothing suitable on the market. She proposed instead that

Figure 5.100: Rosanne Somerson, *Chest of Drawers with Wrap*, 1995. (Dean Powell Photography)

faculty from the Furniture Department design and oversee manufacture of the furniture. Somerson and her colleagues John Dunnigan and Peter Walker formed a small company, DEZCO, and designed a line of twelve pieces for the student dormitories produced from sustainably harvested and produced materials.

In Somerson's characteristic fashion, the project also became a pedagogical opportunity: "One of the exciting things about this was that it was a chance to show our students that within the furniture field there are real distinctions among the production market, the studio furniture market, and the fine art market." Somerson and her colleagues hope to convey that makers can adapt to different markets if they have the "right principles, right awareness, and understanding and knowledge," she explains. "But we hadn't really shown it ourselves." For these faculty members, the design and manufacture of dorm furniture provided an "opportunity to mirror our teaching mission."

I'm a college president who is also a furniture designer and maker, mother, and partner. My primary role now is as an educator and thought leader. I feel like every college president has a responsibility to not just run their school, but to be a voice in the world about thought leadership. Part of my pleasure in being in this role right now is that I can really push out into the world the importance of art and design, the importance of creativity, the importance of equity and inclusivity, the importance of things done well and over time, and I can humanize technology in interesting ways that we can provide examples for—and new forms of—intelligence. I feel really privileged to be a college president, and I want to use that platform as a cause, to make an impact in the world.

For Somerson, furniture design provided perfect preparation for becoming a college president; the demand to engage in multiple aspects of design and fabrication is a useful ground on which to nourish the skills for administrative and leadership roles. "I had a really fortunate career as an artist, and I wanted to help provide, make conditions for the next generation to have opportunities—different opportunities—but a field of opportunities like I had." The demands and time pressures are many, but "the skills that I learned as a young mother and a professional have really helped me to be a much better president because I have learned how to use time well, how to build strategies, and how to engage collaboration to get things done."

For Somerson, success was never about financial markers; it is about making an impact. That, she says, is about believing in yourself. "Now

Figure 5.101: DEZCO dormitory furniture, 2006. (RISD)

I'm more interested in leaving behind a legacy of impact, creating circumstances for others. My definition of success is much more about creating new kinds of knowledge, reversing inequities, and making impact—opening pathways for others to have opportunities to use their capabilities to bring new ideas to life."

FOLAYEMI WILSON
Time for the future

Figure 5.102: Folayemi Wilson in her studio at Djerassi, fall 2018

Djerassi Residency, Woodside, California

I ain't got time, I got things to do.

Djerassi, the renowned artist residency at home on a several hundred-acre site on the California coast south of San Francisco, is a staggeringly beautiful place, a mix of redwood forest, oak woodlands, and coastal grasslands. The density and complexity of the city to the north and the tech capital to its south are geographically close but a world away. Without an imperative for production, time there feels as expansive as the space.

Artist Folayemi "Fo" Wilson is a couple weeks into a six-week Djerassi residency, where a multi-disciplinary group of artists spends four to six weeks together—working, dreaming. In the beautiful rolling hills not far from the Pacific Ocean, Wilson is relaxed and discursive about her work and in particular her relationship to time, the passing of those she loves, and her own mortality. Having lost so many loved ones—including her three siblings, both parents, and her best friend—she takes nothing for granted. The very real threads of grief and loss that have permeated her adult life lend Wilson a measurable urgency. She's conscious and intentional, acutely aware of what she will leave behind: First and foremost her work, which she approaches with a fierce discipline.

> I'm very work focused. I can't live without it. It's how I make my life meaningful. Relationships are important and I treasure them; when I'm with you, I'm with you and you have my full attention. When I'm at work, I'm working.

~

Eliza's Peculiar Cabinet of Curiosities

Twelve miles from downtown Milwaukee, Lynden Sculpture Garden is a lush, rolling, beautifully maintained forty-acre home to a collection of large-scale sculptures, including works by familiar names like Henry Moore and Barbara Hepworth. Unexpectedly, we arrived during "Home," a free, community-led family day celebrating Milwaukee's refugee communities. The mostly mid-century modernist sculptures were blanketed with happy children climbing, sliding, and playing hide and seek. Around a landscaped lake, off the mowed grass and into a less manicured area through high prairie grass and trees, there's a clearing: Straight ahead is *Eliza's Cabinet*, a small, white clapboard structure with a covered porch along one side.

Encountering a facsimile nineteenth-century slave cabin juxtaposed with a celebration of refugee families is an entirely chance but complex conjunction of past, present, and possible futures in ways that are characteristic of Wilson's work, which is informed by *The Black Atlantic*, Paul Gilroy's influential 1993 text that explores the Atlantic Ocean as a transnational and intercultural framework to understand the movement of peoples of African descent around the globe, and the complexity and possibility of hybrid,

Figure 5.103: Folayemi Wilson, *Eliza's Peculiar Cabinet of Curiosities*, Lynden Sculpture Garden, Milwaukee, 2016. (Chipstone Foundation)

contemporary, Black diasporic identities (encyclopedia.com, unknown). Wilson dives into the relationship between hybridity and the conception of time as mutable. This informs her interest in Afrofuturism which, like the science fiction of Octavia Butler, reimagines a liberatory art-, science-, and technology-filled future steeped in African traditions and Black identity.

Eliza's Peculiar Cabinet of Curiosities was first installed at Lynden in 2016. The title and concept refer to the sixteenth-century *wunderkammer* or *cabinet of curiosities*, densely arranged rooms that exhibited the material evidence of that collector's interests, commonly holding both real and fake natural history artifacts, religious relics, bits of art, and curious antiquities. *Eliza's Cabinet* is masterfully constructed of reclaimed oak framing with pegged mortice and tenons. Oak is hard and strong, more difficult to work than some other woods but durable and resistant to rot. The individual pieces of oak are larger than they would be in contemporary stud construction, allowing the use of fewer boards. Two walls "fold" out

335

Figure 5.104: Folayemi Wilson, *Eliza's Peculiar Cabinet of Curiosities*, detail, Lynden Sculpture Garden, Milwaukee, 2016. (Chipstone Foundation)

and lay flat, forming decks that invite the visitor into Eliza's material reality and imaginative space, with more than a hundred objects placed on built-in shelves around the small cabin. Each shelf on the open framework wall projects forward from the plane of the wall and is dadoed into the vertical stud and then pegged with square pegs. A rough-hewn ladder pierces the roof, and projections of water play in both a bucket on the floor and in the attic, a contemplation of water as a metaphor for resistance, survival, and struggle.

The cabin is characteristic of Wilson's work in its employment of woodworking traditions, furniture forms, a deep knowledge of history, and an Afrofuturist aesthetic to recontextualize the familiar, complicate a linear sense of chronology, and assert the transformative power of Black imagination. Wilson's approach to time draws on a sensibility common to many African traditions in which timescapes are multiple and permeable, with past, present, and future intersecting and overlapping. A Princess Leia figurine sits under a domed specimen jar adjacent to a *carte-de-visite* of Mary Todd Lincoln. What could Princess Leia represent in this intersection with Lincoln 150 years apart? While Princess Leia resides today in the adult visitor's adolescence, she is future-time for Eliza. As observer, anthropologist, collector, and naturalist, the unseen Eliza is subject rather than object, the curator of her own collection, commentator on the lives of her European captors, and agent of her imagination. Thus, the visitor experiences multiple subjective positions: Their own, Eliza's, and Wilson's. "With *Eliza's Cabinet*, Wilson positions the Black imagination as an essential element in Black survival and self-determination" (Lynden Sculpture Garden, 2016).

From Rye to the Bay and east to Chicago

Wilson was born in 1955 and raised in suburban Rye, New York, where, she recalls, her "first friend was a pine tree in the yard. I would sit under that pine tree and contemplate and think. That was my safe zone." Tragically, Wilson's mother died when she was thirteen, and she moved with her father and siblings to Queens. A shy and bookish teen who devoured her father's magazines, she developed an early interest in print media and design. However, to help her be more comfortable around people, her brother encouraged her to join the National Black Theater of Harlem, which offered her a place to dance, learn about theater, and come into herself as a person in a community where she felt accepted. "I felt odd and weird and didn't find a lot of friends, so I was kind of a loner. This group, it was the first time I felt like, 'Oh these people are like me and they're Black.'"

Wilson's first role with the theater was to design their posters and flyers. She had gotten into design after reading an article in *Black Enterprise* in which the art director described his work. "Wow. I want to do that," she remembers thinking. "He talked about drawing and commissioning illustrators and working with photographers and laying out the pages and working with the editors and reading the stories. I like all of that. I could do all of that in one job?" Eager to finish high school, Wilson doubled up on English classes, graduated early, and started at City College of New York. She had a child at age 20 and was soon a single mom, working, studying, and raising her son. She took some design classes at Parsons to get the basics of typography and composition and started working freelance in advertising.

Figure 5.105a, b, c, and d: Folayemi Wilson, *Eliza's Peculiar Cabinet of Curiosities*, interior details, Lynden Sculpture Garden, Milwaukee, 2016

The environment for young women in the field was much like *Mad Men*, a television series Wilson says she didn't watch because she "lived it."

> I was carrying my portfolio around, and I was going into Macy's, and I remember some man said, "Oh, you have a portfolio. You're a designer, an artist." I said, "Yes." They said, "You look like you'd be

a good model." I'm like, "Model for what?" "Oh, well we have some lingerie that my advertising agency needs." I was like, "Get out of my face. Goodbye."

Wilson moved toward art direction, beginning at *Ms.* magazine, where she found a more equitable environment and staff policies that supported working mothers. She also got to sit in meetings with early feminist luminaries like Alice Walker and Angela Davis. Over the next decade or so Wilson worked at, among others, *Essence, Condé Nast, House & Garden*, and the *New York Times Magazine*. The work engaged Wilson at multiple levels: Intellectually stimulating, it required allying the visual with both content and concept. The work—suited to single parenthood—was also collaborative, requiring meeting and liaising with editors, illustrators, photographers, and printers. By then in her mid-thirties, Wilson opened her own design studio, specializing in print publishing, particularly redesigns and new magazines. The world of print media was thriving and her studio was very successful; she worked with high-profile clients like BET, among others. Despite a growing economy, Wilson felt that the studio—totally reliant on print publication— was vulnerable; she wanted to diversify into product design. She signed up for an executive MBA program at New York University, took classes on Fridays and Saturdays, and ran the business the rest of the week. Less than a year into the program personal tragedy hit hard: Within six months she lost two siblings, one to suicide and the other to leukemia.

Grieving and needing a fresh start, Wilson closed her design office and moved to San Francisco. She took an art direction job with Pottery Barn, did a lot of therapy, took long hikes, did yoga, and—a longtime meditator— started studying Buddhist philosophy. She also started woodworking classes at UC Berkeley. Though she was making good money and had great clients, she wasn't happy. She remembers a phone conversation with her best friend in New York, who said, " 'I'm really sick of you complaining. What would you rather be doing?' "

I said, "I love being in the wood shop. I go in there in the morning and it closes at 5, and I'm like, I don't know where the time has gone." She said, "Well, figure out how you can do that," and hung up.

That was a light bulb moment.

Figure 5.106a, b, c, and d: Folayemi Wilson, (clockwise from top L) *Boa Bedside Table*, 2015. (Folayemi Wilson); studio detail, 2019. (Folayemi Wilson); *Dark Matter*, detail, 2019. (Folayemi Wilson); studio detail, 2019

Wilson decided to go back to school to get an MFA in Furniture Design. She opted for Rhode Island School of Design, partly because—when asked about African aesthetics—then-Chair of the Furniture Department Rosanne Somerson was straightforward in acknowledging she didn't know enough but was equally enthusiastic to learn alongside her potential student. Wilson did three years in the RISD program, with extra credits in woodworking and art history, and stayed to teach as an adjunct for another two years. Realizing that part-time and adjunct professors are typically neither paid nor treated well, Wilson started looking for full-time positions in academia, and soon had two good offers on the table. She took the better one and spent four years teaching at the University of Wisconsin, Milwaukee.

With her experience in both graphic design and furniture making, Wilson engages with the meanings signified by material culture, specifically furniture. Historic furniture forms like nineteenth-century French parlor chairs can stand in for a conversation about the socio-economic and colonial relations of that period. Chairs can also operate as a stand-in for the body—particularly adorned and suspended at eye-level as *Jezebel's ch(l) air* (Figure 5.107a).

We construct and organize our domestic and public spaces with furniture, shaping and constraining social relations. For her 2006 *Seeing Series* (Figure 5.108) Wilson created three iconic furniture forms—a chair, a lamp, and a table—and paired the simply crafted pieces with her own performances

(a)   (b)

Figure 5.107a and b: Folayemi Wilson, (L–R) *Jezebel's ch(l)air*, 2011; *Improv*, with Norman Teague, 2018. (Folayemi Wilson)

as those objects. Wilson uses this construct to explore the markers that define us to others, in this case pointing to the ways that unrecognized and unresolved attitudes about race and gender can limit our ability to see each other. Though clearly speaking to the metonyms of the color black and our construct of a racialized blackness, she writes that the series is all about grey, the spaces between.

> How should one read these images? What responses are solicited by the collision of multiple and potential meanings and representation in body, object, color, and gender in a single work? Is black seen as a formal color, a race, or a culture? Have women and women of color in particular, indeed risen beyond identities of servitude in society's and our own minds?

~

Chicago, Illinois

The lobby of Columbia College in Chicago during a Fourth of July heatwave was deserted but for security staff and a few technicians. Wilson, who got rid of her smartphone when Trump got elected, was reclining on the couches in the lobby texting on an old flip phone. Her heavy backpack was filled, we imagined, with a multitude of projects. Warm and welcoming, she immediately brings us up to the college's tenth floor woodshop and gives us a quick tour of the organized and systematic shop, occasionally flashing a big smile, a glimpse of the energy she draws from life. Wilson began her tenure at Columbia College in 2011, where she is now co-directing the Diversity, Equity, and Inclusion Office, and running Undoing Racism (The People's Institute for Survival and Beyond) workshops for 650 faculty and staff members. In fact, Columbia College is making a commitment to creating an inclusive learning environment in ways—and with a degree of success—that few other universities today can claim. Wilson is fully aware of the significance of her identity for the student body, and vice versa. "I'm still here … because it's got a majority of students of color; it's more diverse than any other school I've ever taught at," she explains. "Whereas in other art schools I've taught I might, if I was lucky, have one or two students of color, here I have at least a third students of color in my classes. The student body is kick ass and very diverse, very progressive, very socially focused."

Figure 5.108: Folayemi Wilson, *Seeing Series*, 2006. (Folayemi Wilson)

However, Wilson is also well-acquainted with what she calls the snake pit of academic politics. She doesn't think about breaking barriers because "it just is, it's ever present." In one position she held, a colleague ran the woodshop like a personal fiefdom, even criticizing her teaching methods in the middle of one of her classes. It became bad enough that she had to invoke the Equal Opportunities Commission (EOC) to the college administration. At another institution a colleague repeatedly mistook her for the only other African American woman who attended various meetings. And, like many of her Black academic colleagues, the emotional cost and additional labor of constantly educating her white colleagues in histories and cultures outside of their narrow fields of expertise wears her down.

This is a really weird thing to say but I feel like I need to be paid a Black tax. I have an experience that my other colleagues don't have and they're asking me to help them go into territory that they have never explored. I have a whole lifetime of understanding race. I can't get away from it.

Ever mindful of the ticking clock and of moving forward with knowledge of the past, it is in young people and the transformative power of their imaginations where Wilson finds hope for change.

blkhaus-studios, Chicago

A couple years ago Wilson and collaborator Norman Teague formed blkhaus-studios, a reference to the Bauhaus desire to make design accessible. "We want design to be an agent of change for people of color." From the outset Wilson and Teague were looking for a storefront on the Southside so that kids can walk by and say, "What are you guys doing in there?"

When I was coming up, I didn't know that much about design, and it was that George Nelson table that was in our living room that didn't belong that kind of got me curious about it. So I just feel like if we have a store front and kids walked by and see shit happening and dust flying and whatever, that maybe they'll figure out that that might be something they'd want to do. Making.

Wilson's belief in the power and importance of learning about your body and your self-worth through making is rooted in her own childhood, watching the confidence young boys gained when they worked at the local gas station learning to fix cars. "The sense of self-worth has become so intellectualized and monetized that the idea of using your hands to have the satisfaction of making something is not that valued." Even the pig cutting board we all made in shop class mattered. "Every kid had a pig cutting board. Every young boy knew how to fix a car. It was kind of a rite of passage." In the absence of this kind of education, our relationships to objects and our own bodies atrophy, and we forget, "My body can make shit. My body can do things. My hands can actually have knowledge in them."

To bring this to life and make it sustainable, Wilson and Teague have formed an L3C corporation, a hybrid, low-profit business structure that will combine income from their own commissions with manufacture by other makers, as well as youth training in design and fabrication. Wilson and Teague are conscious to avoid helicoptering into a community that's not their own. Though they both live in Chicago South Side, Wilson says, that means bringing in the aldermen to help do community engagement right.

Wilson and Teague were recently invited by the Design Museum of Chicago to develop an object that's made collaboratively by the community. The idea will be to look critically at museum collections, exposing collection practices to the community, and in the process amplify the collaborative engagement, with process here as important as product. "What is a collection? How do you maintain it? How would a community decide what should be collected in the community, if they had an opportunity?" Their goal in this particular project is to demystify the collections practices of the institution and create context for the community to challenge the museum.

> How do you decide who's worth something? All those questions are great for museums to talk about with communities if they can challenge them on an institutional process. And then why does it (a collection) have to stay in this building? You know, why can't it be out with the people? Why do the people have to come to the building to enjoy the collection?

This community dialogue intersects with both Wilson's pedagogy and her own creative work, which always addresses history: Representing it and correcting it, particularly correcting and contextualizing the role and history of Black women using Afrofuturism as an expansive framework to bridge past and future. "Before we can imagine a new world for our students, we have to imagine a new world for ourselves, so that's the problem right now. It's not the students. The students are there. The students, they actually operate in that place. We don't operate in that place. We have to catch up with *them*."

References

Brenner, C. B. and Zacks, J. M. (2011, 13 December). Why Walking through a Doorway Makes You Forget. *Scientific American*. Retrieved December 2020, from https://www.scientificamerican.com/article/why-walking-through-doorway-makes-you-forget/

Chicago, J., de Bretteville, S., and Raven, A. (1972). "Women and Social Movements, How did the Los Angeles Women's Building Keep Feminism Alive, 1970–1991, 'Feminist Studio Workshop,' ca 1972." *Alexander Street*. Retrieved December 19, 2020, from https://documents.alexanderstreet.com/d/1001001881

Chrinian, E. (2017, 22 February). *This Is How the Furniture Industry Is Going Green*. Retrieved June 2021, from eugenechrinian.wordpress.com: https://eugenechrinian.wordpress.com/2017/02/22/this-is-how-the-furniture-industry-is-going-green/

City of Stockton. (2016, 28 January). *History: A Look into Stockton's Past*. Retrieved December 2020, from http://www.stocktongov.com/discover/history/hist.html

Collectively Authored. (2015). *A Long Engagement: Wendy Maruyama and Her Students*. San Diego, CA: Furniture and Woodworking, San Diego State University.

enclopedia.com. (unknown). *Black Atlantic*. Retrieved February 2020, from https://www.encyclopedia.com/history/dictionaries-thesauruses-pictures-and-press-releases/black-atlantic

Fire, N. (2020). *Sustainable Improvement*. Retrieved February 2021, from https://www.highpointmarket.org/products-and-trends/sustainable-improvement

Hiller, N. (2017). *Making Things Work: Tales from a Cabinetmaker's Life*. Edited by Meghan Fiztpatrick. Bloomington, IN: Putchamin Press.

Hiller, N. (2018). *English Art & Crafts Furniture: Projects & Techniques for the Modern Maker*. Cincinnati, OH: Popular Woodworking Books.

Hudnall, K. (2019, 1 October). *@katiehudnall*. Retrieved December 2019, from https://www.instagram.com/katiehudnall/

Jahoda, S., Murphy, B., Virgin, V. and Woolard, C. (2014). "Artists Report Back." *BFAMFAPhD*. Retrieved December 2020, from http://bfamfaphd.com/wp-content/uploads/2016/05/BFAMFAPhD_ArtistsReportBack2014-10.pdf

LaFarge, A. (2019). *Louise Brigham and the Early History of Sustainable Furniture Design*. Cham, Switzerland: Palgrave McMillan.

Lynden Sculpture Garden. (2016, 26 June). *Lynden Sculpture Garden*. Retrieved February 2021, from https://www.lyndensculpturegarden.org/press/fo-wilson-elizas-peculiar-cabinet-curiosities-opens-lynden-june-26

Maruyama, W. (n.d.) *Turning Japanese.* Retrieved January 2019, from https://wendymaruyama.com/section/24989-Turning-Japanese.html

Pritam Johnson, B. and Eames Johnson, W. (2013). *Speaking of Furniture: Conversations with 14 American Masters.* North Adams, MA: Artist Book Foundation.

SIOSI. (n.d.) *SIOSI Design.* Retrieved June 2020, from https://siosidesign.com/

Somerson, R. (2006). Oral history interview with Rosanne Somerson, 2006, August 7, and 2007, June 22. (T. Michie, Interviewer). Archives of American Art, Smithsonian Institution.

Soul Fire Farm. (2020, 1 January). *Soul Fire Farm.* Retrieved November 2020, from https://www.soulfirefarm.org/

Strasser, S. (1999). *Waste and Want, A Social History of Trash.* New York: Metropolitan Books, Henry Holt.

Takumi Juku. (2021). Retrieved November 10, 2019, from https://takumijuku.com/

The World Counts. (2021). Retrieved June 2021, from https://www.theworldcounts.com/

US Census Bureau. (2019, 1 July). *Quick Facts, Hudson City, New York.* Retrieved November 2020, from https://www.census.gov/quickfacts/hudsoncitynewyork

USDA. (2015, 1 January). *USDA Forest Products Laboratory.* Retrieved December 2020, from https://www.fpl.fs.fed.us/products/publications/specific_pub.php?posting_id=72842&header_id=p

Woolf, V. (1929). *A Room of One's Own.* New York: Harcourt Inc.

WORKBENCHcon. (2020, 1 January). Retrieved December 2020, from https://www.workbenchcon.com/

Bamboo   A woody grass, this fast-growing plant shares many characteristics with wood—hardness and stainability among them—but because it's more sustainable to grow for harvest, it's increasingly popular for use in applications that call for sheet material.

Band saw   A power saw with a continuous, flexible blade with teeth on one side. The blade is a loop that runs across two or three wheels, through a slot in a table, which can often be tilted to cut a bevel.

Bent lamination   A technique for forming curves in which several thin strips are glued together face-to-face against a rigid form. The laminated strips retain the curve of that form.

Butt joints   A very basic woodworking joint in which elements are glued end-grain to face-grain or end-grain to long-grain. Not a strong joint, this technique usually requires fasteners or mechanical support for durability.

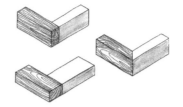

Caning   A furniture technique commonly used for weaving chair seats. The material used is derived from the rattan vine, native to Indonesia, the Philippines, and Malaysia.

Computerized Numerical Control (CNC)   Refers to automated machining tools (drills, lathes, or mills) that are controlled by means of a computer with programmed instruction and without a manual operator.

5-axis CNC   5-axis CNC machining indicates that the cutter can move across five different axes, including the X, Y, and Z linear axes as well as the A and B axes, allowing rotation to approach the workpiece from any direction.

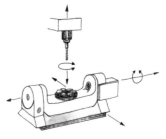

Compound curve   In woodworking this refers to bending material or cutting curves simultaneously in two or more directions. The surface of a sphere, for example, is a compound curve.

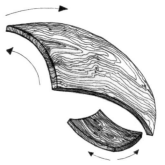

Computer-aided design (CAD)   For engineers, architects, designers, and even construction managers, CAD has replaced manual drafting as the tool of choice to create both 2D and 3D designs.

Coopering

Traditionally refers to making wooden casks, barrels, buckets, or tubs from wooden staves.

Crisp edge/ soft edge

These terms refer to the edge where adjacent planes meet, whether the maker has eased, softened, or left a hard or crisp edge. Though some part personal style and fashion, treatment of edges can change how the piece takes finish and how welcoming it is to the touch.

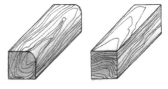

Doorway effect

The doorway effect grew in prominence after a 2011 study by researchers at the University of Notre Dame found that people who passed through doorways were prone to forgetting. They suggested that crossing the threshold caused the brain to refresh. A follow-up study at Bond University found this effect limited to subjects whose working memory is already overloaded.

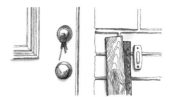

Dovetailed carcass (carcase)

The frame (or box) of a cabinet (carcass) with dovetail joints at the corners providing great strength.

Dovetails/ Half-blind dovetails

A dovetail joint consists of trapezoidal "pins" extending from one board interlocking with "tails" in the end of another. This joint is mechanically very strong and is commonly used in box construction such as drawers, boxes, and cabinets. There are different types of dovetail joints, including half-blind dovetails, used when the maker prefers that end grain isn't visible from the front of the joint.

Glue joint   Glue is very effective for joining wood long-grain to long-grain and can be as strong as a single piece of wood. Glue is far less effective on end grain surfaces, as the pores of the wood act like drinking straws, taking up the glue.

Grain/graphics The visual effect of a piece of wood, which is dependent on a number of factors, including the species, how the piece was cut from the trunk of the tree, and speed of growth.

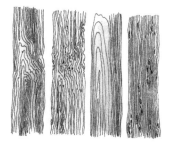

Inlay   (Verb) To insert or apply layers of material in the surface of an object; for example, contrasting woods can be inlaid into a table surface in a pattern or descriptive scene.

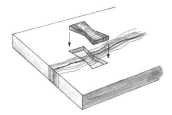

Joist   Traditionally a length of
              timber that supports part of
              the structure of a building,
              typically arranged in parallel
              series to support a floor or
              ceiling. Today they might
              also be steel for larger
              construction projects.

Knolling Categorizing objects and
              arranging then in parallel
              or at 90-degree angles.
              Andrew Kromelow—then
              janitor at Frank Gehry's
              furniture fabrication shop—
              coined the term to describe
              the angular furniture
              created by Knoll, the
              company for whom Gehry
              designed chairs.

Live edge The live edge of a piece of
              wood is the outside of the
              tree. Usually, lumber is
              milled to remove this and
              create rectilinear planks
              or beams. In live edge
              furniture the designer or
              maker incorporates the
              natural edge or periphery of
              the slab into the design of
              the piece.

MDF   Medium-density fiberboard (MDF) is an engineered sheet material composed of the fibers of hardwood or softwood scraps bound with glues and then formed into panels under pressure. It's stronger, more dense, and heavier than particle board. It has no voids, no grain structure, and wears poorly when exposed to water.

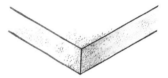

Milling   Tree milling is the process by which logs are cut into slabs and then lumber.

Mortise and Tenon   Joints that connect two pieces of wood, most commonly at right angles. In use for thousands of years, they are strong and stable and variable in form. What they have in common is the hole (mortise) and the tongue element (tenon) that is scaled to insert tightly into the mortise.

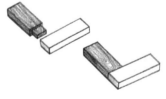

Particle board Like MDF, particle board is an engineered sheet material composed of soft and hardwood fibers adhered with glues and resins and then formed into panels under pressure. It is lighter than MDF and breaks down quickly when exposed to water.

Piecework Piecework (or piece work) is any type of labor in which a worker is paid a fixed rate for each unit produced or action performed, regardless of time. Though it often refers to factory production, today it can also be care providers paid by procedure or technicians paid by unit installed.

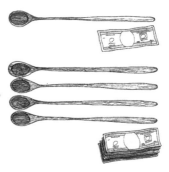

Plywood Plywood is a structural sheet material created with multiple thin sheets of wood layered at right angles to each other and adhered with glues. Unlike particle board, masonite, or MDF, plywood has grain structure and is subject to voids, depending on quality. It is structurally stronger and more durable as well.

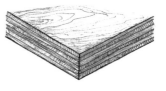

Rabbet/ rabbeting

A very basic joint for box building, the rabbet has more strength than the butt joint. The open recess along the end or edge of a board that receives the end of the perpendicular board adds extra gluing surface and protects against racking.

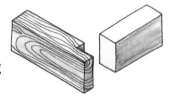

Rattan

Rattan (ratan) describes a large group of climbing palms found most often in tropical Asia and Africa. Most are considered lianas due to their climbing habit. In furniture, rattans are often woven into seats and chair backs.

Shaping

Broadly, shaping includes any effort to make the natural form of the wood conform to a designed or imagined shape for structural or aesthetic reasons. Shaping can be achieved with power tools or hand tools, and with varying degrees of detail depending on desired outcome.

Steam bending   Steam bending is a way of creating curves that involves applying both heat and moisture to soften wood fibers enough that they bend and stretch. The wood is then clamped or fastened in place so that it retains the curved form as it dries and cools, when the shape can be refined with other tools.

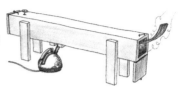

Tolerances   Tolerances refer to how exacting the measurement of pieces or the fit of a joint should be. This can be a question of structure and strength, or a question of personal preference and appropriate craft.

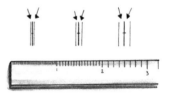

Tool marks/ evidence of the process/ hands of the maker   Makers can choose how much evidence of their labor will remain visible in a finished piece.

Turning   Turning wood is the process of carving a block of wood into a symmetrical object, most often a spindle, bowl, vase, or platter, while using a motor-driven lathe to spin the wood at varying speeds. The turner uses cutting tools, knives, and chisels, to shape the wood as it rotates on a central axis.

Veneer   (Noun) A veneer is thin decorative covering of fine wood applied to another wood, or to a sheet material like plywood used as the underlying structural element. Veneered elements are less prone to warping and wood movement than solid wood elements.

Whipsaw   A whipsaw is a large, two-person saw with a narrow blade that cuts only in one direction. They were originally used to mill logs into lumber.

Wood movement/ warping

Wood is a hygroscopic material: It absorbs and loses moisture in relation to the humidity of its environment. It expands in damp environments and shrinks in dry environments, and will warp in relation to its grain structure and moisture content.

Index